This edition produced for Prospero Books, a division of Indigo Books & Music.

First published in 2003

05 04

3 5 7 9 10 8 6 4 2

FLAME TREE PUBLISHING
Crabtree Hall, Crabtree Lane, Fulham,
London, SW6 6TY, United Kingdom
www.flametreepublishing.com

Flame Tree is part of
The Foundry Creative Media Company Limited

Copyright © 2003 Flame Tree Publishing

ISBN 1 904041 94 9

A copy of the CIP data for this book is available from the British Library

Printed in China

Kings & Queens

Paul Cheshire

INTRODUCTION: PROFESSOR DAVID LOADES

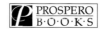

PROSPERO
B·O·O·K·S

CONTENTS

Each chapter is divided into entries and organized chronologically

INTRODUCTION

TRADITIONALLY there have been two ways of looking at British History; from the top down, and from the bottom up. Roughly speaking, these are now expressed through political and ecclesiastical history on the one hand, and religious and social history on the other.

Even the earliest chronicles show a mixture of these two approaches; on the one hand the *gestes* or deeds of kings, princes and princesses; and on the other destructive storms, monstrous births and cattle plagues. We must also remember that the written chronicles which survive were only the tip of an enormous iceberg of interest. Before the sixteenth century, very few people could read or write, and these chronicles represent generations of folk myths, stories and traditions, filtered eventually onto parchment by a monk or some other clerical scribe. The reasons for the absorbed interest shown in the doings of royal families were rather different from those shown today. There was the same kind of voyeurism; but also an awareness that these people exercised real power. The wars of princes were defining episodes in the lives of their peoples, particularly if they happened to get caught up in them.

The balance between the 'real' and the voyeuristic has, of course, shifted dramatically in recent years. Firstly, the number of royal families (or families calling themselves royal) declined sharply between the ninth and the thirteenth centuries, from more than a dozen to three or four. By the seventeenth century it was down to one, both simplifying and elevating the process of study. Until the eighteenth century monarchs wielded real power; and then it became influence, and has so remained, more or less concealed. Since the beginning of the twentieth century, political, and even constitutional interest has declined, but recent events have shown that personal interest flourishes as never before. Once upon a time, when the king was believed to be the mediator of divine authority to his people, his behaviour was of critical interest to those who wanted the country to keep on the right side of God; now the behaviour of the royal family is treated as a kind of social thermometer. It may come as a shock to learn that the present practice of succession, whereby the oldest surviving child of the monarch inherits the Crown was not always followed. In the early days (and particularly in Wales and Ireland, where the rules were different), siblings often succeeded, even when there were direct heirs. It was normal for the most suitable member of the royal family to be promoted, irrespective of his exact relationship to the deceased king. As late as the end of the fifteenth century Richard III attempted such an approach, and got away with it for a while. Unlike France, none of the British monarchies operated a so-called 'Salic Law', barring women from the succession; but women were frequently pushed aside, even when they were the direct heirs – as happened to Matilda in the twelfth century.

So how do we know about all these things? For the recent monarchy there is a great wealth of literature, both scholarly and popular, based upon State papers, private cor-respondence, and the memoirs of those who were involved. For the early modern monarchy, from the late fifteenth century to the eighteenth, much the same applies, although the sources are less abundant. However, before that the nature of the material is different. There are very few letters before the sixteenth century, either official or personal, but contemporary chronicles or annals are important, and a good deal can be deduced from the legal and financial records, where these survive. Such records are good for England, less good for Scotland, and almost non-existent for Wales and Ireland, where (as we have seen) the monarchies came to an end at an earlier date. For the early period, we are heavily dependent upon such annals as have survived, usually either embroidered *gesta* of the kings themselves, or the lives of contemporary churchmen, particularly those with any claim to sanctity. Many of these annals are redactions of long-running oral traditions. For the Celtic kingdoms, there are also some early bardic writings, particularly hero stories and genealogies; while some of the early English kings issued charters which have survived. Archaeological evidence is mainly contextual. We can deduce that a large building was a royal hall or fortress, but not who built it, or exactly when. Only coins really contribute to the histories of kings, but early examples are rare.

This brief Source Book should give the reader some idea of the richness of the history which the royal dynasties of these islands represent, and satisfy most curiosity about such matters.

PROFESSOR DAVID LOADES
Research Professor, University of Sheffield,
Director of the British Academy John Foxe Project

IRELAND

MÁEL SECHNAILL I (D. AD 862)

King of Tara (AD 846–62). One of the southern Uí Neill family centred on the ancient site of Tara in County Meath, Máel Sechnaill came to power in AD 846. He was later acknowledged as Ireland's 'high king' and during his reign he fought off challenges from Vikings and native kings and extended the borders of his kingdom.

◆ *see* House of O'Neill

O'NEILL, HOUSE OF

A dominant force in the north of Ireland for four centuries, the Uí Néill dynasty took its name from Niall Noígallach. A semi-legendary figure who flourished in the fifth century, Niall of the Nine Hostages lived and died as a celebrated raider of various British locations.

A possible descendant of Niall was the fifth-century figure, Lóegaire mac Néill, who may have been king of Ireland during St Patrick's time. Thereafter, various Uí Néill rulers expanded the clan's realms, one branch extending south to become an independent dynasty. The northern Uí Néills also gained a separate identity as the O'Neill family claimed its line of descent from the mighty high king of Ireland, Niall Glúndub. Forced to take up arms against Viking raiders, he died in battle at Dublin in AD 919.

Following his demise, the northern Uí Néills were never quite the same force until the emergence of Áed Méith and then Áed's nephew, Brian O'Neill. Like his great ancestor, Niall Glúndub, he became Ireland's high king, Brian claiming this title in 1258, some 20 years after he had become head of the Cenél nEógain clan, but just two years before his death at the Battle of Down.

His successor was Áed Buidhe O'Neill, but in 1283 Brian's son, Domhnall, became king after fending off a challenge from Áed Buidhe's brother. Deposed just three years later, Domhnall enjoyed a brief return to the seat of power in 1291 before fully regaining control in 1296. Then reigning until his death in 1325, Domhnall O'Neill sided with Edward Bruce in 1315, supporting the Scot in his vain bid to overturn English power in Ireland and so become the country's king.

The last true chief of the family was Hugh O'Neill (1550–1616). The Earl of Tyrone, he led a brief Catholic revolt against the English before heading into exile as part of the Flight of the Earls. Taking place in 1607, traditionally the exodus of Hugh O'Neill, Rory O'Donnell (the Earl of Tyrconnel) and Cúchonnacht Maguire (the Lord of Fermanagh), this has been viewed as a critical event in Ireland's history. After the earls fled, their estates were seized and the so-called 'plantation' in Ireland of non-Catholics began in earnest.

◻ *see* Niall Glúndub

NIALL GLUNDUB (D. AD 919)

King of Cenél nEógain, king of Tara and later high king of all Ireland. A son of Aed Findliath Mac Néill, the king of the northern Uí Néill clan, Niall Glúndub ('Niall Black-knee') became king of Tara in eastern Ireland in AD 916. Reigning in both kingdoms at a time of regular Viking raids, the Norsemen landed at Waterford in AD 914 and attacked Munster in AD 915. Back in increasing numbers in AD 917, two years later Niall Glúndub was killed in battle when attacking the Vikings of Dublin, his name living on in the O'Neill surname.

◻ *see* House of O'Neill

DÁL CAIS, HOUSE OF

In the ascendancy in Ireland during the first half of the tenth century, the Dál Cais remained a major influence until the early years of the twelfth century. With its roots in Munster, the 'Seed of Cas' first announced itself as a force to be reckoned with under the leadership of Rebachán mac Mothlai (d. AD 934) and its influence did not wane until the death of Muirchertach Uá Briain in 1119.

Following the reign of Rebachán, a key figure in establishing this southern clan was Cennétig, the son of Lorcáin. It was Cennétig who led his people to the brink of greatness. Previously one of a number of minor sub-kingdoms in Southern Ireland, under Cennétig the Dál Cais began to eat away at the long-held authority of the Eóganacht confederacy. Following Cennétig's death, his eldest son, Mathgamain, made further gains until his murder in AD 976.

▲ ABOVE: Brian Bóruma after the Battle of Clontarf

He was succeeded by his younger brother, Brian Bóruma (Boru), and it was under his dynamic leadership that the most dramatic advances were made. In little more than a quarter of a century as the Dál Cais king, Brian Bóruma claimed many notable scalps and several titles. He became king of Cashel, the acknowledged king of the south and latterly the self-proclaimed 'Emperor of the Irish'. In 1002 his election as his country's high king (or king of kings) established the high-water mark in the rise of the Dál Cais.

Brian Bóruma was killed in the aftermath of his most celebrated battle, at Clontarf in 1014. He was succeeded by a line of rulers who remained potent figures in Irish affairs for more than a century after the death of their mighty ancestor. Remaining a leading light in Thomond, North Munster, later members of the Dál Cais family bore the names Uá Briain, Briain or O'Brien, their surnames reflecting their descent from Brian Bóruma.

�» *see* Brian Bóruma, Cennétig, Eóganacht, Máel Sechnaill II, Mathgamain

CENNÉTIG (D. AD 951)

King of the Dál Cais. Son of Lorcán and father of Mathgamain and of the celebrated high king of Ireland, Brian Bóruma. The king of North Munster, also known as Cennétig mac Lorcin, he did much to establish the Dál Cais tribe as a powerful, rising force in and around their South Ireland home.

�» *see* Brian Bóruma, House of Dál Cais, Eóganacht, Mathgamain

MATHGAMAIN (D. AD 976)

King of the Dál Cais (AD 964–76); son of Cennétig mac Lorcán. Building on the success of his father, who he succeeded in AD 964, Mathgamain consolidated his dynasty at the expense of the fading Eóganacht confederation. Fighting many battles in Munster and beyond, he was killed in AD 976 and succeeded by his younger brother, the famed Brian Bóruma.

�» *see* Brian Bóruma, Cennétig mad Lorcán

BÓRUMA, BRIAN (C. 926–1014)

High king of Ireland (1002–14); son of Cennétig. Brian Bóruma (also known as Brian Boru), a king from southern Ireland, was a great Dál Cais ruler. He seized Limerick in AD 968, then became king of Munster after the murder of his brother, Mathgamain (AD 976). Chief of Cashel by AD 978, he later advanced into Connacht and Leinster. Striking a deal with Máel Sechnaill II in AD 997, the kings agreed to divide Ireland between them. Brian Bóruma took Dublin in AD 999 and was elected as Ireland's high king in 1002. 'Emperor of the Irish' from 1005, he led his warriors into battle at Clontarf in 1014, but was killed a short time later.

Already a political and military veteran (he had won notable victories against Viking opponents at Limerick and Waterford), Brian Bóruma succeeded his elder brother, Mathgamain, as king of the southern province of Munster in AD 976. Munster's new chief launched successful retaliatory raids against his brother's killers, before turning his attentions to the neighbouring

▲ ABOVE: Brian Bóruma is killed by Brodar, a Dane, after the Battle of Clontarf kingdoms of Connacht (to the north of Munster) and Leinster (to the east). Eventually he agreed an uneasy truce with the powerful eastern king, Máel Sechnaill II, and after overrunning Dublin's Norsemen Brian Bóruma became high king of Ireland in 1002. Recognised as such in a ceremony held on the hallowed Hill of Tara in County Meath, Irish kings and Viking leaders beat a path to Kincora, by the banks of the River Shannon, to pay homage there to Ireland's king of kings at his royal residence.

MÁEL SECHNAILL II (D. 1022)

King of Tara (AD 980–1022); also known as Malachy and Máel Sechnaill II mac Domnaill. Máel Sechnaill II enjoyed a long reign and for much of it his destiny was interlinked with that of the great Brian Bóruma. The two had been allies since AD 997 and five years later Máel Sechnaill II and other Irish kings were forced to accept Brian Bóruma as 'high king'. However, after the latter's defeat at the Battle of Clontarf in 1014, Máel Sechnaill II assumed his long-time rival's role as high king of all Ireland.

◆ *see* Brian Bóruma

MAC MÁEL NA MBO, DIARMAIT (D. 1072)

King of Leinster. Rising to prominence in 1046, he fought for the right to become king following the death of the Leinster ruler. A warrior-king, he continued to fight in neighbouring provinces. Defeating the Vikings of Dublin by 1054, he took control of that kingdom, placing his son, Murchad, in command there. Later forming alliances with the kings of Connacht and Munster, in the latter province he helped Toirrdelbach Ua Briain to become ruler in 1063. Said to have offered sanctuary to the sons of Harold II following the Battle of Hastings in 1066, King Diarmait was himself killed in battle six years later.

UA BRIAIN, TOIRRDELBACH (D. 1086)

King of Munster (1063–86); grandson of Brian Bóruma and a son of Teige. Also referred to as Turlough O'Brien, he was king from about 1063. Later seizing Leinster and Dublin, at his death he was the most powerful ruler in Ireland. He was succeeded by his son, Muirchertach Ua Briain.

Toirrdelbach was already a seasoned campaigner when he succeeded his uncle, Donnchad, in 1063. Having won power in Munster with the aid of his cousin, Diarmait Mac Máel Na Mbo, when the Leinster king died in 1072 Toirrdelbach then pressed his claim to be called high king of Ireland by asserting his control in southern Ireland. Taking Leinster, he overran Dublin and appointed as ruler his son and eventual successor, Muirchertach Ua Briain, but found Connacht and Meath tougher nuts to crack.

◀ *see* Muirchertach Ua Briain

UA BRIAIN, MUIRCHERTACH (D. 1119)

King of Munster and Dublin (1075–1119); son of Toirrdelbach Ua Briain. Also referred to as Muirchertach O'Brien, he ruled in Dublin from 1075 and in Munster from 1086 following the death of his father. Controlling Connacht, Leinster and Meath by 1096, he was unable to conquer the north, but remained the most powerful ruler in Ireland. A Christian king and religious reformer who passed the ancient Celtic site of Cashel to the Irish Church in 1101, he fell seriously ill in 1114, dying of his illness five years later.

◀ *see* Toirrdelbach Ua Briain

MAC CARTHAIG, CORMAC (D. 1138)

King of Munster (c. 1122–38). Reigning from about 1122, Cormac mac Carthaig took on the might of the Connacht king, Toirrdelbach Ua Conchobair, and the Ui Briain clan. He was deposed and sent into exile in 1127. Although he was later restored, relations with rival kings such as

Diarmait Mac Murchadha remained tense. Cormac's chapel at Cashel in County Tipperary was consecrated in 1134, four years before Cormac Mac Carthaig was killed.

🔹 *see* Diarmait Mac Murchada, House of Uí Briain, Toirrdelbach Ua Choncobair

O'CONNOR, HOUSE OF

Sharing the same name as the County Offaly clan, which was well to the fore in central Ireland during the fifteenth century, the O'Connors of Connacht were the descendants of Conchobar (or Connor). A ruler of the Uí Briain Aí, a line said to have descended from the fifth-century king Brión (Brian), Conchobar's small kingdom covered part of modern-day County Roscommon.

Retaining this Roscommon heartland, later leaders extended the borders to the north and south-west. Established in this expanded kingdom by the early eleventh century, one of the first kings of note was Gaí Bernaig (or Aedh). He was one of a number of Irish kings who joined forces to fight Brian Bóruma's son, Donnchad, before being killed in 1067 by his northern rival, Art Uí Ruairc (O'Rourke). Later, Gaí Bernaig's son Ruaidrí na Soíde Buide briefly succeeded in becoming the king of all Connacht, but after he was blinded in 1092 by the Uí Fhlaithbertaig (O'Flaherty) tribe, the dynasty's fortunes faded.

However, power returned in spectacular fashion with the rise of Toirrdelbach Ua Conchobair. Also known as Turlough O'Connor, he was chosen as king of Connacht in 1106. Retaining this title for the next 50 years, by 1138 he had conquered Munster and other provinces and was duly recognised as Ireland's high king.

After Toirrdelbach's death in 1156, his Connacht crown passed to his son, Ruaidrí Ua Conchobair (Rory O'Connor). Like his father, he also rose through the ranks of Irish rulers to succeed Muirchertach Mac Lochlainn as Ireland's last-ever high king.Henry II campaigned in Ireland in 1171 before defeating the king of Leinster, Diarmait MacMurrough. Successful in forcing into submission other Irish kings, in 1175 Henry persuaded Ruaidrí to acknowledge him as his overlord.

Deposed a short time later, no O'Connor king after Ruaidrí Ua Conchobair would ever again hold so much power. His brother or half-brother, Cathal Crobderg, was recognised as Connacht's king by King John in 1204, but in the last years of his reign he had to fight hard against the powerful Anglo-Irish landowners, Richard de Burgh and Hugh de Lacy. Cathal was succeeded by his son, Fedlimid, who was reduced to the role of tenant-king after 1235, the year in which de Burgh won full possession of Connacht.

◆ *see* Toirrdelbach Ua Conchobair, Muichertach Mac Lochlainn

UA CONCHOBAIR, TOIRRDELBACH (C. 1088–1156)

King of Connacht (1106–56); high king of Ireland. Also known as Turlough O'Connor, he became king in 1106. Seizing Munster and other provinces, from 1138 he claimed the title of high king. Later challenged by Muirchertach Mac Lochlainn, he ruled over Connacht for 50 years and was succeeded by his son, Ruaidrí.

Supported by his uncle, Muirchertach Ua Briain, in 1106 he was elected king of the O'Connor province of Connacht in western Ireland. Continuing to broaden his horizons, Toirrdelbach became ever more powerful. Then, when Muirchertach Ua Briain died in 1119, the Connacht king took advantage of the power vacuum created by his death. He gained more territory during the next 12 years, but was then pegged back.

On the offensive again from 1138, it was at this time that Toirrdelbach assumed the role of high king. He was challenged in his declining years by the Cenél nEógain ruler, Muirchertach Mac Lochlainn. A warrior-king on land and sea, who famously built castles and bridges, he died at the age of 68 and was buried at the holy site of Clonmacnois in County Offaly. Toirrdelbach Ua Conchobair was succeeded by his son Ruaidrí.

MAC LOCHLAINN, MUIRCHERTACH (D. 1166)

King of Cenél'nEógain; high king of all Ireland (1156–66). Ruling in Cenél nEógain from 1145, four years later he moved south from his kingdom in modern-day Donegal to invade Dublin. Then winning the support of the Leinster king, Diarmait Mac Murchadha, in 1156 he succeeded Toirrdelbach Ua Conchobair as high king. Subduing the threat posed by Toirrdelbach's son, Ruaidrí, in 1161, after he blinded the King of Ulaid (in the north of Ireland) an invasion force poured into Muirchertach's kingdom and killed him.

◆ *see* Diarmait Mac Murchada, Toirrdelbach Ua Conchobair

MAC MURCHADA, HOUSE OF

Reigning in the eastern province of Leinster, the Mac Murchada (or MacMurrough) stronghold was Ferns, County Wexford, and the surrounding area. It was there in the south of Leinster that the Uí Chennselaig lived. Periodically this tribe had provided Leinster with kings, but it was only with the emergence of Diarmait mac Máel na mBó in the eleventh century that the Uí Chennselaig took centre-stage again in Leinster.

Ninety years after this great ruler died, Diarmait Mac Murchadha (or Dermot MacMurrough) rose to power. Like his famous predecessor, he too was a member of the Uí Chennselaig clan, which had retained power throughout Leinster since the death of Diarmait mac Máel na mBó. Becoming king of Leinster in 1132 Diarmait Mac Murchadha was a Christian who founded religious houses such as the Augustinian abbey at Ferns (where he died in 1171), but he was also an ambitious, sometimes ruthless king who abducted the wife of the king of Bréifne and raped the abbess of a Kildare nunnery.

King until 1166, shortly after his great rival Muirchertach Mac Lochlainn became high king, the king of Bréifne took revenge on the man who had stolen his wife by driving Diarmait from Ferns and into exile. Eventually reclaiming his kingdom in 1170 with the help of his future son-in-law, Strongbow, he then died the following year.

Much later another Mac Murchada became king of Leinster. Ruling there from 1375, Art Mac Murchadha became a staunch opponent of Richard II. Aggrieved at having his wife's inheritance seized in 1391, three years later the English king responded by sailing to Ireland to force Art to back down. However, the Leinster ruler soon bounced back and by 1399 he was proclaiming himself to be the king of all Ireland.

▲ *ABOVE: Viking boats attacking the coast of Ireland*

MAC MURCHADHA, DIARMAIT (D. 1171)

King of Leinster (1132–66, 1170–71); also known as Dermot MacMurrough. He reigned from 1132 to 1166 and 1170 to 1171. Abducting Devorguilla in 1152, he was overthrown and banished in 1166, but returned to power in 1170 with the help of Strongbow and the support of Henry II. The founder of many religious houses, he has often been represented as a pro-English king.

Fighting his way to the kingship of Leinster by 1132, 12 years later the 'high king' Toirrdelbach Ua Conchobair divided up an area of land in Meath between Diarmait and the Bréifne king, Tigernán. In 1144 Diarmait abducted his rival's wife, Devorguilla). He continued to rule over Leinster for another two decades.

▲ ABOVE: Henry II agrees to help Diarmait Mac Murchada

Diarmait was a devoutly Christian king, who worked to reform the Irish Church and founded many religious houses. Secure in his kingdom until 1166, it was in that year that King Diarmait's world and his reputation were changed by a series of setbacks. The first of these was the death of the 'high king' Muirchertach Mac Lochlainn, the second was the selection of Ruaidrí Ua Conchobair instead of Diarmait as his successor. Immediately going on the warpath Ruaidrí took Dublin, while Tigernán forced Diarmait to leave Ferns (in County Wexford), the place the Leinster king had made his capital.

Leaving Ireland, he sailed to England, where he was soon given the permission of Henry II to raise an army to help him recover his kingdom. Partially successful in 1167, he returned three years later with a larger force, which included in its ranks Diarmait's future son-in-law and successor, Richard de Clare (alias Strongbow). Winning Waterford in August 1170, in September Dublin was recaptured. King of Leinster once more, the second reign of Diarmait Mac Murchadha lasted only a few months as he died early in 1171.

◆ *see* Henry II, Toirrdelbach Ua Conchobair

UA CONCHOBAIR, RUAIDRÍ (D. 1198)

King of Connacht (1156–85); the last high king of all Ireland and son of Toirrdelbach Ua Conchobair. Also known as Rory O'Connor, he succeeded his father in 1156. Ten years later, he became high king following the death of Muirchertach Mac Lochlainn. Driving out Diarmait MacMurrough, the Leinster king returned with Strongbow and other English forces. He acknowledged Henry II as overlord in 1175, but relinquished power in 1183 and was deposed in 1185 or 1186.

The heir of Toirrdelbach Ua Conchobair following the death of his brother, Conchobar, Ruaidrí became king following his father's death in 1156. Little is known about the first decade of the new ruler's reign, but by 1166 he was powerful enough to take over as high king of Ireland when Muirchertach Mac Lochlainn was killed in battle. Soon moving to defeat the threat of Leinster's king, Diarmait MacMurrough, when the exiled Diarmait tried to recover his lost kingdom he was beaten back.

Continuing to take the fight to Ruaidrí, the exiled Diarmait was supported by Henry II, who then campaigned in Ireland from September 1171. With nothing settled by fighting, in 1175 England's sovereign and the ruler of Connacht signed the Treaty of Windsor, which allowed Ruaidrí to rule in Connacht and keep his position as high king. For his part Ruaidrí recognised Henry as overlord and agreed to pay him a percentage of his income. However, as Henry had previously beaten the Irish Church and most of Ruaidrí's fellow Irish kings into submission, the appointment of his son, John, as Lord of Ireland marked the beginning of centuries of English rule in Ireland.

Retiring to a monastery in 1183, Ruaidrí attempted a comeback a short time later, but was permanently deposed in 1185 or 1186. Dying at an

◀ *LEFT: Henry II presents papal bull to Irish clergy*

Augustinian abbey at Cong in County Mayo, Ruaidrí Ua Conchobair was buried alongside his father at Clonmacnois in Offaly.

◆ *see* Toirrdelbach Ua Conchobair

UA CONCHOBAIR, CATHAL (D. 1224)

King of Connacht (1198–1224). Also known as Cathal O'Connor and nicknamed 'Crobderg' ('The Red-Handed'), he was the son of Toirrdelbach Ua Conchobair. Becoming king after the death of his brother Ruaidrí, he fought off challenges to hold power in Connacht until his death.

Possibly an illegitimate son of the great high king, Toirrdelbach Ua Conchobair, he struggled with his elder brother (or half-brother), Ruaidrí, for control in Connacht from 1189. He had to wait his turn, though, as the ruling king stood down in favour of his son, Conchobar. Finally becoming the Connacht ruler after Ruaidrí's death in 1198, during his reign he smoothed the way for the accession of his son by recognising King John's position as Irish overlord, but he resisted attacks by Richard de Burgh, the nephew of Henry III's regent. Cathal also fought the rebel, Hugh de Lacy, Earl of Ulster, in 1220 and again in the year of his death.

NÉILL, BRIAN (D. 1260)

King of Cenél nEógain (1238–60). Brian Néill was later proclaimed high king of all Ireland. He became ruler of the northern kingdom from 1238 and three years later he asserted his authority by attacking and defeating the Mac Lochlainn clan. Continuing to fight for supremacy in the north, the chief of the Uí Néills forged various alliances with native Irish leaders, which culminated in 1258 in his claim to be high king of Ireland. However, two years later Brian Néill was killed in the Battle of Down.

◆ *see* House of O'Neill

BRUCE, EDWARD (C. 1276–1318)

Brother of Robert the Bruce, Edward fought alongside his famous sibling at the Battle of Bannockburn in 1314. Appointed heir presumptive in Scotland in 1315, that same year he sailed to Ireland and there proclaimed himself king. He fought for three years to assert his claim, but was killed in battle in 1318 at Faughart near Dundalk, the town where he had won his first major success on Irish soil just three years before.

◆ *see* House of Bruce, Robert Bruce, House of O'Neill

NÉILL, DOMHNALL (D. 1325)

King of Cenél nEógain; also known as Donal O'Neill. This son of Brian Néill had three spells as king.

First claiming power in 1283 following the death of his father's successor, Buidhe Néill, his initial reign lasted three years. King again in 1291, after 1296 he reigned unopposed until losing territory to the 'Red Earl', the powerful Richard de Burgh. Then linking up with Edward Bruce in 1315, he supported the brother of Robert the Bruce in his bid to become king in Ireland. However, after the death of Edward at the Battle of Faughart in 1318, retribution soon followed and Domhnall was deposed. Recovering some territory in the years that followed, he died in 1325.

◆ *see* Edward Bruce

MAC MURCHADHA, ART (D. C. 1416)

King of Leinster (1370s–1416); also known as Art MacMurrough. He ruled in eastern Ireland from the 1370s until his death. An enemy of Richard II, after Art's marriage to the heiress, Elizabeth Calf, the English king attacked in 1394. Conceding defeat, the Leinsterman refused to give up his lands and so retained his independence despite a fresh English attack in 1399.

◆ *see* Richard II

AD 834–1034 House of Mac Alpin
AD 834   Death of Alpin
AD 858   Death of Kenneth I Mac Alpin
AD 862   Death of Donald I
AD 877   Death of Constantine I
AD 900   Death of Donald II
AD 952   Death of Constantine II
AD 954   Death of Malcolm I
AD 971   Death of Kenneth II
1034   Death of Malcolm II
1034–1371 House of Dunkeld
1040   Death of Duncan I
1057   Death of Macbeth
1093   Death of Malcolm III
1099   Death of Donald III
1107   Death of Edgar
1124   Death of Alexander I
1153   Death of David I
1165   Death of Malcolm IV
1214   Death of William I The Lion
1249   Death of Alexander II
1286   Death of Alexander III
1290   Death of Margaret
House of Balliol
1313   Death of John Balliol
1364   Death of Edward Balliol
House of Bruce
1329   Death of Robert I the Bruce
1371   Death of David II
1371–1567 House of Stuart (later Stuart)
1390   Death of Robert II
1406   Death of Robert III
1437   Death of James I
1460   Death of James II
1488   Death of James III
1513   Death of James IV
1542   Death of James V
1587   Death of Mary, Queen of Scots
1625   Death of James I (James IV of
          Scotland)

ALPIN (D. C. 834)

King of the Scots of Dalriada; possibly the son of Eochaid. The territory of Dalriada encompassed modern-day Argyll, Kintyre and various west-coast islands, and here Alpin reigned for approximately three years. He was killed around AD 834 while on a raiding mission in Galloway. Little is known about Alpin (or Alpín), the Scottish royal who was reputedly the father of Kenneth mac Alpin, the man who later ruled over Dalriada and the former kingdom of the Picts.

▲ *ABOVE: Eochaid, Kenneth I mac Alpin*

◀▶ *see* Eochaid, Kenneth I mac Alpin

KENNETH I MAC ALPIN (D. C. AD 858)

King of the Scots (AD 840–58); son of Alpin. Also known as Cinaed mac Alpín, in AD 843–47 the ruler of the Scots of Dalriada defeated the Picts and formed the new nation of Alba. At a time of persistent Viking raids, little is known about his life or reign, but his descendants flourished. Succeeded by his brother, Donald I, later kings included Kenneth's sons, Constantine I and Aed.

He was an all-conquering king, who ruled over Dalriada from AD 841 and united the Scots and the Picts. With Pictish ancestry of his own, King Kenneth I took seven years to bring the Picts' land under his control within a united kingdom known as Alba or Scotia.

Leading Alba in its fight against Viking assaults, Kenneth moved the centre of his operations from the west to new fortresses at Forteviot,

Dunkeld and Scone where, legend has it, Kenneth I mac Alpin set the sacred coronation stone in AD 850. Moved from Dunstaffnage Castle to Scone, there the stone remained until, more than three centuries later, it was removed by England's warrior-king, Edward I, and taken south to Westminster Abbey.

The father of Constantine I and King Aed, Kenneth I died at Forteviot and was succeeded by his brother, Donald I.

▲ *ABOVE: Edward I steals the stone from Scone*

☼ *see* Aed, Constantine II, Donald II

DONALD I (D. AD 862)

King of the Scots (AD 858–62), son of Alpin. Donald (or Domnall) succeeded his brother, Kenneth I mac Alpin, and reigned for about four years. His appearance was unfavourably described by some medieval writers, who looked more favourably on his record as ruler instead. Consolidating the gains won by his predecessor, he died near Scone. Perhaps struck down by illness, or possibly murdered, Donald I's death saw power pass to Kenneth mac Alpin's son, Constantine I.

☼ *see* Kenneth I mac Alpin, Constantine I

CONSTANTINE I (D. C. AD 877)

King of the Scots and Picts (AD 863–77); also known as Constantin. The son of Kenneth mac Alpin and the brother of Aed, Constantine became king in AD 863 after the death of his uncle, Donald I. He spent much of his reign fending off a stream of Viking attacks. He was able to extend his realm southwards, claiming Strathclyde in AD 871 or 872 following the murder of his own brother-in-law, Artgal (whose death Constantine may have ordered). By this time the dominant ruler in central and southern Scotland, Constantine I did not always use force to get the better of his enemies and often preferred

▲ *ABOVE: Constantine I and St Helen*

to buy peace. In AD 875 he was defeated by Halfdan, a Viking enemy of Alfred the Great, who was then launching raids from Northumbria. Two years later Constantine again locked horns with Norse warriors, but was killed in action at Inverdovat on Tayside. His death sparked a power struggle in Scotland that was to last for more than two decades, but his immediate successor was his little-known brother, Aed, while his son reigned later as Donald II.

◼ *see* Aed, Donald II, Kenneth mac Alpin

AED (D. AD 878)

King of the Picts and Scots (AD 877–78). Aed, sometimes known as Aed the Furious, or Whitefoot, was the son of Kenneth mac Alpin. He was the brother of Constantine I, who he succeeded as king of the Scots and Picts. Aed reigned for barely a year before he was killed, while in the Strathallan region, by his cousin, Giric. The murdered monarch was succeeded by Giric, who may have ruled jointly with Aed's nephew, Eochaid.

🔹 *see* Constantine I, Eochaid, Kenneth I mac Alpin

EOCHAID (D. C. AD 879)

King of the Scots (AD 878–79); grandson of Kenneth mac Alpin and son of the Strathclyde ruler, Rhun. Succeeding his father as king of the Britons of Strathclyde, Eochaid may or may not have become king of the Scots following the murder of Aed in AD 878. Possibly sharing the duties of kingship with Giric in the Scots' kingdom, the fortunes of Eochaid after the accession of Donald II in AD 879 are not known.

🔹 *see* Donald II, Aed, Kenneth mac Alpin

DONALD II (D. AD 900)

King of Scotland (AD 889–900); son of Constantine I. Also referred to as Domnall II, Donald II was the first man to be described by chroniclers as Ri Alban (King of Scotland). Although he was monarch for 11 years, little is known about his reign. He was succeeded by his cousin, Constantine II.

Facts concerning the reign of Donald II are scarce, but some historians believe that he succeeded the co-rulers Eóchaid and Giric, the latter being sent into exile by the new king. However, if Donald successfully established himself as chief of the Scots and the Picts, he made little impact further north, as his reign coincided with the rise to power of the Orkney-based Viking known as Earl Sigurd the Mighty.

Donald was possibly murdered at Dunnottar, near Stonehaven on Scotland's east coast; legend has it that the body of the first king of Scotland was buried on the island of Iona.

◆ *see* Constantine I

CONSTANTINE II (D. C. AD 952)

King of Scotland (AD 900–43). Constantine II fought against Viking

▲ *ABOVE: Constantine II*

raiders during his reign and was twice defeated by Athelstan of England. By retaining inherited lands and conquering new territory he became the first Scottish ruler to hold power south of the Forth river.

There was no Scottish crown in AD 900, but Constantine's accession ceremony took place on Moot Hill at Scone. With the stone of destiny (which was to become such a potent symbol of Scottish national pride) a centrepiece of the ceremony, the new king was 'married' to the land. His bloodline was recited and members of the nobility swore their allegiance to the new sovereign.

In the often troubled reign that followed, Constantine II had to contend with a series of Viking raids, but in AD 937 he joined forces with Olaf, king of Dublin's Norsemen, and with Strathclyde's ruler, King Owen. However, this alliance of kings was comprehensively routed at the Battle of Brunanburh by Athelstan. This defeat, at the end of a day-long battle fought on an unknown site, led to Constantine II offering his second 'submission' to the victorious Athelstan. Ten years earlier he had bowed down before the English king following his invasion of Northumbria.

Defeat at Brunanburh and his subsequent submission proved to be the last notable events of Constantine's reign as he abdicated in about AD 943. During his reign, though, he had successfully consolidated his kingdom, extending its borders into Strathclyde and Lothian. He lived out the rest of his life in a monastery at St Andrews, Fife.

◆ *see* Athelstan, Malcolm I

MALCOLM I (D. AD 954)

King of Scotland (AD 942–54); son of Donald II; also known as Mael Coluim I. Malcolm succeeded his cousin, Constantine II, and two years later he concluded a deal with Edmund of England, in which they agreed that Malcolm I would retain sovereignty over Strathclyde and Cumbria, lands that Edmund had previously invaded.

Forced like his predecessors to tackle the threat of Viking attacks, Malcolm's main foe was Eric Bloodaxe. However, the king of the Scots was killed not by Norsemen, but by the natives of Moray, a region he had earlier captured. Although he was the father of King Dub and Kenneth II, he was succeeded on his death by his cousin, Indulf.

◆ *see* Constantine II, Donald II

INDULF (D. AD 962)

King of Scots (AD 954–62); son of Constantine II. Indulf succeeded his cousin, Malcolm I, in AD 954 thanks to the tanistry system, which saw monarchs elected from the male successors of Indulf's own father and those of Donald II. He was previously ruler of the sub-kingdom of Strathclyde, and during his eight-year reign as king of the Scots their kingdom was enlarged. Parts of Lothian were annexed, while one of Indulf's last conquests was the city of Edinburgh. Killed in AD 962 by Vikings, he was succeeded by Dub, who had earlier replaced him in Strathclyde. However, Dub's reign was brief as he was killed, possibly by Indulf's son, Culen.

▲ ABOVE: Indulf

◆ see Constantine II, Culen, Malcolm I

DUB (D. C. AD 966)

King of the Scots (AD 962–c. 966); son of Malcolm I. Dub (also known as Dubh or Duff) succeeded the murdered King Indulf in AD 962, but came to a grisly end himself just four years later. Kidnapped by a band of assassins Dub's corpse was discovered in a ditch at Kinross on the banks of Loch Leven. He was succeeded as king of the Scots by Culen, the shadowy son of Indulf and the man alleged to have ordered the murder of King Dub.

◆ see Culen, Malcolm I

CULEN (D. AD 971)

King of Scotland (AD 966–71); son of King Indulf. Sometimes referred to as Cuílán the Whelp, like his father Culen also came to a bloody end. He was murdered in Lothian in AD 971 by Rhydderch, the king of Strathclyde. Enthroned only five years earlier, Culen was said by some to have been the man who ordered the capture and murder of his predecessor, King Dub, while his own death avenged the earlier murder of Rhydderch's brother and the abduction or rape of the Strathclyde ruler's daughter. After this spate of revenge-seeking was over, Culen was succeeded by the new king of Alba: Kenneth II.

◆ *see* Dub, Kenneth III

KENNETH II (D. AD 995)

King of the Scots (AD 971–95); son of Malcolm I. Also known as Cinaed II, he succeeded Culen who was murdered in AD 971. Ceded Lothian by Edgar of England, his reign was marked by the royal in-fighting that probably cost Kenneth II his life. The father of Malcolm II he was succeeded by Constantine III.

Becoming king in AD 973, Kenneth II bowed down before Edgar at Chester, his reward for recognising the English king as overlord being the valuable territory of Lothian. Such a deal with a southern sovereign cut little ice closer to home, however, as his 24-year reign was scarred by the fight to choose a successor. His life came to a brutal, if mysterious end in AD 995

▲ *ABOVE: Kenneth II*

37

Possibly killed on the orders of his successor, Constantine III, one tale tells of how the king was killed as an act of revenge by the mother of a son that Kenneth II had killed. This noblewoman named Finvela was said to have lured Kenneth to her home by telling him that she would there unveil a band of men who had betrayed their monarch.

However, after a drunken feast, Finvela led the king to a room containing a statue. On this statue was placed a golden apple, which Finvela offered up as a token of peace. Accepting this gift, as Kenneth II plucked the apple from the statue he unwittingly triggered his own death, for the apple had been connected to a series of hidden crossbows; the bolts they fired killing the unlucky king.

◆ *see* Constantine III, Culen, Malcolm I

CONSTANTINE III (D. AD 997)

King of Scotland (AD 995–97). This son of Culen, also known as Constantine the Bald, probably came to power in AD 995 following the death, in suspicious circumstances, of his distant relative, Kenneth II. Sometimes cited as the man behind Kenneth's demise, Constantine III reigned for just 18 months before he too was killed. The sixth successive Scottish monarch to die a violent death, his murder may have been ordered by Kenneth III, the man who next ascended the throne.

◆ *see* Culen, Kenneth II, Kenneth III

KENNETH III (D. 1005)

King of the Scots (AD 997–1005). In the violent world of eleventh-century politics he who lived by the sword often died by the sword. Thus, Kenneth III, who was implicated in the death of his predecessor, Constantine III, was himself killed by an enemy force led by Kenneth's own successor,

Malcolm II. Ruling from AD 997 to 1005, Kenneth, the grandson of Malcolm I and the son of King Dub, died in battle alongside his son, Giric.

⬕ *see* Constantine III, Malcolm II

MALCOLM II (C. AD 954–1034)

King of Scotland (1005–34); son of Kenneth II; also known as Mael Coluim II. In 1005 Malcolm killed Kenneth III and seized his throne to become king of the Scots a decade after the death of his father and ruled for 29 years.

Three years after his ascension, Malcolm's daughter married the Norse Earl of Orkney, Sigurd the Stout. With Sigurd's realm encompassing Caithness, Sutherland and the Western Isles, this marriage effectively extended the influence of the Scots, particularly in the Western Isles, where the Norse inhabitants had remained largely outside the control of either Scottish or Scandinavian kings for more than 100 years.

In 1018 Malcolm II seized Lothian and Strathclyde by routing the army led by his long-standing enemy, Earl Uhtred. The Northumbrian had put together a fighting force of English and Viking warriors, but at the Battle of Carham, by the banks of the River Tweed, Malcolm and his ally, Owen the Bald of Strathclyde, won the day. Later King Owen's death enabled the Scots monarch to establish his rule in Strathclyde, while the Northumbrian land of Lothian also came under his complete control.

▲ *ABOVE: Malcolm II*

39

Hailed by his fellow Scots as the 'honour of all the west of Europe', it was only in his last years that Malcolm II suffered a major setback, when an attack by Cnut in 1027 forced the king of the Scots to recognise Cnut as his overlord. He died seven years later from injuries sustained in battle. Malcolm II was succeeded by Duncan I, the son of his daughter, Bethoc.

◖ *see* Cnut, Duncan I, Kenneth I, Kenneth II

DUNCAN I (C. 1010–40)

King of Scotland (1034–40); grandson of Malcolm II; also known as Donnchad I. Duncan I was the son of Crinan, the Abbot of Dunkeld, and Bethóc, the daughter of Malcolm II. He succeeded Owen the Bald as king of Strathclyde in 1018. Married to a cousin of the Earl of Northumbria, Duncan I became king of the Scots after the murder of his grandfather by rivals in the Scottish royal family. His accession signalled the end of tanistry in Scotland. An often divisive system, choosing a future king from within the royal

▶ *RIGHT: Duncan I*

ranks became a thing of the past once Duncan, Malcolm's nominated heir, succeeded to the throne unopposed.

Young and ambitious, the new king's forays to north and south gained him little, with even his siege of Durham in 1139 proving unsuccessful. Heading north in 1040, in Moray the king met his nemesis: Macbeth. Caught up in a feud that had claimed lives in both men's families, Duncan's raid on Macbeth's home territory ensured that still more blood would be spilt. In the skirmish, Duncan I was mortally wounded, leaving Macbeth as the new king.

◆ see Macbeth, Malcolm II

MACBETH (1005–57)

King of Scotland (1040–57). Immortalised by William Shakespeare in his play of the same name, Macbeth killed and then succeeded Duncan I. The son of Findlaech of Moray in North-East Scotland, Macbeth's mother was a sister of Malcolm II. Coming to power in Moray in 1032, his marriage to Gruoch further strengthened his hand, as she was the granddaughter of Malcolm II. Soon caught up in a struggle for power with the new king, Duncan I, the Mormaer (or king) of Moray eventually killed his enemy when Duncan led a raiding party into Macbeth's home territory in 1040.

▲ ABOVE: Macbeth

But Macbeth was unable to rest on his laurels and during a battle fought in 1045 King Macbeth killed Duncan's father, Abbot Crinan. There were more challenges to face, however, not least those launched by Duncan's sons, the future kings, Malcolm III and Donald III. Nevertheless Macbeth still felt confident enough to make a pilgrimage to Rome. But then at Dunsinane in 1054, his forces, bolstered by Norman recruits, were routed by the combined English, Scandinavian and Scottish armies led by the Northumbrian Earl Siward. Suffering such a crushing defeat deep in the heart of his kingdom, Macbeth could only look on in dismay as the eldest son of Duncan I, Siward's nephew, Malcolm, was installed as ruler in Lothian and Strathclyde.

The net was closing in on the king and in 1057 Malcolm launched the fateful strike that claimed his life at Lumphanan to the west of Aberdeen. Avenging Duncan's death, Malcolm III Canmore did not become king until 1058 when Macbeth's stepson and successor, Lulach, was killed.

◘ *see* Lulach, Malcolm III

LULACH (D. 1058)

King of Scotland (1057–58); stepson of Macbeth and the son of Macbeth's wife, Gruoch, by her first marriage to Gillacomean. Also known as Gille Comgáin, he was a cousin of Macbeth and, until his death in 1032, the Mormaer (or Earl) of Moray. Twenty-five years later his son, Lulach, was proclaimed king of the Scots at Scone following Macbeth's murder, but his reign was ended almost before it had begun. Ambushed in 1058 at Essie in the Strathbogie region to the north-west of Aberdeen, the young king was killed by his successor, Malcolm III.

◘ *see* Macbeth, Malcolm III

▶ RIGHT: Lulach

MALCOLM III (C. 1031–93)

Kings of Scots (1058–93); son of Duncan I; also known as Mael Coluim III Cenn Mór (or Bighead). Malcolm III had been king of Strathclyde before he murdered his father's archenemy, Macbeth, and Macbeth's stepson, Lulach, to claim the throne in 1058. By 1069 Malcolm III was firmly established as Scotland's king. In that year he married the Wessex princess, Margaret, his second wife. Margaret was a granddaughter of Edmund Ironside and a sister of England's would-be king, Edgar the Atheling. A learned and devoutly Christian woman, Scotland's queen set about reforming the Scottish Church at the same time as her husband was fighting to win land in northern England. She was sanctified in 1250.

Attacking Northumbria in 1070, Malcolm braced himself for the retaliatory attack he knew would come. Pushing north, the soldiers of William I swept aside all opposition, eventually forcing the humiliated Scottish king to concede defeat to the Normans. Bowing down before William at Abernethy, near Perth in 1072, the king of the Scots then looked on helplessly as England's king rode south with two prize hostages: Malcolm's son, Duncan, and his brother-in-law, Edgar the Atheling.

Malcolm, however, refused to give up the struggle and launched assaults on Northumbria in 1079 and again in 1090. This last attack provoked England's new king, William II, and he marched into Scottish territory during 1092. Malcolm then launched yet another attack the following year, but was killed in an ambush by Arkil Morel, the nephew of Robert Mowbray, Earl of Northumberland. Also killed was Edward, the king's eldest son, while Queen Margaret died a short time later, reputedly of a broken heart. A great, long-reigning monarch, Malcolm III was succeeded by his brother, Donald III.

▲ *ABOVE: Malcolm III*

☐ *see* Duncan I, Donald III, Lulach, Macbeth

DONALD III (C. 1031–99)

King of Scotland (1093–97); son of Duncan I. The younger brother of Malcolm III, Donald (known as Donald Ban), had ascended the throne left vacant by Malcolm's murder. Donald had been in exile at the time of his brother's death and on hearing of it he leapt into the breach. He was already an old man, however, and found that retaining power was more difficult than seizing it. His right to the throne was soon challenged by Duncan, Malcolm's son by his first wife, and in 1094 the younger man successfully ousted Donald. However, later that year Duncan was murdered, most likely on the orders of Donald. The death of his usurper allowed Donald to reclaim the throne.

▲ ABOVE: Malcolm is hunting when a serf complains that his daughter has been raped

Dividing his kingdom in two, Edmund, a half-brother of Duncan, was appointed to help him govern. But then in 1097 yet another son of Malcolm III and Margaret stole Donald's crown. This time there was no way back. Cruelly blinded and imprisoned by the new king, Edgar, the forlorn figure of Donald Ban died in 1099. He is believed to have been laid to rest on Iona – the last in a long line of Scottish kings to be buried on the Inner Hebridean island.

◆ see Duncan I, Duncan II, Malcolm III

DUNCAN II (C. 1060–94)

King of Scotland (1094); son of Malcolm III by his first wife, Ingeborg. Duncan II spent his childhood as a hostage in England; after 22 years in exile he returned to his native land to claim the Scottish crown worn for so long by his father. The English king, William II, provided Duncan with an army and with this support behind him, the challenger succeeded in overthrowing his uncle, Donald III Ban, in May 1094. However, he enjoyed the briefest of reigns. On 12 November 1094, just six months after he became king, Duncan II was murdered and Donald, the likely orchestrator of his death, became Scotland's sovereign for the second time.

◆ see Normans, Donald III

EDGAR (1074–1107)

King of Scotland (1097–1107); Edgar was the fourth son of Malcolm III and Margaret and great-grandson of England's Edmund II. He is reputed to have been a generous ruler, and a strong supporter of the Church.

Edgar first came to the fore in 1095, when the English king, William II, declared himself to be Scotland's overlord and Edgar to be the country's king. In 1097, with an army paid for by William II and led by his uncle, Edgar the Atheling, Edgar won a decisive battle at Rescobie, to the east of

Forfar. Defeating, overthrowing and blinding the reigning Scottish sovereign, Donald III, Edgar claimed the throne and remained there for the next decade. Links with England were maintained during this period and, in November 1100, his sister Matilda married the newly crowned English king, Henry I. On the negative side, Iona, the ancestral burial ground of Scottish kings, was given up, while Norway's Magnus Barelegs captured the Western Isles.

Edgar died in 1107 and was buried at Dunfermline. He was succeeded by his younger brother, Alexander I.

◆ see Alexander I, Donald III, Edgar the Atheling, Henry I, William II

ALEXANDER I (C. 1077–1124)

King of the Scots (1107–24). One of four sons of Malcolm III to be crowned, Alexander I earned the nickname Alexander the Fierce by taming northern clans. In 1100 a younger sister married England's Henry I, thus Alexander I became the English king's brother-in-law and subsequently his son-in-law when he married one of Henry's illegitimate daughters, Sibylla.

Ascending the throne in 1107, following the death of his half brother, Edgar, his realm included central and eastern lands south of the Spey river and South Scotland where, grudgingly, he allowed his brother, David, to hold sway. A

▶ RIGHT: Alexander I

devoutly Christian monarch, he supported the Scottish Church in its efforts to fight the combined threats posed by paganism and the English archbishops at Canterbury and York. The king's 17-year reign ended with his death in 1124. Scotland's crown passed to Alexander's younger brother, David I.

◄ *see* David I, Henry I, Malcolm III

DAVID I (C. 1084–1153)

King of Scotland (1124–53); son of Malcolm III. David I succeeded his brother, Alexander I, in 1124 and extended his kingdom farther south than any previous Scottish king.

The youngest son of Malcolm III and his second wife, Margaret, David was still a child when both his father and mother died in 1093. He therefore spent much of his youth in England, where he became an important and powerful landowner. He also gained the earldoms of Northampton and Huntingdon by virtue of his marriage to the widow Maud. His sister, Edith (also known as Matilda or Maud), married Henry I, while another sister, Mary, wed the Count of Boulogne and gave birth to a daughter, who married the man who would later become King Stephen of England. However, despite his many English connections, David returned to his native country during the reign of his elder sibling, Alexander I, and he continued the tradition of all heirs to the Scottish throne by ruling southern Scotland.

▲ *ABOVE: David I*

David shared many of his brother's qualities and as king was a modernising force in Scottish affairs. He introduced new, Norman methods to Scotland's government and to the judiciary and he encouraged trade, agriculture and education. Under David many churches and abbeys were built and monastic orders flourished. Anglo-Normans were appointed to bishoprics old and new and Norman families settled in Scotland, among them the de Brus (later Bruce), de Bailleul (Balliol) and fitzAlan (or Fitzalan) clans.

David also generally managed to maintain good relations with England. During the civil wars between Stephen and Matilda he recognised Matilda's claim to the English throne and in 1138 he was

▲ ABOVE: The Norman Priory on Holy Island, Northumberland

beaten by Stephen at the Battle of the Standard, which was fought on Cowton Moor, near Northallerton. Eleven years later, though, he gained English lands stretching from Tyneside to the Tees.

David died in May 1153, outliving his son and heir by a year. The throne passed to his grandson, Malcolm IV.

➲ see House of Balliol, House of Bruce, Henry I, Malcolm IV, Matilda, Robert I, Stephen, Alexander I

MALCOLM IV (1141–65)

King of Scots (1153–65); grandson of David I; also known as Mael Coluim IV and nicknamed Malcolm the Maiden. Malcolm succeeded his grandfather in 1153 at the age of 11.

Malcolm was the son of Henry, Earl of Northumbria, who was David's acknowledged heir from 1144. Malcolm rose to become king of the Scots after the deaths in quick succession first of his father in 1152 and then of his grandfather just a year later. The accession of a minor caused a flurry of activity in Scotland. The Norwegian king attacked Aberdeen and there were other attacks and uprisings in other parts of the kingdom.

Order was eventually restored, but in 1157 England's new king, Henry II, ordered Malcolm IV to return lands in Cumbria and Northumbria to him. As part of the deal, Henry made Malcolm the Earl of Huntingdon. A devout Christian who died unmarried, Malcolm the Maiden reigned for 12 years before his death brought to the throne his brother, William I 'the Lion'.

➲ see Henry II, William I, David I

WILLIAM I THE LION (C. 1142–1214)

King of Scotland (1165–1214); grandson of David I. The younger son of Henry, Earl of Northumbria, William was just a child when his father died and his elder brother was crowned Malcolm IV. Then, when Malcolm died young, in 1165 William ascended the Scottish throne. Promptly agreeing a deal with France to forge what would later come to be known as the Auld Alliance, the new king of the Scots did not make his first attack on England until 1174. After a disastrous assault led by William himself, at Alnwick in Northumbria, the Lion-King was tamed. Taken prisoner by his enemy, he was then led away to meet Henry II in Normandy, where he was made to sign the Treaty of Falaise, a treaty that completed William's humiliation.

Surrendering the independence of the kingdom and its church, further crushing blows were dealt to the Scots by the enforced garrisoning of castles and the concession of Northumbria to English rule. Eventually William I regained control of his realm, but before that occurred he had to put down uprisings led by Scottish rebels. In Galloway, in the south-west of the country, there were insurrections, while a sustained attack on William's crown was led by Donald MacWilliam. A descendant of Malcolm III Canmore and his wife, Ingeborg, his challenge was not extinguished until he was put to death in 1187.

Two years after the death of Donald MacWilliam, the king of the Scots, William I the Lion, entered into a deal with England's new king, Richard I the Lionheart. Needing money to fund a crusade, in an agreement known as the Quitclaim of Canterbury, Richard agreed to give Scotland back its independence and its castles in exchange for 10,000 marks. Finally freed from English oppression, William I enjoyed 25 more years as king, his death in 1214 coming just two years after he had defeated and killed Donald MacWilliam's son, Guthred. Married to Ermengarde de Beaumont from 1085, William was succeeded by their son, Alexander II.

◆ *see* Alexander II, David I, Malcolm IV

ALEXANDER II (1198–1249)

King of the Scots (1214–49). The only legitimate son of William the Lion, who he succeeded in 1214, Alexander's early reign was dominated by raids on England, with King John retaliating by invading Lothian. Later, Scotland's sovereign married John's daughter, Joan, but the union produced no children. Queen Joan died in 1238, one year after Scotland and England had signed the Treaty of York. Alexander took his second wife, Marie de Courcy, in 1239. Their son succeeded to the throne as Alexander III in 1249.

▲ *ABOVE: Alexander II*

Born at Haddington in Lothian, the son of William the Lion and Ermengarde de Beaumont, Alexander II ascended the throne on the death of his father in 1214, at the age of just 16. Three years later he signed an Anglo-Scottish treaty and on 19 June 1221 the seal was put on this treaty with Alexander's marriage to England's Princess Joan, the eldest daughter of John and the sister of the new English monarch, Henry III. A Christian king, Alexander promoted the Scottish Church, founded abbeys and built castles. The man King John called the 'red fox cub' was also said to have ordered the brutal maiming of 80 men who had been witnesses to the murder of a Caithness bishop; each man had his hands and feet hacked off.

Alexander II strove to assert his authority in the north (Caithness and Moray), west (Argyll) and south-west (Galloway), made a vain bid to purchase the Hebrides and the kingdom of Man from Norway and, in 1237, put his name to the Treaty of York, an attempt to end border disputes. The new borderline between Scotland and England stretched from Gretna in the west to just north of Berwick in the east. The agreement saw Alexander renounce his claim to Northumbria and Westmorland in exchange for money and other territories.

Ten years later, while on his way to attack Viking settlers on the Western Isles, Alexander II fell ill with a fever. Dying on the island of Kerrera on 8 July 1249, he was buried at Melrose Abbey.

◆ *see* Alexander III, Henry III, John

ALEXANDER III (1241–86)

King of the Scots (1249–86). Only eight years old when he inherited Scotland's crown from his father, Alexander II, two years later the boy-king married Princess Margaret of England. The passing of Margaret in

▲ *ABOVE: Alexander III is rescued from the fury of a stag*

1275 was followed by the deaths of two sons and his daughter Margaret, the mother of his successor, Margaret the Maid.

Born at Roxburgh in 1241, by the time Alexander was 10 years old he was king of the Scots and married to Margaret, the eldest daughter of Henry III. The wedding took place in York on 26 December 1251. Sending an army to attack Norse settlers in the Hebrides, in 1263 the Scots engaged Haakon of Norway's forces at the west-coast port of Largs. Three years later the Treaty of Perth saw Norway hand over control of the Hebrides to Scotland's king.

Alexander fell out with his English in-laws in 1278, but good relations were restored when Alexander agreed to pay homage to his brother-in-law, Edward I. In 1283 relations with Norway improved when Alexander's daughter, Margaret, married Haakon's grandson, King Eric II. Then, just as the Scots were beginning to reap the benefits of their sovereign's largely successful rule, the king was killed. On 18 March 1286, while riding home from Edinburgh to his second wife, Yolande (also known as Joleta) of Dreux, the king's horse fell, throwing its royal rider to his death. With all three of Alexander's children and his first wife having predeceased him, this fatal accident brought to the throne the late king's infant granddaughter, Margaret.

◀ see Edward I, Henry III, Margaret

MARGARET (1283–90)

Queen of Scotland (1286–90); granddaughter of Alexander III; known as 'the Maid of Norway'. The daughter of Eric, King of Norway, and Margaret, daughter of Alexander III, Margaret was still a baby when she was acknowledged as heir to the Scottish throne after a series of deaths in the royal family put her first in line. The first wife of Alexander III, his two sons and then Margaret's mother had all died before the king himself passed away.

She was still an infant at the time of her grandfather's death in March 1286, but the Maid of Norway was soon the subject of a marriage deal proposed by England's sovereign, Edward, suggesting that little Margaret be married to his own young son, the future Edward II. The proposal was ratified by the signing of the Treaty of Birgham in 1290.

Sadly, though, Scotland's queen-in-waiting did not live long enough to marry her English prince. Sailing from her Norwegian home to Scotland the seven-year-old Margaret got no further than the Orkneys before she died. The death of the young girl caused Scotland to be thrown into a state of turmoil and it was not until 1291 that Margaret's successor, John Balliol, was appointed by Edward I, the man who, had she lived long enough, would have become her father-in-law.

◆ *see* John Balliol, Edward I, Edward II, Alexander III, Alexander II

BALLIOL, HOUSE OF

Originally the de Bailleul family of Picardy, France, the Balliol émigrés who settled in the British Isles following the Norman Conquest became wealthy and influential members of the Scottish nobility. With estates in both Scotland and England, it was during the twelfth century that the Scots' king, David I, had given lands north of the border to Bernard de Bailleul. Firmly established by the reign of William the Lion, in 1174, at the Battle of Alnwick, Bernard 'The Younger' Balliol tamed the lion. Handed over to England's Henry II, William was then forced to sign the Treaty of Falaise, which acknowledged English suzerainty over Scotland.

A man of substance, Bernard Balliol was the grandfather of John. His father's namesake, the younger John Balliol flourished in the middle years of the thirteenth century, when he was one of the most powerful landowners of the period. Married to Devorguilla (Dearbhfhorghaill), the daughter of Alan, Lord of Galloway, when the minor Alexander III ascended the throne, John Balliol was one of the regents appointed to rule Scotland. Accused of treason in 1255 John was forced to give up his vast estates, but by siding with Henry III against Simon de Montfort he regained his former status.

In 1263 John founded a college at Oxford University as a penance. After her husband's death in 1269 John's widow donated further funds to Balliol College and it still bears the family name more than seven centuries later. Living until 1290 Devorguilla suffered the loss of two sons during her lifetime, but a third boy lived long enough to become king of the Scots.

Nominated as Scottish monarch by Edward I of England, John Balliol endured a short and difficult reign. Caught between the Scottish nobility and the English monarchy, the king, later derided by Scots as Toom Tabard ('Empty Coat'), made his last stand in 1296. Beaten by the English at Berwick in March of the same year, four months later England's forces were established as an army of occupation and at Montrose on 10 July John Balliol was dethroned.

However, the demotion of Toom Tabard did not mark the end of the Balliol dynasty as, in 1332, the former king's son, Edward, succeeded David II as king of the Scots. John Balliol's eldest boy, like his father, Edward Balliol, relied heavily on English support in his bid to win Scotland's crown. Beating the king's regent in battle on Dupplin Moor in August 1332, six weeks later Edward was crowned at Scone. No sooner was his

▶ RIGHT: *John of Balliol's Seal*

coronation concluded, however, than Edward Balliol was forced into exile. Returned to the throne in 1334, the following year he was ousted once more. Continuing to lead various raids in his attempt to regain power, in 1346 he fought his way to Glasgow. But the tide had turned and Edward was doomed never again to rule in Scotland, although the second and last Balliol king of the Scots did not finally renounce his claim to the throne until 1356.

◆ *see* Edward Balliol, John Balliol, David II Edward I, Henry III

BALLIOL, JOHN (C. 1250–1313)

King of the Scots (1291–96). A leading candidate for the Scottish crown after the death of Margaret the Maid in 1290, John Balliol was appointed king of the Scots by the English king, Edward I.

A son of John and Devorguilla (Dearbhfhorghaill) Balliol, the deaths of his father and elder brothers led to John's inheritance of large estates in both Scotland and England. John was married to Isabelle, the daughter of the Earl of Surrey, and their son, Edward Balliol, was to fight an intermittent battle for the Scots' crown between 1332–56. In 1290, however, John Balliol was one of more than a dozen contenders for Scotland's throne and as tensions surfaced and infighting broke out amongst the clans, the Scottish lords called on Edward I of England to choose their nation's next monarch. A meeting was called and in November 1291 the English king announced that John Balliol would be Scotland's next sovereign.

Crowned at Scone in 1292, from the first the new king struggled. Torn between his demanding English master and his resentful subjects, in 1294 John Balliol rejected a summons to join Edward on a campaign against England's old enemy, France. He compounded this rejection by signing a treaty with the French. Two years later, in 1296, he declined to pay homage to Edward: the consequences of this insubordination were swift and savage. Marching north with a large army, Edward the 'Hammer of the Scots' struck the first of several blows. In November 1291 Berwick had been the setting for the grand assembly at which Edward I conferred kingship on John Balliol, but five years later the city was razed to the ground by English forces. Continuing northwards, Edward's army reached the eastern seaport of Dunbar, where it inflicted a humiliating defeat on the Scottish king and his supporters.

Stripped of his crown, John Balliol was sent to the Tower of London while Edward I continued his victory procession through the Scottish heartland. Held prisoner in the Tower for three years, eventually John Balliol was placed in papal custody and returned to his ancestral homeland in Picardy, France, where he died in 1313.

◆ see House of Balliol, Edward Balliol, Constantine III, Edward I

▲ ABOVE: John Balliol surrenders his crown to Edward at Kincardine, Scotland

BRUCE, HOUSE OF

Descendents of the de Brus family of Bruis (Brix), near Cherbourg, France. It was in the early years after the Norman Conquest that the first members of this clan arrived in the British Isles, where they were granted 43 manors in Yorkshire. Ennobled as Lords of Annandale in South-West Scotland early in the twelfth century, in 1238 Robert de Bruce (nicknamed 'The Competitor') was made heir presumptive to the Scottish crown. Appointed as one of the 15 regents in Scotland in 1255, 35 years later he was a prime candidate to be chosen as monarch in succession to Margaret the Maid. Passed over in favour of John Balliol, in 1294 Robert the Competitor died and the fight to become king of Scotland was carried on by his grandson: Robert the Bruce.

▶ RIGHT: The seal of David II
▲ ABOVE: Robert the Bruce statue, Stirling

Robert the Bruce was famed for his legendary encounter with a spider and for his great victory against the English at Bannockburn in 1314. Taking up arms against Edward I, he was crowned Robert I at Scone in 1306. The following year his brother, Edward, became his heir. Younger than Robert, Edward then proclaimed himself 'King of Ireland', but was killed in battle in 1318 and so, when Robert I died in 1329, he was succeeded by his young son, David II, who in turn was succeeded by the grandson of Robert I the Bruce: Robert II.

The younger King Robert was Scotland's first Stewart king (the name was changed later to Stuart). He ruled until 1390 and was followed as king of the Scots by his son, Robert III, who handed over the reins of power to a younger brother, Robert, Duke of Albany. The duke was duly appointed as regent, while the brother's sister, Jean, married Sir John Lyon. The Thane of Glamis, Lyon was a distant ancestor of Queen Elizabeth, the Queen Mother.

◐ see David I, Edward Bruce, Robert Bruce, Edward I, Edward II, Elizabeth the Queen Mother

ROBERT I (THE BRUCE) (1274–1329)

King of Scotland (1306–29); elder brother of Edward Bruce. One of the greatest names in Scottish history, legend has it that this triumphant king of the Scots was inspired to fight on against the might of England by the persistence of a spider weaving its web.

Born at Turnberry in West Scotland, he was the eldest son of Robert Bruce, Lord of Annandale, and Marjorie, Countess of Carrick. Becoming Earl of Carrick, when he was 18 years old he married his first wife, Isabel. After her death, he remarried, his second wife being Elizabeth de Burgh, the daughter of the Earl of Ulster. For many years a loyal supporter of England's king, waging war with Edward I against John Balliol, Robert the Bruce's loyalty had seen his family granted many privileges. However, in 1297, two years after recognising Edward as Scotland's king, Robert the Bruce allied himself with William Wallace, the celebrated freedom fighter who was leading the struggle for Scottish independence.

Briefly back in the English fold (1301–02), following Wallace's execution in 1305, he declared himself Scotland's king and was crowned Robert I at Scone on Palm Sunday

▲ ABOVE: Before Bannockburn Robert the Bruce kills Sir Henry de Bohun
▲ ABOVE: Robert the Bruce monument, Stirling

1306. Angering England's king, his accession was doubly audacious because, just a short time before, he had been excommunicated by Scotland's Church for killing a rival noble in a Dumfries kirk. So, disowned by the Church and set on a collision course with Edward I, Robert I was then assailed by a large army led by Aymer de Valence. This intimidating force, which had marched to Methven, to the west of Perth, promptly annihilated the Scots' forces. Further defeats followed, causing Robert the Bruce to take to his heels. For months he roamed from place to place, as Edward's henchmen rounded up and killed his supporters, including three of Robert's brothers. A testing time for the toppled king, it was during this period that he lay low on Rathlin, the island where, it is said, he was inspired to begin his fightback by a persistent spider, which he watched weave and re-weave its web.

Returning to the fray in 1307, that year Robert I started a sequence of victories, while in June that year the ailing Edward I led a vast army on the long trek northwards, only to die en route. Continuing to make gains, he won at Inverary in 1308, subjugating the rest of northern Scotland by 1309. He won the support of the Scottish Church in 1310, while cross-border raids ravaged towns in North-East England in 1311. A good situation improved still further on 24 June 1314 when the king of the Scots annihilated the English enemy at Bannockburn near Stirling. After Bannockburn Edward II struggled in vain to retain even a foothold in Scotland. Robert captured Berwick in 1318. Then, in 1320, the Declaration of Arbroath was signed by prominent Scottish bishops and leading lords. This declaration called for recognition of Robert's kingship and for Scotland's independence, but was ignored south of the border, hostilities continuing unchecked, despite a truce agreed in 1323.

Then, in 1327, with English barons turning on Edward II, the Scottish sovereign launched a major offensive in northern England, which led to the treaties of Edinburgh and Northampton. Acknowledging Robert the Bruce to be Scotland's rightful king, England also recognised Scotland's independence. However, native delight at these gains was soon tempered by the passing of the Scottish king. Possibly struck down by leprosy, the 53-year-old Robert the Bruce died at Cardross on 7 July 1329 and was succeeded by his young son, David II.

see House of Bruce, Edward Bruce, Edward I, Edward II

DAVID II (1324–71)

King of Scotland (1329–32, 1341–71). At Berwick on 16 July 1328 David, the four-year-old son of Robert the Bruce and his second wife, Elizabeth, was married to Joan, the seven-year-old daughter of England's former king,

Edward II, and younger sister of Edward III. Succeeding his father the following summer, David's coronation was staged at Scone on 24 November 1331. With power in the hands of the regent, Thomas Randolph, Earl of Moray, a successful coup in 1332 by Edward Balliol saw the latter become king. David settled in France and it was not until 1341 that he was restored to the Scottish throne.

◀ LEFT: David II

David retained his country's traditional allegiance with France and in 1346 he attacked England while Edward III was away fighting French forces. Despite this distraction, the Battle of Neville's Cross on 17 October 1346 was a personal disaster for David II, who was injured and taken prisoner by Edward's men. David remained in England for more than a decade. In 1357 the Treaty of Berwick was negotiated, guaranteeing a decade of peace between Scotland and England. In addition the Scots regained their sovereign in exchange for a king's ransom of 100,000 marks. A crippling sum that the Scots struggled to pay even as their pro-English king negotiated a deal with Edward III, one that would have seen the heir to England's throne become heir to Scotland's too.

Queen Joan died on 7 September 1362 and her widowed husband later married Margaret Drummond. However, no legitimate heir resulted from either marriage and so, on David's death, the crown passed to his step-sister's son, who became Robert II.

◗ *see* Edward Balliol, House of Bruce, Edward III, Robert II, House of Stewart

BALLIOL, EDWARD (C. 1283–1364)

King of the Scots (intermittently 1332–56); son of John Balliol. Assuming power in 1332, Edward regained the Scottish crown that had been snatched from his father's head 36 years previously. While in exile, his successful move to dethrone David II was backed by Edward III of England in exchange for land. Victorious at Halidon Hill in 1333, the following year Berwick and Lothian were ceded to England. Driven from Scotland in 1335, prior to the restoration of David II, he made sporadic returns to attack successive Scottish regents.

Edward was the eldest son of John Balliol and his wife, Isabelle, and he spent many years living on his family's estates in France. He settled in England in 1324 and six years later he sailed to Scotland at the head of a large fleet of warships in an attempt to reclaim the Scottish throne for the

Balliols. He defeated a Scottish force at Dupplin Moor, near Perth, in August 1332, and the following month Edward was crowned at Scone. He was soon forced to beat a hasty retreat from Annan, however, after a surprise attack by a militia led by the regent and the future Scots king, Robert II.

Edward was not to be deterred, though. By 1334 he was back in Scotland and as English armies won notable victories at the battles of Halidon Hill and Berwick, Edward Balliol must have rejoiced. However, with England then given vast tracts of land, supporters loyal to the deposed king, David II, struck back and, in 1235, a surprise attack at Culblean Hill in the Grampian mountain range caused Balliol to hurry south to seek sanctuary in England. Thereafter, he led various English-sponsored raiding parties, only renouncing his claim to the Scottish throne in 1356.

◆ *see* House of Balliol, Constantine III, David II, Edward III, Robert II

STEWART, HOUSE OF

Scotland's royal house for almost 350 years, the first monarch from this dynasty was crowned Robert II in 1371. Becoming king of the Scots in succession to David II, he was the grandson of Robert I the Bruce and the son of Walter fitzAlan, who was the sixth high steward of Scotland. From this hereditary title was derived the family name of Stewart. Later still, the name changed to Stuart from the French-style 'Steuart'.

Robert II Stewart reigned for 19 years, having previously served two terms as regent in the reign of his predecessor. An old man when he finally stepped aside, Robert's eventual successor was his son, John, who adopted the title Robert III. He was king of the Scots for just nine years. Then, like his father before him, he stood down. Handing power to his son, David, after David's death in suspicious circumstances, the king's brother, the Duke of Albany, ruled. However, when Robert III died in 1406 he was succeeded by his son, James I.

At the time of his accession young James was a prisoner in the Tower of London. Kept in England for the next 18 years, when he returned to Scotland he set about establishing his control in a kingdom that had been ruled over in his absence by the Duke of Albany and his son, Murdoch.

James I was a reforming ruler, a monarch who introduced many new laws. In 1437 he was assassinated. Succeeded by his son, James II became the first of six successive monarchs to ascend the throne as a minor.

Six years old when he became king, James II did not assume full control over his kingdom until he reached maturity. Early in his reign he was supported by the Douglas family, but later the king cut down to size the Douglases and other powerful opponents. Killed when a cannon exploded, James II was succeeded by his young son, James III. Like his grandfather and his father before him, James III had to fight hard to establish his kingship in the face of strong opposition from Scottish nobles. He was even forced to imprison his own brothers, while himself briefly taken captive in 1482. Restored the following year, he was killed by rebels in 1488 and became the third Scottish king in a row to die an early and violent death.

Once again a young prince ascended the Scottish throne, but James IV, like his predecessors, lived long enough to rule without regents. A popular, educated king with a worldly approach to government, it was James IV who linked the Scottish royal house with the ruling family in England by marrying Margaret Tudor, a daughter of Henry VII. Killed at Flodden Field when fighting the forces of his brother-in-law, Henry VIII, James's death led to the coronation of his baby son, James V.

Able to seize control only after he had escaped the clutches of his mother's second husband, the Earl of Angus, James V was forced to tackle many of the same problems that had confronted his Stuart predecessors, putting down various uprisings and fighting the English. However, shortly after the Scots were routed at Solway Moss in 1542 James V died, the crown then passing to his infant daughter, Mary, Queen of Scots.

One of the most famous Scottish monarchs, Mary spent very little of her adult life in Scotland. Briefly queen of France, after the death of her husband, François I, she returned home in 1561. The next four years passed off without incident, but Mary's life was turned upside down following her marriage to her cousin, Henry Stuart. Better known as Lord Darnley, in 1566 he killed his wife's secretary, yet within a year he too had been murdered.

By then the mother of a young son, James, Mary soon married for the third time, but five months after Darnley's death she was forced to abdicate and was imprisoned. Escaping from custody, Mary, Queen of Scots, made one last attempt at reclaiming her crown before heading south to England, remaining there in the kingdom of her cousin, Elizabeth I, for the rest of her life. In Scotland her place as monarch was taken by her baby son, who was crowned James VI in 1567. Somehow reaching adulthood with his crown intact, James VI ruled over Scotland until his death in 1625.

In 1603, James VI united the Scottish and English crowns for the first time. Known as James I in England, after his coronation at Westminster Abbey the Stuart king returned just once to the land of his birth.

ROBERT II (1316–90)

King of Scotland (1371–90). The son of Walter, the Great or High Steward of Scotland and Marjorie, daughter of Robert I the Bruce, he was just a baby when he became heir presumptive to his grandfather's throne. Passed over when King Robert's second wife gave birth to the future David II, during the reign of his young uncle Robert the Steward married Elizabeth Muir and raised a family The couple's eldest son would later become Robert III, while their daughter, Jean, wed Sir John Lyon, the Thane of Glamis in eastern Scotland and an ancestor of Queen Elizabeth the Queen Mother.

First pushed into the spotlight when he was appointed regent at the age of 17, he stepped aside in 1338 having paved the way for King David's return to power in 1341. However, he was reinstated for a second term in 1346 following his uncle's capture at the Battle of Neville's Cross. With David II in the custody of Edward III, Robert deputised until 1357, when the king was released under the terms of the Treaty of Berwick.

Eventually gaining power in his own right after David's death in 1371, his reign was marked by unrest and infighting among the Scottish nobility, by a succession of border raids and by a depressed economy. Unable or unwilling to tackle the problems facing his kingdom, Robert II stood aside in 1384 giving day-to-day control to his eldest son, John. Then, in 1388, power effectively passed to the king's second son, Robert, Duke of Albany and Earl of Fife. However, Robert II was nevertheless succeeded two years later by John, who chose to be crowned as Robert III.

▲ ABOVE: Robert II

◘ see Edward Balliol, Robert III, Robert the Bruce

ROBERT III (C. 1336-1406)

King of Scotland (1390–1406); son of Robert II. Given the name John at birth, he succeeded his father in 1390, six years after he had been placed in day-to-day charge of the Crown's affairs. Badly injured when kicked by a horse in 1385, his continuing ill health did not prevent him from being crowned as Robert III. However, just as his younger brother, Robert, Duke of Albany, had been the power behind the throne in the last years of their father's reign, so the duke wielded considerable influence in the first years of the new reign.

In 1399 Robert III stepped aside to be replaced by his eldest son, David, Duke of Rothesay. Regent for just three years, in 1402 David died in suspicious circumstances. The Duke of Albany was implicated, but not charged, and so regained the hold on power he had so briefly lost. Four years later, as fears about the safety of his young son, James, continued to mount, Robert III sent the boy into exile. However, when the ship carrying James to France was intercepted by English pirates, the heir to Robert's throne was kidnapped. Later passed into the hands of England's monarch, Henry IV, James soon became a king in exile, while Robert III died within a month of his son's capture.

see James I, Robert II, Henry IV

JAMES I (1394–1437)

King of Scots (1406–37). The second son of Robert III and Queen Annabella, James I was still a child when his elder brother, David, died in 1402 making James heir to his father's throne. James was just 12 years old when he was seized by pirates as he made his way to France to escape assassination attempts in his native Scotland. Handed over to Henry IV, the English king promptly imprisoned his prize hostage, while news of his son's capture was said to have brought on the death of James's father later that year. A king in exile, James I would have to wait 18 long years before sitting on the throne. Scotland's interim rulers were the king's uncle, Robert, Duke of Albany, and from 1420, the Duke's son, Murdoch.

Four years later, though, James I returned to Scotland and asserted control by executing his cousin, Murdoch, and other members of the Scottish nobility. The same year James married Joan, a cousin of England's reigning monarch, Henry V, and a member of the influential Beaufort family. In 1430 Queen Joan gave birth to the royal couple's first child, James.

As king of the Scots, James I demonstrated his passion for law and

order, introducing many new laws covering a wide area, from finances to fishing; in this way he effectively curbed the power of Scotland's lords. He also banned football games and restricted the hours in which alcohol could be consumed. However, with his rule characterised by a reforming zeal, James I made enemies among his subjects and the king had to combat rebellions in both the Highlands and the Lowlands. On 20 February 1437 a band of assassins gathered in Perth to stab the king to death in the presence of his queen. With James I dead the crown passed to his young son, James II.

◆ see James II, Robert III

▲ ABOVE: Catherine Douglas tries to protect James I from the conspirators threatening his murder

JAMES II (1430–60)

King of Scotland (1437–60). The son of James I and Queen Joan, the younger James became king following the murder of his father while he was still a child. James II had to wait 12 years before winning the right to rule over his kingdom. Aided and abetted in his bid for power by the mighty Douglas family, in November 1440 the two young sons of the recently deceased 5th Earl of Douglas were murdered as they dined with the boy-king, James II. From that time James was on a war footing

▲ *ABOVE: James II of Scotland*

with the 'Black' Douglases, and in 1452 at Stirling Castle the 8th Earl of Douglas was killed, allegedly by the sovereign himself.

By this time the minority of James II had come to an end and he was ruling in his own right. In 1449, the same year that his minority ended, he married the niece of the Duke of Burgundy, Mary of Guelders. Continuing to hound the Douglas family and its supporters and to move against other

challengers such as John of the Isles, by the end of his reign James II was in full command of his kingdom.

Later switching his attentions to the border country, in 1460 the king laid siege to Roxburgh Castle. However, James II was killed when one of his own cannons exploded, his early death bringing to the throne yet another royal child, the late king's eight-year-old son, James III.

◆ *see* James I, James III

◀ *LEFT: Edinburgh Castle*

71

JAMES III (1452–88)

King of Scotland (1460–88). James was the son of James II and Queen Mary and for the first few years after he succeeded while still a minor his mother acted as regent. She was replaced as regent shortly before her death in 1462 and a succession of regents governed Scotland until James III came of age in 1469. That same year his marriage to Margaret, the daughter of Christian I of Denmark and Norway, brought the Orkneys and the Shetland Islands under Scottish control.

Despite asserting his power throughout the 1470s, James III was persistently troubled by rebellious Scottish nobles. The 'Red' Douglas clan, spearheaded by the Earl of Angus, was one foe, while the faction led by the king's brothers, the Duke of Albany and the Earl of Mar, was especially troublesome. With matters coming to a head in 1479, James III imprisoned his brothers. However, while the earl died a suspicious death in custody, the duke escaped and headed for England. Returning three years later in the company of an English army, at Lauder to the north of Galashiels the king was seized and taken to Edinburgh, where he was imprisoned at the city's castle, while the English force captured Berwick. Restored to the throne in 1483, the monarch struggled to impose his authority, his confidence further dented by the death of his wife, Margaret, in 1486.

Two years later the king was forced to put down a revolt led by the leaders of the Campbell clan and the 'Red' Douglas family. However, forced to fight at Sauchieburn near Stirling on 11 June 1488, James III died during or shortly after the battle and was succeeded by his son, James IV.

◆ *see* James II, James IV

JAMES IV (1473–1513)

King of Scotland (1488–1513). Orphaned and crowned by the time he was 15 years old, James was the son of James III and Margaret of Denmark.

▲ ABOVE: James IV

Required to put down a rebellion in his first year as king, later he led successful military campaigns in the Highlands and islands before turning his attentions to the south. Offering his support to the Yorkist pretender, Perkin Warbeck, with Warbeck's defeat James IV made his peace with Henry VII, the first Tudor king, who later gave his blessing for the wedding of his eldest daughter, Margaret, and the king of the Scots. A hugely important alliance for the long-term future of both Tudor and Stuart dynasties, in the short-term the marriage produced a son and heir, James.

At home the king proved to be a well-liked figure, who promoted the arts and education and the introduction of the first Scottish printing presses. He also lavished vast sums of money on palaces and a huge warship known as the Great Michael.

Renewing the Auld Alliance with France in 1512, the following year the Scots responded to England's attack on the French by sending the largest Scottish army ever assembled into battle. Marching south in 1513, James IV led his men into England. Crossing the River Tweed, on 9 September 1513 the Scots and the English clashed. Doing battle at Flodden Field, 16km (10 miles)

▶ RIGHT: Margaret Tudor, wife of James IV

73

south-west of Berwick, many Scottish lords, earls, chiefs and thousands of foot soldiers were cut down. Also killed was James IV, his body taken to England by the victorious army of Henry VIII and the late king's brother-in-law was reputedly sent the bloodied tunic James had worn at Flodden.

Meanwhile, up in Scotland the crown sat uneasily on the head of yet another royal minor, the late king's baby son, James V.

◐ *see* Henry VII, James V

JAMES V (1512–42)

King of Scotland (1513–42). James V was the son of James IV and Margaret, daughter of Henry VII and sister of Henry VIII. He was no more than a baby when he ascended Scotland's throne in September 1513. Initially his mother was nominated to act as regent, but after the queen married the Earl of Angus in 1514, she was replaced by John, Duke of Albany, who maintained this position until 1524. When Albany went back to France control over the child-king and the country shifted to Angus.

Having spent his childhood years at Stirling Castle, James V escaped the clutches of the Earl of Angus. By this time the earl was separated from James's mother and in the summer of 1528 he was holding the king under lock and key. One day, however, James V managed to slip free and return to his childhood home at Stirling Castle to stake his claim to rule alone.

▲ ABOVE: *James V of Scotland*

The king was just 16 years old when he first took the reins and began to rule in his own right, but it was not long before James V showed his determination to be a strong ruler. In revenge for the insult shown to his mother and for the way he had been treated as a child, he sent the Earl of Angus scurrying into exile in England. When forced to deal with unrest in the north of his kingdom, he succeeded in putting down the uprisings there. He then turned his attention to other areas in which he felt the need to assert his authority. In 1532 he founded the central court, the College of Justice, while another major feature of his reign was the increasing wealth of the Crown, which was greatly enriched by taxing the Scottish Church.

During the period of the regency two main factions had arisen in Scotland: those who were pro-English, who later supported the Protestant Reformation, and those who were pro-France and therefore Catholic. James knew where his loyalties lay and proved them by concluding a marriage alliance with France in 1537. James V then wed his first wife, Madeleine, the daughter of François I. However, when Madeleine died just a few months later, the king of the Scots swiftly took another French bride, Mary of Guise-Lorraine. She bore him two sons, both of whom died in 1541. The following year she fell pregnant again.

Meanwhile, her husband was busy launching a fateful attack on England. Fighting a much larger English army, on 24 November 1542 the Scots were routed at the Battle of Solway Moss, near Gretna. The English won the day. Two weeks later James V died amid the splendour of his palace at Falkland. He was only 30 years old. Tragically, his death occurred just a few days after the birth of his daughter, the heir he had longed for to perpetuate his line. This was to be the ill-fated Mary, Queen of Scots.

◆ *see* James IV, Mary Queen of Scots

MARY, QUEEN OF SCOTS (1542–87)

Queen of Scotland (1542–67) and briefly queen of France. Mary was the daughter of James V of Scotland and his second wife, Mary of Guise. The younger Mary was just six days old when her father died in December 1542, his death following hard on the heels of the Scots' crushing defeat at the Battle of Solway Moss. Left to grow up without a father, in 1543 it was decided that the infant Mary would marry the young son of Henry VIII, the future King Edward VI. In the meantime England continued to attack its northern neighbour. During Edward VI's reign, France's king declared war on England after landing 6,000 soldiers in Scotland, having first evacuated Mary. In the jostling for power that followed, the young Scottish queen was betrothed to the French dauphin.

In 1558 Mary's marriage to the dauphin at the age of 16 was closely followed by the death of the English queen, Mary I. With her namesake's passing an opportunity arose for the Scottish monarch to press her claim to be the second successive queen of England. However, passed over in favour of her cousin, Elizabeth, the potential for seizing the English crown by force was soon bolstered when Mary's husband, François, became king of France in July 1559

Mary was briefly queen of France while her mother Mary of Guise acted as regent in Scotland. By the end of 1560, however, her mother and her husband were both dead. Earlier that same year a prolonged siege of Leith, near Edinburgh, had led to English success and the Treaty of Edinburgh, which acknowledged Elizabeth as the rightful English monarch, while a short time later the Scottish parliament renounced the pope's authority in Scotland. A bad year for Mary came to a sorry end when her husband, François II, was taken ill and in December 1560 died.

She returned to Scotland in 1561, at a time when the country was changing fast under the increasing influence of the Calvinist strain of

Protestantism preached by zealots such as John Knox. The queen was a continuing target for Knox's attacks. At the same time, Mary herself remained a thorn in the side of her cousin, Elizabeth I of England.

In July 1565 Mary married another cousin, Henry Stuart, Lord Darnley. On March 1566 the queen's secretary, David Rizzio, was stabbed to death by the jealous Darnley and his accomplices. Three months later, on 19 June 1566, Mary gave birth to her son and heir, James. Darnley himself was murdered in February 1567, strangled at Kirk-o'-Field outside Edinburgh. His death was followed two months later by Mary's third marriage to James Hepburn, 4th Earl of Bothwell.

The dramas still came thick and fast as, with Hepburn (and possibly Mary) implicated in Darnley's downfall, Mary was seized by a band of Scottish nobles, who imprisoned her at Loch Leven Castle. Soon her reign as queen of Scots would be over and so too her relationship with Bothwell. Forced to abdicate on 24 July 1567, Mary was succeeded by her one-year-old son, who was crowned James VI of Scotland.

Returned to prison on the banks of Loch Leven, the former queen of Scots escaped to mount one last attack in the hopes of reclaiming her crown. Defeated, however, she headed for England, where she threw herself on the mercy of Elizabeth I. The English queen permitted her to stay in England, but the price Mary had to pay was a lifelong sentence of house arrest.

Frequently linked to pro-Catholic plots against the Protestant Elizabeth, she was moved from country house to country house. But then, with the uncovering of the Babington Plot in 1586, the Stuart queen was arrested, found guilty of involvement in the plot to murder Elizabeth I and then beheaded.

◆ *see* James V, James VI, Elizabeth I

◀ *LEFT: Mary, Queen of Scots*

WALES

▲ ABOVE: Edward I

GWYNEDD, HOUSE OF

One of the leading Welsh kingdoms during the Middle Ages, Gwynedd's heartlands were Anglesey and Snowdonia in North-West Wales, but from the ninth century onwards its borders extended occasionally to the east and down to the south of Wales.

With their origins stretching back to the days of the Romans, by the sixth century the Gwynedd kings were well established. However, it was only after Rhodri Mawr (Rhodri the Great) succeeded his father, Merfyn Frych, in AD 844 that Gwynedd became a national power. Extending his kingdom to take in all but the south-east and south-west tips of Wales, by AD 872 Rhodri had taken control of approximately two thirds of a country still regularly attacked by Vikings based in Ireland and on the Isle of Man.

After Rhodri's death in AD 878, Gwynedd's large kingdom was divided in two, Cadell reigning in Deheubarth in the south, with his elder brother, Anarawd, reigning in Gwynedd in the north. The two kingdoms then remained more or less separate entities, although Gwynedd rulers such as Gruffudd ap Llywelyn and Owain Gwynedd reigned briefly over much of Wales.

Llywelyn ap Iorweth (Iorweth the Great) and Llywelyn ap Gruffudd (Llywelyn the Last) were similarly successful in the thirteenth century, but the overwhelming force of the English king, Edward I, finally ended the era of Gwynedd and its long line of kings.

Dafydd ap Gruffudd enjoyed six months as king of Gwynedd, but with his execution in October 1283, the kingdom he had so briefly ruled over was no more. Formally broken up the following year by the Statute of Rhuddlan, from 1294 Gwynedd disappeared to be replaced by three English-style counties: Anglesey, Caernarvonshire and Merioneth.

RHODRI MAWR (D. AD 878)

King of Gwynedd (AD 844–77); son of Merfyn Frych. Rhodri was the first Welsh king to earn the mantle 'Mawr' (meaning 'Great').

Born Rhodri ap Merfyn, when his father, King Merfyn, died in AD 844 after 19 years as ruler in North Wales, the new sovereign inherited a

▲ *ABOVE: Anglesey*

sizeable kingdom: Gwynedd from his father and Powys from his mother. Eight years later Rhodri sent shock waves reverberating throughout northern Europe by killing the feared Gorm and defeating his Viking force at Anglesey. Then in AD 872 the Welsh king further reinforced his hold on power by marrying Angharad, the sister of the Ceredigion (Cardigan) king, Gwygon ap Meurig.

Said to have built a castle at the great Deheubarth capital of Dinefwr in AD 876, Rhodri was forced into exile during AD 877 by invading Vikings. Soon mounting a challenge to take back his Gwynedd kingdom, in AD 878 he died in battle at Prestatyn. Possibly killed when fighting an alliance of Norsemen and Mercians led by Ceowulf, for much of his reign Rhodri Mawr had been the most powerful of all Welsh kings.

Succeeded in Gwynedd by his son, Anarawd ap Rhodri, after Rhodri's death no native-born ruler would ever again rule over such a large realm, the kingdom the monarch passed on then being divided into two regions: Gwynedd (north) and Deheubarth (south). A younger son, Cadell ap Rhodri, reigned in the former, while Rhodri Mawr's grandson was the famed Deheubarth king, Hywel Dda.

◆ see Hywel Dda, Anarawd ap Rhodri

DYFED, HOUSE OF

An independent kingdom in South-West Wales. Once the homeland of the Demetae people and later a setting for the fabled tales known as The Mabinogion, Dyfed was ruled over by its own line of kings until the death of Llywarch ap Hyfaidd in AD 904. With his passing, the kingdom was absorbed into the new kingdom of Deheubarth by Hywel Dda, the husband of Llywarch's daughter, Elen.

◆ see House of Deheubarth, Hywel Dda

CADELL AP RHODRI (D. AD 909)

King of Deheubarth (AD 878–909). A son of Rhodri Mawr, after his father's death Cadell was created joint ruler, with elder brother Anarawd, of the lands bequeathed them. Cadell reigned over the southern region known as Deheubarth and was given considerable help in defending his territory by Alfred the Great. However, with the English king's passing in AD 899, troubled times befell Wales and the gloom did not lift until the reign of Cadell's acclaimed son, Hywel Dda.

◼ *see* Anarawd ap Rhodri, House of Deheubarth, House of Gwynedd, Hywel Dda, Rhodri Mawr

ANARAWD AP RHODRI (D. AD 916)

King of Gwynedd (AD 878–916). Son of the celebrated Welsh king, Rhodri Mawr, like his father, Anarawd, reigned for more than three decades. Coming to power in AD 878 following Rhodri's death, Anarawd ap Rhodri established his own royal house, Deuheubarth, centred on the Gwynedd capital, Aberffraw. At Conwy in AD 881 the Gwynedd king notched a notable victory against Ethelred of Mercia. He later acknowledged Alfred the Great as his overlord and before his death in AD 916 Anarawd repelled a number of Viking raids and declared war on his brother, Cadell. He was succeeded by his son, Idwal ap Anarawd.

◼ *see* House of Deheubarth, House of Gwynedd, Idwal ap Anarawd, Rhodri Mawr

DEHEUBARTH, HOUSE OF

With its capital at Dinefwr, the medieval kingdom of Deheubarth ('south part') was the traditional southern ally of Gwynedd. The realm covered much of southern and western Wales, incorporating the south-western regions of Dyfed, Ceredigion (Cardigan) and Ystrad Tywi (south of Carmarthen to the Gower), while occasionally reaching into Brycheiniog (Brecon) in the south-east.

Once part of Rhodri Mawr's vast empire, after his death in AD 878 the region was ruled over by its own line of kings. Rhodri Cadell reigned until AD 909 and Hywel ap Cadell to AD 950. The latter, better known as Hywel Dda, merged his Seisyllwg territory with Dyfed in AD 904 to create Deheubarth. At the end of the eleventh century Rhys ap Tewdwr, son of Tewdwr the Great, forged an alliance with the Gwynedd king, Gruffudd ap Cynan. Previously living in exile in Brittany, Rhys made a triumphant return home, winning back Deheubarth.

Inextricably linked with Gwynedd since the ninth-century heydays of Merfyn and his son, Rhodri Mawr, in the twelfth century the then king of Deheubarth, Rhys ap Gruffudd, accepted the English title 'Lord Rhys' and the role of Justice of South Wales. After his death the Deheubarth line lived on through men such as Maredudd and his son, Rhys ap Maredudd, while later descendants included Owain Glyndwr and Henry VII.

◖ *see* House of Gwynedd, Maredudd, Rhodri Mawr, Early Rulers of Wales

IDWAL AP ANARAWD (D. AD 942)

King of Gwynedd (AD 916–42); son of Anarawd ap Rhodri and grandson of Rhodri Mawr. Also known as Idwal Foel (Idwal the Bald), it is thought he succeeded his father following Anarawd's death in AD 916. Together with other contemporary Welsh kings such as Hywel Dda of Deheubarth he paid homage to Athelstan, regularly visiting the great king of all England at his court. He also supported Athelstan in the attack that he launched against the Scots' king, Constantine II, in AD 934. Eight years later, Idwal's death brought to power his sons, Iago and Ieuaf, however they were soon driven from Gwynedd by Idwal's cousin, Hywel Dda.

◖ *see* Anarawd ap Rhodri, Constantine II, House of Deheubarth, Athelstan

HYWEL DDA (D. AD 950)

King of Deheubarth (c. AD 908–50); son of Cadell ap Rhodri and grandson of Rhodri Mawr. Hywel Dda enjoyed a long and successful reign that began c. AD 909, the year of his father's death. Hywel 'the Good' gained control of Gwynedd in AD 942, four years after he had made a pilgrimage to Rome. He was best-known for codifying his country's laws, for expanding his realm and for his pro-English outlooks.

With his power base in Ceredigion (Cardigan), Hywel forged an enduring alliance with the great English sovereign, King Athelstan, while at home in Wales the man who came to be called the 'head and glory of the Britons' eventually gained control in Dyfed, Gwynedd and Powys. Blessed with the same energy and drive as Rhodri Mawr, like his grandfather he also realised the advantages to be gained from securing a good marriage. So it was that he married Elen, the daughter of Llywarch ap Hafaidd, King of Dyfed, this marriage alliance gaining the Deheubarth king control over much of South Wales, while the death of his cousin, Idwal ap Anarawd, in AD

▲ *ABOVE: Hywel Dda proclaims the laws of Wales to the Welsh parliament*

942 left the way clear for Hywel to assert his authority in Gwynedd. The south-eastern territory of Morgannwg (Glamorgan) remained elusive, but still his territorial gains made him the dominant power in Wales.

The first Welsh king known to have issued his own coinage, Hywel Dda also set about establishing throughout his realm a uniform system of laws. This codification programme began in AD 930 at Whitland in South-West Wales. A major advance, the laws covering six main legal areas were so well framed that they endured more or less unchanged right up to the invasion by England's Edward I almost four centuries later. Shrewd, sometimes ruthless, Hywel Dda died in AD 950 after ruling over his kingdom for 41 years. He was succeeded in Gwynedd by his son, Owain ap Hywel.

�‹› *see* House of Gwynned, Owain ap Hywel, Rhodri Mawr

IAGO AP IDWAL (D. C. AD 979)

King of Gwynedd (AD 950–79); son of Idwal ap Anarawd. Driven into exile after his father's death by his second cousin, Hywel Dda, and his English allies, Hywel's death in AD 950 gave Iago and his brother, Ieuaf, the opportunity to reclaim Gwynedd, which they did by defeating Hywel's son and successor, Owain. However, in the years that followed Iago's accession, a family feud led to years of unrest. Iago defeated and imprisoned Ieuaf in AD 969 to establish an authority over his kingdom, that was recognised four years later when Iago was one of the select band of British rulers that paid homage to England's King Edgar at Chester. Also present at that great royal gathering was Ieuaf's son, Hywel.

The following year the two rivals would meet again with the nephew, Hywel, defeating his uncle, Iago. Five years later Hywel ap Ieuaf won again to bring to an end the long and difficult reign of Iago ap Idwal.

◹› *see* Hywel Dda, Idwal ap Anarawd, Hywel ap Ieuaf

HYWEL AP IEUAF (D. AD 985)

King of Gwynedd (AD 974–85); son of Ieuaf. Hywel twice defeated his uncle, Iago ap Idwal, in battle, on the second occasion (in AD 979) with Viking assistance. Capturing and overthrowing Iago in that conflict, in AD 980 he resisted a counterattack by Iago's son, Cystenin. Dying in AD 985, he was briefly succeeded by his brother, Meurig. The last of Ieuaf's sons, he died in AD 985.

◆ *see* House of Deheubarth, Iago ap Idwal

CADWALLON AP IEUAF (D. AD 986)

King of Gwynedd (AD 985–86). Cadwallon succeeded his brother, Hywel ap Ieuaf, after his death in AD 985. Little is known about Cadwallon prior to his gaining the throne of Gwynedd and even when he did his reign was so short-lived that not much information can be gleaned. It is likely that he supported his brother in his struggles during his lifetime. Cadwallon was murdered by Maredudd ap Owain, who united the houses of Deuheubarth and Gwynedd.

◆ *see* House of Deuheubarth, House of Gwynedd, Hywel ap Ieuaf, Maredudd ap Owain

OWAIN AP HYWEL (D. AD 988)

King of Deheubarth (AD 950–88); son of Hywel Dda. Owain succeeded his famous father in AD 950. Despite carrying out several invasion attempts in Gwynedd in the first part of his reign, it was only after his younger son, Maredudd, assumed control in his father's later years that Gwynedd was annexed by Deheubarth. Owain's eldest son, Einion, had been killed in AD 984, so Owain ap Hywel was succeeded by Maredudd.

◆ *see* Hywel Dda, Maredudd ap Owain

MAREDUDD AP OWAIN (D. AD 999)

King of Deheubarth and Gwynedd (AD 986–99); son of Owain ap Hywel and grandson of Hywel Dda. Maredudd ruled jointly in Deheubarth with his father until Owain's death in AD 986. After taking sole command he attacked Gwynedd, killing Cadwallon ap Ieuaf and banishing Cadwallon's heir, Idwal. From that time on Maredudd reigned supreme in both Deheubarth and Gwynedd despite regular Viking attacks. The grandfather of Gruffudd ap Llywelyn, Maredudd was succeeded by his son-in-law, Llewelyn ap Seisyll.

 see Gruffudd ap Llywelyn, Llewelyn ap Seisyll

CYNAN AP HYWEL (D. 1005)

King of Gwynedd (AD 999–1005); son of Hywel ap Ieuaf. After the death of Maredudd ap Owain, Cynan retook the throne of Gwynedd. Maredudd had restored the glory of the kingdom after years of war between Hywel and his enemy, Iago ap Idwal, but under Cynan's six-year rule the realm was plunged into chaos once more. Little is known of Cynan, but he was succeeded by Llywelyn ap Seisyll.

 see Hywel ap Ieuaf, Iago ap Idwal, Maredudd ap Owain

LLYWELYN AP SEISYLL (D. 1023)

King of Deheubarth and Gwynedd (1005–23). Following years of unrest in which battles had been fought and kings deposed, he became ruler in Deheubarth following the death of his father-in-law Maredudd ap Owain, in AD 999. Then seizing Gwynedd in 1016, he retained possession of it until his violent removal in 1023. Possibly killed and buried near Pentrefoelas in North Wales, Llywelyn was succeeded by his son, Gruffudd ap Llywelyn.

 see Gruffud ap Llywelyn, Maredudd ap Owain

 ◀ *LEFT: Llwelyn is defeated and beheaded*

RHYDDERCH AP IESTYN (D. 1033)

King of Deheubarth (1023–33). Hailing from South Wales, Rhydderch seized power after the death of Llywelyn ap Seisyll in 1023 and then ruled over Deheubarth for the next 10 years. Succeeded by the brothers, Hywel and Maredudd ap Edwin, 14 years after his death, Rhydderch's son, Gruffudd ap Rhydderch, became Deheubarth's king.

◐ *see* Gruffudd ap Rhydderch, Hywel ap Edwin, Maredudd ap Edwin

HYWEL AP EDWIN (D. 1044)

King of Deheubarth (1033–44); son of Edwin. After the death of Rhydderch ap Iestyn in 1033 Hywel reigned jointly with his brother, Maredudd. However, when Maredudd died in 1035 he was left to rule alone. Later repelling attacks by Viking raiders, in 1042 Hywel was defeated by the Gwynedd king, Gruffudd ap Llywelyn. In exile for the next two years, on his return Hywel was killed in a battle fought beside the Towi river by Gruffudd, who then fought Gruffudd ap Rhydderch for control of Deheubarth.

◐ *see* Gruffudd ap Llewelyn, Gruffudd ap Rhydderch

GRUFFUDD AP RHYDDERCH (D. 1055)

King of Deheubarth (1033–55); son of Rhydderch ap Iestyn. A feared warrior-king, he defeated Gruffudd ap Llywelyn to claim Deheubarth, but was later killed and succeeded by Gruffudd who thus became the first king of Wales.

Campaigning fiercely in the east and south-east of his kingdom, his greatest victory came in 1045 when he defeated Gruffudd ap Llywelyn. This victory forced the Gwynedd king to give up control of most of Deheubarth. However, in 1047 the northern king struck back. Aided and abetted by an English army led by Svein, a son of Earl Godwin of

Wessex, Gruffudd ap Llywelyn's men slaughtered 140 of Gruffudd ap Rhydderch's family and retainers. The Deheubarth king escaped with his life, but in 1055 Gruffudd ap Llywelyn headed south once more, defeating and killing Gruffudd ap Rhydderch to become the first king of all Wales.

◆ *see* Rhydderch ap Iestyn, Gruffudd ap Llywdyn

GRUFFUDD AP LLYWELYN (C. 1000–63)

King of all Wales (1039–63). The son of Llywelyn ap Seisyll and his wife, Angharad, Gruffudd took control in Gwynedd from Iago ap Idwal, whom he murdered in 1039. That same year he underlined his power by defeating the Mercians at Rhyd-y-groes (or Crossford) on the banks of the River Severn. Launching his assault on the kingdom of Deheubarth, in 1042 he fought and won a battle with the Deheubarth king, Hywel ap Edwin. Defeating and killing Hywel in a second skirmish in 1044, still Gruffudd could not fully establish his rule in the southern kingdom. Losing in battle to Gruffudd ap Rhydderch in 1045, a whole decade would pass before the Gwynedd king gained his revenge on his opposite number in Deheubarth.

Gruffudd also blazed a warlike trail across the border. He beat the men of Herefordshire at Leominster in 1052, before returning to Wales,

◀ LEFT: Gruffudd, son of Llewelyn

93

where in 1055 he finally won control in Deheubarth. Another victory came Gruffudd's way that year, when he joined forces with Elfgar of East Mercia to attack Hereford, while the following year Leofgar, the Bishop of Hereford, was at the head of a small band of men when he was killed close to Glasbury-on-Wye. Reprisals followed, but Gruffudd continued to make gains before a peace deal was agreed. This recognised Gruffudd's supremacy in Wales, while the Welsh king pledged his loyalty to Edward

the Confessor. The deal was sealed by Gruffudd's marriage to Elfgar's daughter, Eldgyth.

In 1058 Gruffudd was on the warpath once more, but then following Elfgar's death in 1062 the mighty English noble Earl, Harold Godwinson, attacked Gruffudd at his court at Rhuddlan Castle in North Wales. The Gwynedd ruler lived to fight another day, but as Harold and his brother, Tostig, conquered Gruffudd's kingdom, the king himself was killed. Murdered by his former

◀ LEFT: Harold II

supporters on 5 August 1063, according to some accounts they sent his severed head to Harold Godwinson, the soon-to-be-crowned Harold II, who then married Gruffudd's widow, Eldgyth. Once described as the 'head and shield and defender of the Britons', Gruffudd's death led to a succession struggle in Gwynedd that was eventually won by Trahearn.

◩ *see* Llewelyn ap Seisyll

BLEDDYN AP CYNFYN (C. 1025–75)

King of Gwynedd and Powys (1063–75). Bleddyn was installed as king of the northen regions of Wales by the English king, Edward the Confessor, after the death of Gruffudd ap Llewelyn and he proved to be worthy of the position. He ruled there with his brother, Rhiwallon, and together they ran the provinces of Powys and Gwynedd during one of the most turbulent times in British history: the Norman Conquest. The Welsh kings supported the English against the Normans and forced William the Conqueror to take military measures to control the Welsh.

The conquest over, internal wranglings in Wales caused problems as the sons of Gruffudd ap Llewellyn challenged for the throne. At the Battle of Mechain in 1070 they both died, along with Rhiwallon, leaving Bleddyn solely in charge of the two kingdoms. For some time after this Bleddyn was able to turn his attention to the things he cared about most and he earned the love and respect of his people through his generosity and his just rule. This period of respite lasted just three years, however, and in 1073 the Normans made their move into Wales. The ensuing struggle allowed kings of other Welsh provinces to move in on the powerful areas of Gwynedd and Powys, and Bleddyn was mudered in 1075.

◩ *see* Edward the Confessor, Gruffudd ap Llewelyn, William I the Conqueror

RHYS AP OWAIN (D. 1078)

King of Deheubarth (1072–78); brother of Maredudd ap Owain. Rhys proved to be an ineffectual ruler, unable to defend his kingdom from the marauding Normans in their attacks in 1073 and 1074. He is remembered as the man who arranged the murder of the Gwynedd king, Bleddyn ap Cynfan, although he gained nothing from this death.

◆ *see* Maredudd ap Owain

TRAHEARN (D. 1081)

King of Gwynedd (1063–81); son of King Caradog of Arwystli. Trahearn seized power following the murder of Gruffudd ap Llywelyn in 1063. Ruling over his kingdom for 18 years, in 1078 he extended its borders by defeating the Deheubarth king, Ryhs ap Owain. However, three years later Gruffudd ap Cynan and his Deheubarth ally, Rhys ap Tewdwr (a cousin of Rhys ap Owain) killed Trahearn when winning the Battle of Myndydd Carn.

RHYS AP TEWDWR (D. 1093)

King of Deheubarth (1078–93), a descendant of Hywel Dda, also known as Rhys the Great. Once in exile in Brittany, Rhys ap Tewdwr fought with Gruffudd ap Cynan and his cousin, Rhys ap Maredudd, when winning the Battle of Mynydd Carn, which was fought near Tenby in South-West Wales in 1081. However, Rhys ap Maredudd was killed during the heat of battle and so Rhys ap Tewdwr succeeded him in Deheubarth, while Gruffudd took control in Gwynedd.

Forced to submit to William the Conqueror, after England's king had marched into his kingdom in 1082, Rhys ruled for six more years before being chased out of Deheubarth by raiders from neighbouring Powys. Sailing to Ireland, he remained there until returning to Deheubarth in 1091 with a Viking army and taking back his kingdom. Two years later, however, Rhys ap Tewdwr was killed.

◆ *see* Hywel Dda, William I, Gruffudd ap Cynan, Rhys ap Maredudd

▲ ABOVE: Powys Castle

MAREDUDD AP BLEDDYN (D. 1132)

King of Powys (1116–32). Maredudd followed his brothers into the rulership of Powys and proved himself less worthy than they had been. He had been held prisoner by the English for five years, but escaped in 1108. When Henry I launched his invasion of Wales in 1114, Maredudd paid homage to the English king and in return was allowed to rule the area as overlord. Later invasions by Henry, however, resulted in Maredudd's flight to Gwynedd to seek sanctuary. The Gwynedd king, Gruffudd ap Cynan, would not risk annoying the English king by taking Maredudd in, however, and was forced to sue for peace to his own detriment. Maredudd died in 1132, having lived well into his sixties. He was succeeded by his son, Madog.

◨ *see* Madog ap Maredudd, Henry I, Gruffudd ap Cynan

GRUFFUDD AP CYNAN (C. 1055–1137)

King of Gwynedd (1081–1137); son of Cynan ap Iago. The only Welsh king known to have inspired a biography written during the Middle Ages, Gruffudd reigned twice in Gwynedd. Dying in 1137 he was succeeded by his son, Owain ap Gruffudd.

Spending his early years in Dublin, in 1075 he sailed to Wales where he made an unsuccessful attempt to seize power in Gwynedd by attacking Rhuddlan Castle in North Wales. However, six years later, with the support of men such as Rhys ap Tewdwr, he killed and succeeded the Gwynedd ruler,

▲ *ABOVE: Manuscript showing Norman warriors*

Trahearn, at the Battle of Myndydd Carn. Continuing to lead an eventful life, during which he was imprisoned in a Norman gaol, later he became an ally of the Norman king, Henry I.

After his capture by Norman forces, he was ransomed in 1094. Driven westwards, he returned to Dublin in 1098. Back in Wales again the following year, Gruffudd made his peace with Henry I. Initially a client-king based in Anglesey, before his death in 1137 he extended his power throughout Gwynedd. Succeeded by his son, Owain, his daughter, Gwenllian, was the wife of Gruffudd ap Rhys, the Deheubarth king.

◆ *see* House of Deheubarth, Norman Dynasty

GRUFFUDD AP RHYS (D. 1137)

King of Deheubarth (1116–37); son of Rhys ap Tewdwr. In exile after his father's death, Gruffudd did not rule in Deheubarth until he was granted limited powers there by Henry I. Killed in a rebellion, he was succeeded by his sons, Anarawd and Cadell ap Gruffudd.

Following the death in battle of his father in 1093, Gruffudd fled Deheubarth and spent his early childhood in Ireland while the Normans continued their occupation of central and southern Wales. Not returning to his native kingdom until 1113, three years later he made a vain attempt to wrest control of his kingdom from Henry I. Submitting to England's monarch, in return for his support Gruffudd was given a manor by Henry, who also allowed him to remain as the nominal head of Deheubarth.

Killed in the rebellion that followed the accession of England's King Stephen in 1135, his death in 1137 may have been hastened by the treachery of his second wife.

◆ *see* Cadell ap Gruffudd, Gruffudd ap Cynan, Henry I, House of Gwynedd, Rhys ap Tewdr

MADOG AP MAREDUDD (D. 1160)

King of Powys (1132–60). Madog was the last ruler of the whole of Powys. At the beginning of his reign he held a position of great authority, but this declined throughout his time as king of Powys. Aiming to retain good relations with Henry I and King Stephen of England, he worked hard to gain equally good relations with his neighbours in Wales. He married the daughter of Gruffudd ap Cynan and for a while harmony was established between Powys and Gwynedd. Later, though, Madog was forced to fight it out with Gruffudd's successor, Owain, in 1149. This was the start of the decline of his power: Owain won the day and by the end of the year much of Powys was in his hands. It was not until 1157 that Henry II of England rewarded Madog's former loyalty by restoring him to power in Powys. The remainder of Madog's reign was relatively peaceful and he was much mourned on his death.

◆ see Henry I, Henry II, Stephen

OWAIN AP GWYNEDD (C. 1100–70)

King of Gwynedd (1137–70); son of Gruffudd ap Cynan; also known as Owain ap Gruffudd. Owain succeeded his father with the aid of his brother in 1137. He went on the warpath in Wales in his early years when he was untroubled by English opposition. During this campaign Owain captured Carmarthen, Mold and the kingdom of Powys. But after 20 years as ruler of Gwynedd, he was attacked and defeated by England's new king, Henry II. Beaten again by Henry in 1163, from then on Owain of Gwynedd continued to side with the English monarch against the Deheubarth king, Rhys ap Gruffudd.

CYNAN AP OWAIN (C. 1140–74)

King of Gwynedd (c. 1170–74). When Owain Gwynedd died his kingdom was divided between his sons, thus intiating sibling rivalry and a period of turmoil in Gwynedd. Little knowledge of Cynan exists, other than that he established enough claim to serve as king for a few brief years. His sons, Gruffudd and Maredudd, succeeded in expelling Rhodri from Anglesey.

◆ see Gruffudd ap Cynan

RHODRI AP OWAIN (D. 1195)

King of Gwynedd (1170–90); son of Owain ap Gwynedd. Rhodri joined his brother, Dafydd, in their attack on the elder sons of Owain, Gwynedd to throw them out of the territories they had inherited and claim them for themselves. Although their mission was successful, Dafydd turned on his brother and imprisoned him in 1174. Rhodri escaped the following year and sought his revenge, driving Dafydd into the east and seizing most of the kingdom of Gwynedd. He ruled until 1190 when his nephews conspired against him and drove him into exile. Rhodri is buried at Holyhead.

◆ see Owain ap Gwynedd, Dafydd ap Owain

RHYS AP GRUFFUDD (C. 1130–97)

King of Deheubarth (1155–97). The son of Gruffudd ap Rhys and his wife Gwenllian, Rhys first made his mark in 1157, helping Welsh kings to begin the fightback against Henry II of England. He brought to this long campaign the experience of war he had gained when fighting with his half-brothers, Anarawd and Cadell, against the Clares of Ceredigion (Cardigan) and the Cliffords of Llandovery. Battling with the Clares and Cliffords again in 1159, four years later the struggle against the English enemy took a turn for the worse when Henry II defeated Rhys and forced him to surrender his hold on Ceredigion and to forsake the title of king.

Then dubbed the Lord Rhys, the Deheubarth leader was down, but not out and he retook Ceredigion in 1164. Next assuming power in Cyfeiliog, in 1171 Rhys made his peace with Henry II

Allowed to retain his lands in South Wales, Rhys was also given the rôle of justiciar (or chief justice) in his native territory. From that time on Rhys ruled in peace over his domain until 1189. With his capital at Dinefwr, near Carmarthen, he introduced Plantagenet ways and built castles, while also establishing the Welsh tradition of eisteddfods, where poets met and recited verse.

Despite family in-fighting, Rhys ap Gruffudd retained his hold on power until his death. However, with the end of his long life, so the kingdom he ruled over disintegrated. Survived by his sons, Gruffudd ap Rhys, Maelgwyn and Rhys Gryg, after his death the fortunes of the kingdom of Deheubarth went into a slow, but terminal decline.

LLYWELYN AP IORWERTH (C. 1173–1240)

King of Gwynedd (1200-40); son of Iorwerth Drwyndwn and grandson of Owain Gwynedd. Also known as Llywelyn the Great, he succeeded Dafydd ap Owain.

Growing up in the Powys homeland of his mother, Llywelyn first served notice of his ambitions when he took on and defeated the Gwynedd ruler, Dafydd ap Owain, at the Battle of Aberconwy in 1194. However, he did not find it easy to build on this victory and so it was not until the beginning of the thirteenth century that he secured control over all Gwynedd.

◀ *LEFT: Welsh hero, Iorwerth is murdered*

Ever conscious of the powerful presence of England, Llywelyn paid homage to King John in 1203, the year that he pledged to marry John's illegitimate daughter, Joan. With English support, the next few years saw Llywelyn push south from his base in North-West Wales, gradually overwhelming Powys, where Gwynwynwyn and later his son, Gruffudd, led the resistance to the attacks from the north.

LLYWELYN AP GRUFFUDD (C. 1228–82)

King of Gwynedd (1247–82); the first leader to be styled Prince of Wales. The grandson of Llywelyn ap Iorwerth and son of Gruffudd ap Llywelyn, his father had died while making his escape from the Tower of London in 1244. However, Llywelyn did not have long to wait to scale the heights of power in Wales because on 25 February 1246 his uncle and enemy, Dafydd ap Llywelyn, died, the death of the Gwynedd king opening the door to Llywelyn and his brothers.

However, an even more powerful opponent than Dafydd lived on in the form of Henry III and in 1247 the English king forced Llywelyn to sign

▶ RIGHT: Head of Llwelyn ap Gruffydd is paraded through streets

the Treaty of Woodstock. Conceding land and control, the fightback began in 1255. First winning a struggle with his brothers, Owain and Dafydd, in 1256 he set out to take back the lands seized earlier by the English by winning battles and forging alliances with other Welsh rulers and with Simon de Montfort, the leader of the English rebellion against Henry III.

Then in September 1267 came the climax of Llywelyn's campaign of attacks when the Treaty of Montgomery saw him recognised by the English Crown as the Prince of Wales. This recognition was only granted in exchange for a huge monetary payment and so it was not long before Llywelyn was fighting to win more territory. But then in 1272 Edward I became the new king of England, his accession marking the beginning of the end for Llywelyn the Last.

Deserted again by his brother, Dafydd, Llywelyn's defiantly independent stance tired Edward who took arms against him in 1277. Soon defeating him, in October 1277, Llywelyn was faced with the option of signing the Treaty of Aberconwy or watching helplesly as his people starved. He signed the treaty. Then confined to one part of his former kingdom, he married Simon de Montfort's widow, Eleanor, before being reunited with his brother, Dafydd.

However, Llywelyn's comeback bid was soon ended as in December 1282 he was killed in a skirmish at Cilmeri, near Builth Wells, and was succeeded by Dafydd.

◖ *see* Dafydd ap Llwyelyn, Gruffudd ap Llywelyn

OWAIN GLYNDWR (C. 1355–C. 1416)

Self-styled Prince of Wales (1400–16); also known as Owen Glendower. He was descended from the royal families of Powys and Deheubarth and was an ancestor of Henry VII. Forming alliances with French collaborators and English barons such as Mortimer, Northumberland and his son,

Hotspur, he seized towns and land. Later pegged back as the future Henry V asserted his dominance, Owain Glyndwr evaded capture to ensure his status as a great Welsh rebel hero.

Possibly born at Little Treffgarne near Haverfordwest, Owain Glyndwr was a Welshman of royal blood, a man who in his younger days had fought for the English king, Richard II. In 1400, however, his life was transformed. Holding a grudge against Henry IV for not ruling in his favour in a dispute over land, Glyndwr was declared the Prince of Wales on 16 September 1400 and led attacks against several English towns in North-East Wales.

After that little more was heard of the rebel until 1402 when his first major victory was made sweeter still by the capture of Sir Edmund Mortimer, who was a potential challenger to Henry IV. Then, in 1403 near Shrewsbury, the Welsh-born son of the English king, Prince Henry, restored the balance by killing Glyndwr's ally, the feared warrior Hotspur. However, this was a minor setback as strong new alliances were sealed, with France providing military support, while in 1405 he joined forces with Mortimer and Henry Percy, the Earl of Northumberland and father of Hotspur.

▶ RIGHT: Owain Glyndyr

SAXONS

ETHELRED II (D. AD 911)

Lord of the Mercians (AD 883–911). Firm knowledge of this less famous Ethelred II is scant. He is likely to have been Mercian or West Saxon by birth. Doubt surrounds his royal status and although some records accord him the title of king, he is more frequently referred to as the Lord of the Mercians. He probably acknowledged the overlordship of Alfred the Great and he was married to Alfred's daughter, Ethelflaed. Ethelred indulged frequently in border battles with the Welsh and was responsible for the fortification of Worcester and Gloucester. On Alfred's death, the security of Ethelred's position declined and in his last years much of the administrative responsibility of the kingdom fell to his wife.

◨ *see* Alfred the Great, Ethelflaed

EADWULF (D. AD 913)

King of Bernicia (AD 888–913). Eadwulf ruled the area of Bernicia, which lay between the rivers Tyne and Tweed, during the reign of Alfred the Great and forged a good relationship with the king of Wessex throughout his campaigns against the Vikings. It is likely that Eadwulf pledged allegiance to and acknowledged the overlordship of Alfred.

◨ *see* Alfred the Great

ETHELFLAED (C. AD 868–918)

'Lady of the Mercians' (AD 911–918). Ethelflaed was the first-born child of Alfred the Great and at the age of 18 she married Ethelred of Mercia. She proved to be an able administrator and, as her husband's health began to fail, she took on increasing responsibility for the running of the kingdom. Ethelflaed was truly her father's daughter and she led campaigns not only against the Welsh, but also against the marauding Vikings. Initially she tried to negotiate with the latter, but when they launched an attack on Chester, the queen defended her husband's realm through the construction of fortifications. When Ethelred died in AD 911, Ethelflaed continued to run the kingdom as she had done before. The young Athelstan, son of her brother, Edward the Elder, had spent much of his youth in the court of Mercia and therefore under the influence of Ethelflaed. Her expectation that he would succeed her was eventually fulfilled after her daughter, Elfwynn, had briefly assumed the throne of Mercia.

◆ *see* Alfred the Great, Ethelstan, Edward the Elder

EDWARD THE ELDER (C. AD 870–925)

King of Wessex (AD 899–924). The eldest son of Alfred the Great and Ealhswith, Edward ascended the Wessex throne on his father's death on 26 October AD 899 and was crowned at Kingston upon Thames on 8 June AD 900. Earlier he had fought and defeated his cousin, Ethelwold, in a fight for the throne. The son of Ethelred I, who as a child had been passed over in favour of Alfred the Great, Ethelwold remained a thorn in the king's side for some years until he was killed in battle. This was just one of many military victories enjoyed by Edward the Elder during his 25-year reign and he emulated his father by inflicting a series of defeats on the Danes throughout the period AD 910–18.

▲ *ABOVE: Edward the Elder*

109

Regaining possession of the Danelaw in the East Midlands and Essex, Edward also forced the East Anglian Danes into submission. In the west, Edward's cause was aided and abetted by his formidable sister, Ethelflaed. Known as the 'Lady of the Mercians', she fortified her kingdom's borders in the face of attacks from the Welsh, Danish and Norwegian forces, while her battlefield triumphs included her seizure of Derby in AD 917. The following year Edward received the submissions of the Welsh kings of Dyfed and Gwynedd. Then, in AD 923, Constantine II of Scotland and Raegnald, crowned head of the newly established kingdom of York, added their acknowledgements of Edward's position as British overlord.

Married three times, Edward's marriages to Egwina, Elfleda and lastly to Eadgifu produced many children in the years before his death. Dying in Mercia at Farndon, Cheshire, on 17 July AD 925, he was buried at Winchester in Wessex. He was succeeded by his eldest son, Athelstan. He was also survived by his third wife, Queen Eadgifu, who lived long enough to witness the coronations of her sons, Edmund I and Edred, and her grandsons, Edwy and Edgar.

◆ see Alfred the Great, Athelstan, Constantine II, Edmund I, Edred

ATHELSTAN (C. AD 895–939)

King of England (AD 924–39). Athelstan was the first-born child of Edward the Elder and Egwina and was the eldest of at least 14 offspring born to the king. Some doubt has been cast on his legitimacy, as it is unknown whether Edward the Elder was actually married to Egwina at the time of Athelstan's birth. Whatever the case, Athelstan is reputed to have been doted on by his grandfather, Alfred the Great, although the prince was still a young boy at the time of Alfred's death.

Athelstan spent much of his childhood in Mercia, where he was largely brought up by his aunt, Aethelflaed. He was so much regarded as one of their own that on his father's death in July AD 924, having spent 25 years as heir to the throne, the Mercians immediately proclaimed him their king. His ascension to the throne of Wessex took longer as the witan deliberated on his suitability (another possible indication of his illegitimacy). His coronation as king of Wessex eventually took place at Kingston upon Thames on 5 September AD 925.

Known in his charters as 'King of the English, raised to the throne ... by the hand of the Almighty', it was in AD 927 that Athelstan rose to become the undisputed ruler of England. His authority was acknowledged by the Norse king of York, Sihtric Caech, who no doubt feared the threat that Athelstan's Mercian following might pose to his own kingdom. Terms for

▲ ABOVE: Athelstan, king of the West Saxons

peace were agreed and as part of the deal Sihtric married Athelstan's sister on 30 January AD 926. This marriage alliance foundered with the early death of Sihtric, however, and so did the tentative peace that had accompanied it. The people of Sihtric's realm in Northumbria accepted the selection of the late king's son, Olaf, as his successor and Athelstan was forced to make a decisive move against them. Marching into Northumbria in AD 927, his invasion led directly to the submission of the kings of Scotland and Strathclyde as well as the lord of the English enclave of Bamburgh. This profitable campaign then reaped further dividends when Athelstan seized York.

The first king to bring most of England under his control, within four years of his successful sorties in the north Athelstan had made considerable inroads in the west, thus emphasising his status as the most powerful ruler in the British Isles. Athelstan first attacked and pushed back the Britons in South-West England, and across the Bristol Channel the leading Welsh kings, such as the Deheubarth ruler, Hywel Dda, were also quick to acknowledge Athelstan's greatness and pay homage to him. Later quelling an attempt at invasion by a fighting force of Scottish, Strathclyde and Irish-Viking men, the English sovereign's last great victory was won on the battlefield of Brunanburh in AD 937.

Athelstan was also highly influential throughout Continental Europe and a series of carefully planned marriages of his family members with European royalty helped England's king establish a network of alliances. Fortunately for him, Athelstan had been blessed with no fewer than seven half-sisters. One wed Otto, a German prince who later became Holy Roman Emperor; a second married the king of the West Franks, Charles II the Simple; while other daughters of Edward the Elder became the wives of foreign dukes such as Hugh the Great, Boleslav II of Bohemia and Louis of Aquitaine.

A renowned administrator and lawmaker whose many charters bear witness to the sheer volume of new laws introduced in his reign, Athelstan died at Gloucester on 27 October AD 939. Buried at Malmesbury Abbey, the unmarried king's successor was his half-brother, Edmund I.

◆ *see* House of Deheubarth, Hywel Dda, House of Wessex

EDMUND I (AD 921–46)

King of England (AD 939–46); son of Edward the Elder; known as Edmund the Magnificent. Edmund was the grandson of Alfred the Great and the first-born child of Edward the Elder by his third marriage. In AD 937 Edmund fought alongside his step-brother, Athelstan, at the Battle of Brunanburgh. Two years after this triumph he became king.

Eighteen years old when crowned at Kingston upon Thames on 16 November AD 939, his first task as king was to defend the large confederation of sub-kingdoms over which he claimed sovereignty. Led by Olaf Guthfrithson, Dublin's king and ruler of the Norse kingdom of York, the invasion force of AD 940 swept into the Midlands towards Leicester. There, faced with a formidable army, Edmund was forced to sue for peace and, in so doing, to surrender into Danish hands a swathe of land running from Northumbria south to Watling Street. Worse was to follow as Olaf drove on to conquer more northern territories.

However, the English king rallied in AD 942, beating into submission both Olaf Guthfrithson's cousin, Olaf Sihtricson, and his brother Raegnald II. The Five Boroughs were taken back and English forces marched into Northumbria and took York in AD 944. Finally, in AD 945, Strathclyde was overrun and handed over to England's ally, the Scots' king, Malcolm I. Yet Edmund I had little time to bask in the glory of his military victories. At Pucklechurch, Gloucestershire, on 6 May AD 946, the king and his entourage tried to arrest the outlaw, Liofa. A scuffle ensued and in the confusion

Edmund I was stabbed. Dying of his wounds, he was buried at Glastonbury Abbey and was succeeded as king by his younger brother, Edred.

◆ *see* Athelstan, Edred

EDRED (C. AD 923–955)

King of England (AD 946–55). A grandson of Alfred the Great, Edred was the second son of Edward the Elder's third marriage. Handed the reins of power following the death of his brother, Edmund I, on 26 May AD 946, he was crowned at Kingston Upon Thames on 16 August that year.

Failing in his attempt to defeat the marauding Vikings under Eric Bloodaxe in AD 948, Edred was able to take comfort from the

Northumbrian support he then enjoyed. Later losing this support as a power struggle flared up between Olaf Sihtricson and Eric, it was not until AD 954, the year of Eric Bloodaxe's death, that control of Northumbria reverted to an Anglo-Saxon ruler.

He died after a long illness on 23 November AD 955 at about the age of 32. Edred passed away at Frome in Somerset, but was interred at Winchester. Edred had never married and was succeeded by his young nephew, Edwy.

◆ *see* Edmund I, Edwy, Eric Bloodaxe

◀ *LEFT: Edred*

EDGAR THE PEACEFUL (C. AD 943–75)

King of England (AD 959–75). The second son of Edmund I by his first wife Elgifu (or Elgiva), and great-grandson of Alfred the Great, Edgar was still a babe-in-arms when his father died. Growing up during the reigns of his uncle, Edred, and his brother, Edwy, he was still a young prince when, late in the year AD 957, both Mercia and Northumbria swore their allegiances to him.

On 1 October AD 959 Edwy died and Edgar ascended the throne as king of Wessex and all England. The transfer of power from brother to brother was smooth, with the new monarch effecting few changes in personnel or policy during tranquil years refreshingly free from war. In this climate religious reformers such as Dunstan, Ethelwold and Oswald, all subsequently canonised, were given greater freedom.

Edgar's first wife, Ethelfleda, had given birth to his son and heir, Edward, while his second marriage to Elfrida (also known as Elfthrith),

produced two sons. The eldest boy, Edmund, died in AD 971, but the younger son was later crowned Ethelred II. Having reigned for 16 years, Edgar died on 8 July AD 975 and was buried at Glastonbury Abbey.

◘ *see* Ethelred II

▲ *ABOVE: The barge of Edgar*

ETHELRED II (THE UNREADY) (C. AD 966–1016)

King of England (AD 978–1013, 1014–16). The second son of King Edgar's second marriage, at the age of 10 or 11 Ethelred's half-brother, Edward the Martyr, was killed while on his way to meet Ethelred's mother, Elfrida. Soon Ethelred succeeded Edward, while his mother later became a nun. Ascending the English throne on 18 March AD 978, the young king was crowned by Archbishop Dunstan at the Wessex stronghold of Kingston upon Thames one month later, on 14 April.

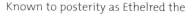

▲ *ABOVE: Ethelred II*

Known to posterity as Ethelred the Unready, the king's nickname was a play on words ('Unrede' meaning 'no counsel') coined in the twelfth century by writers looking back at his time as king. From AD 979 raids by Vikings were a recurrent theme. Initially, the raiders plundered coastal communities, then left as quickly as they had come, but increasingly Danish attackers were paid off with bribes known later as Danegeld. But still the attacks continued and three years after Byrhtnoth of Essex had died a valiant death at Maldon in AD 991, London was besieged by Norway's Olaf Tryggvason and Denmark's King Svein. However, once again a Viking force was paid off. In 1002, it was the turn of Ethelred to go on the offensive as he ordered the murder of every Dane in England. Taking place on 13 November 1002, just a few months after the king had married his second wife, Emma of Normandy, the St Brice's Day Massacre did not go unnoticed in Scandinavia and in 1003 and 1004 hard-hitting Danish attacks were carried out in England.

As more campaigns were launched, the Anglo-Saxons responded by introducing new initiatives, but English resistance was broken in 1013. Beginning in the north, Svein Forkbeard advanced towards the heartland of Ethelred's kingdom. London was defended by Thorkell the Tall, a Viking warrior who had switched sides, but when he was beaten, Ethelred II conceded defeat.

Then, on 3 February 1014, the new king, Svein Forkbeard, died and Ethelred returned to England from Normandy and was accepted as ruler once more. The next year was peaceful, but in 1015 Svein's son, Cnut, made his bid for Ethelred's crown. Yet, just as Cnut made inroads into Anglo-Saxon territories, Ethelred II the Unready fell ill. He died on 23 April 1016 and was buried at St Paul's Cathedral.

The father of many children by his two marriages, he was succeeded by Edmund II, the eldest surviving son of his first marrriage to Elfgiva. Ethelred II was also survived by his second wife, Queen Emma, and their sons, Alfred, and the future monarch, Edward the Confessor.

see Edward the Confessor, Edmund II, Svein Forkbeard

EDMUND II (C. AD 993-1–16)

King of England (1016); known as Edmund Ironside because of his bravery in battle. Edmund was the son of Ethelred II and his first wife Elgiva. After his father had been reinstated as king in 1014 the two men fell out, but were eventually reconciled before Ethelred's death on 23 April 1016.

Ascending the Wessex throne, Edmund II was crowned at St Paul's Cathedral. However, his kingship was immediately challenged by Cnut, the son of Svein Forkbeard, who had briefly deposed Edmund's father three years ealier. In the meantime Cnut had re-established Viking control in the northern Danelaw as he continued the struggle between the Danish kings and their Anglo-Saxon counterparts. His next move was to besiege London.

▲ ABOVE: Edmund II Ironside

Edmund successfully managed to relieve the city, where he enjoyed considerable support, but he soon lost the initiative he had gained, by suffering a heavy and decisive defeat at Ashingdon, Essex. The two warrior kings then came to an agreement by which they would divide England between them: Edmund would rule over Wessex and Cnut was to claim sovereignty in all areas north of the Thames. The arrangement did not last long because on 30 November 1016 Edmund II died. He was buried alongside his grandfather, Edgar, at Glastonbury. Married to Ealdgyth from 1015, Edmund was survived by his wife and their two infant sons, Edmund and Edward. Cnut succeeded him without any opposition.

◗ see Cnut, Ethelred II

EDWARD THE CONFESSOR (C. 1003–66)

King of England (1042–66). Edward was born at Islip, Oxfordshire, when his father Ethelred II, was England's reigning monarch. After the king's death in 1016 Edward and his younger brother, Alfred, sailed to Normandy, the homeland of his mother, Emma. Edward spent his childhood years in the duchy where his uncle Richard, the grandfather of William the Conqueror, was duke. In this age of marriages between the royal families of Europe, Edward, the son of Ethelred, was also the stepson of Cnut, whom Emma had married after the death of Ethelred. Cnut became king of England in 1016 after the death of Edward's half brother, Edmund II. Remaining in Normandy during the reigns of Cnut (1016–35) and Cnut's son, Harold I, (1035–40), Edward became a welcome guest at the English royal court once again when his half-brother, Harthacnut, was crowned king of England. Then, on 8 June 1042, Harthacnut died.

Ascending the throne left vacant by his half-brother's death, it was only right and proper that the devoutly Christian Edward was crowned on Easter Sunday 1043 in a grand coronation service held at Winchester

Cathedral. Edward's accession had been readily accepted, but the new king was soon faced with difficulties. The danger of invasion by King Magnus of Norway remained a threat until 1047 when Magnus's successor, Harold Hardrada, made peace with England.

In 1045 Edward had married Edith, a daughter of Earl Godwin. Later the king became unpopular with some nobles for appointing men from Normandy to important posts. At home, therefore, Edward the Confessor had to cope with the problems posed by three powerful earls: Leofric of Mercia (the husband of the famous Lady Godiva), Siward of Northumbria and Godwin of Wessex. All of them resented the Norman influence that Edward brought to England from his time at the court of Normandy.

As the king grew older and no heir appeared to confirm the line of succession, potential candidates jostled for position behind the throne. Briefly, the Confessor's chosen heir had been Edward the Atheling, son of

▶ RIGHT: *The chapel of Edward the Confessor in Westminster Abbey*
▲ ABOVE: *King Edward the Confessor*

Edmund II, but after his death in 1057, the mantle passed to Edmund's grandson, Edgar the Atheling. Among the other contenders to succeed Edward the Confessor were Godwin's sons, Harold and Tostig, Harold Hardrada and William, Duke of Normandy.

On 5 January 1066, just eight days after the consecration of his beloved Westminster Abbey, Edward the Confessor died. He was buried at Westminster the day after his death. In the immediate aftermath of his funeral the late king was formally succeeded by his wife's brother,

Earl Godwin's eldest son, Harold, whom he had apparently promised the throne while on his deathbed. Queen Edith herself lived on until 1075, when her body was laid to rest alongside her husband. Canonised by Pope Alexander III in 1161, eight years later the mortal remains of Edward the Confessor were reburied with great reverence and humility by Henry III in a new shrine at Westminster Abbey.

◆ *see* Cnut, Edmund II, Ethelred II, Harthacnut, William I

HOUSE OF WESSEX

WESSEX, HOUSE OF

Thought to have been established about AD 495 by Cerdic, the West-Saxon kingdom soon became a force in southern England. King Ceawlin, who ruled in the second half of the sixth century, was so powerful that the monk, Bede, named him as one of the seven English bretwaldas (i.e. king of kings).

Later still Egbert was a dominant ruler. Reigning from AD 802, he extended the Wessex borders defeating Mercia and overrunning Essex, Kent and Sussex. After Egbert's death his son, Ethelwulf, became king. The father of several sons, four of whom went on to wear the Wessex crown. The reigns of Ethelbald, Ethelbert and Ethelred I were all short, but then in AD 871 came the accession of the most famous West-Saxon king of them all: King Alfred.

Establishing and fortifying his kingdom after finally defeating the Danes, the king was also a lawmaker and a writer who promoted literacy. At his death Alfred was succeeded by his son, Edward the Elder. Like his father he fought and defeated the Danes and was acknowledged by other British kings as overlord from AD 917. Edward's son, Athelstan, was also recognised as a king of kings in Britain, while simultaneously forming wedding alliances with Continental royal houses. At home he continued the legal and administrative reforms of his father and grandfather before him.

▶ RIGHT: A Saxon church in Northamptonshire

After Athelstan, the Wessex line was hit by a series of short reigns with five kings ruling in the period AD 939–978. Athelstan's half-brothers, Edmund I and Edred, Edmund's son, Edwy, and Edward the Martyr came and went in the space of a few years, with only Edward's father, Edgar, enjoying a long and peaceful reign during this period, one that lasted 16 years. Then, in AD 978 Ethelred II the Unready ascended the Wessex throne.

Another son of King Edgar, he ruled over Wessex and much of England for 38 years in all, but his troubled reign was interrupted by the brief rule of the Dane, Svein Forkbeard. Ethelred II was later succeeded by his son, Edmund II Ironside, although he died a short time later. There then followed a period of Danish rule with Svein's son, Cnut, reigning until

1035. His successors were his sons, Harold I Harefoot and Harthacnut, but after the latter's death the House of Wessex was restored when Edward the Confessor became monarch.

The longest-reigning king since his father, Ethelred II, Edward the Confessor was the founder of Westminster Abbey and was succeeded by the last Anglo-Saxon king, his brother-in-law, Harold II. King Harold ruled for just nine months, however, before he was killed at the Battle of Hastings in 1066. His death, and the subsequent accession of the Norman duke, William the Conqueror, marked the end of the line for the Wessex dynasty.

▲ *ABOVE: King Ozric of Mercia, early Anglo-Saxon royalty from Gloucester Cathedral*

ALFRED THE GREAT (AD 849–99)

King of Wessex (AD 871–99); son of Ethelwulf. One of the best-loved figures in English history, Alfred was the fourth and last of his father's sons to reign in Wessex. Alfred was born at Wantage in Oxfordshire in AD 849, when his father had already ruled the kingdom of Wessex for almost a decade. Ethelwulf had consolidated the West-Saxon dynasty established by his own father, Egbert. Egbert had once ruled over a kingdom that included the modern-day counties of Sussex, Surrey, Kent and Essex, while even Mercia in the east came under his command. Later, Ethelwulf's death saw the Wessex crown pass in quick succession to Alfred's elder brothers: Ethelbald, Ethelbert and Ethelred I.

In AD 868, Alfred married Ealswith, a Mercian princess. Two years later, on Berkshire Downs, Alfred assisted his brother, Ethelred, in inflicting a heavy defeat on the marauding Danes. However, the 'Great Army' struck back swiftly, bringing Northumbria and East Anglia under their sway and attacking Wessex once again. Alfred had become king of the West Saxons – ascending the throne ahead of Ethelred's young son, Ethelwold – in April AD 871. Within a year he was forced to negotiate a peace settlement with the Danes. After a brief foray into Mercia, however, the Danes returned to Wessex yet again and in AD 878 the invaders launched a surprise attack at Chippenham.

Forced to retreat when a full-scale invasion of Wessex threatened, during Easter AD 878 Alfred sought refuge in the marshlands of Athelney, Somerset. This period in the wilderness has given

◄ LEFT: *King Alfred reading*

126

▶ RIGHT: Statue of Alfred the Great, Wantage

rise to several tales, including the one in which the disguised king was scolded by a swineherd's wife for burning the cakes she had asked him to tend. Also leading raiding parties from his hideaway in the wilds of Somerset, Alfred then won a crucial victory by defeating the Viking, Guthrum, at Edington, Wiltshire. A short time later the Treaty of Wedmore was agreed: acknowledging Danish rights to rule over territory they had already conquered, the deal secured the independence of Wessex.

With peace now assured, Alfred took to strengthening the defences of his kingdom by creating new burgs (fortified towns) and transforming old Roman towns such as Winchester. In AD 886 Alfred's militia captured London. Seven years later a vast Danish army went on the rampage, but the strong fortifications in Wessex held firm. In addition to keeping the Danes at bay, the Wessex king ensured the continuation of his dynasty by diplomatic manoeuvrings with rival kingdoms such as Mercia where, for much of his reign, Burhed (his brother-in-law) and Ethelred (his son-in-law) were rulers.

A popular, resourceful leader who compiled a code of laws, King Alfred also made an important contribution to educating the people of his kingdom. He translated Christian texts, wrote his own original works and was one of the first authors to refer to 'England', the word Angelcynn coined by Alfred meaning 'English folk'. His religious faith and passion for learning underpinned the move to raise levels of literacy throughout the land, while a knowledge of Latin became a necessity for officials of court, Church and the justice system. Dying at Winchester on 26 October AD 899, Alfred the Great was buried at Winchester Abbey. Survived by his wife, he was succeeded as king by his son.

see Edward the Elder, House of Wessex

EDWY (D. AD 959)

King of England (AD 955–59). The eldest son of Edmund I and his first wife, Elgifu, Edwy was still in his teens when he became king. The latest in a series of Wessex monarchs to be crowned as minors, his coronation took place in January AD 956 at Kingston upon Thames. The ceremony itself passed off without incident, but the post-coronation banquet was interrupted by a heated argument. This argument began after the young king decided to steal away from the formal banquet to amuse himself in the company of two women, his wife-to-be, Elgifu, and her mother, Ethelgiva. What happened next is uncertain, but the more sensational accounts suggest that the powerful cleric, Dunstan, was sent by Archbishop Oda to call the king back to the banquet. Flying into a fury at seeing the juvenile king wrapped in the arms of two women, his crown dismissively cast to one side, Dunstan was said to have manhandled both Edwy and the women.

Whether this is what actually happened, the coronation incident preceded a reign as short as it was eventful. Dunstan slipped away into exile, while Edwy wed Elgifu. King in Wessex, Mercia and Northumbria at the time of his accession, in AD 957 the Mercians and the Northumbrians adopted Edwy's brother, Edgar, as king of their

◀ LEFT: Edwy

realms. Worse was to follow for the young king as his marriage to his blood relative, Elgifu, was annulled by Archbishop Oda in AD 958. Then, in September AD 959, his ex-wife died, her death followed on 1 October by that of Edwy. Monarch for less than four years, he was succeeded by his brother, Edgar.

◆ *see* Edgar, Edmund I

EDWARD THE MARTYR (C. AD 962–78)

King of England (AD 975–78). The son of Edgar and his first wife, Ethelflaeda, Edward became king of Wessex after his father's death on 8 July AD 975. Crowned at Kingston upon Thames, Edward was to endure a difficult time as monarch: his troubled reign a marked contrast to the calm of Edgar's years on the throne.

Probably hot-headed and blunt, possibly quick to make enemies, there is little doubt that the teenaged king suffered a violent death. Dying on the night of 18 March AD 978 Edward was murdered by a band of assassins, who intercepted him as he headed for Corfe Castle in Dorset. As he had been travelling there to meet his young half-brother, Ethelred, and his step mother, Elfrida, inevitably she was implicated in Edward's murder. However, no charges were ever brought and, as quickly as Edward's body was buried at the Dorset settlement of Wareham, Elfrida's young son was crowned Ethelred II. Luckless in his short life, in death Edward came to be seen as a saint. Later known as Edward the Martyr, one year after his murder the body of the boy-king was reburied at Shaftesbury Abbey.

◆ *see* Edgar the Peaceful, Ethelred II

▶ *RIGHT: Edward the Martyr*

DANES & VIKINGS

ANGLO-DANES

Viking rulers of the British Isles. Viking raids were recorded as long ago as the end of the eighth century when many battles were fought between native Britons and Danish raiders Lands in all four corners of the British Isles had been seized and many sums paid by native peoples to Norsemen in the form of tribute. Yet it was not until 1013 that Svein Forkbeard became the first Dane to be recognised as king of England.

The eldest son of Denmark's monarch, Harald III ('Bluetooth'), in AD 994 Svein and Norway's Olaf Tryggvason sailed to England at the head of a huge fleet of warships and there besieged London. Eventually peace was exchanged for £16,000, but regular Viking raids continued to afflict English settlements. Svein's sister, Gunhild, was

allegedly one of many English-based Danes to be slaughtered in the St Brice's Day Massacre in 1002. The following year Danish militia sought revenge for this atrocity by fighting their way deep into the heart of England. Another attack in 1004 and a third in 1009 led to Danish assaults on 15 counties before Svein Forkbeard broke the back of native resistance.

Crowned in 1013 following Ethelred II's hurried dash into exile, Svein died just a few months later and Ethelred was reinstated as king until his own death in 1016. Succeeded by his son, Edmund II ('Ironside'), the Danish

▲ *ABOVE: The Anglo-Danish Kings, Canute, Harold I and II with Edward the Confessor, the Anglo-Saxon King* threat showed no signs of abating as Svein's son, Cnut, continued the challenge to Anglo-Saxon rule, which he had helped sustain during his father's lifetime. Overlooked in 1014, two years later Edmund's death saw Cnut add the kingdom of Wessex to the territory ceded him a short time before by King Edmund.

King of Denmark from 1019 and ruler of Norway after 1030, Cnut reigned as England's king until his death in 1035. Succeeded in England by the younger son from his first marriage, Harold I's ('Harefoot') reign was brief. On Harold's death in 1040 he was succeeded by his half-brother, Harthacnut (or Hardicanute). The only son of Cnut and Emma (the widow of Ethelred II), he had been chosen to rule jointly with Harold in 1035, but had forfeited this opportunity by his continued absence from England.

King for just two years, Harthacnut's death brought an abrupt end to the rule of England's Danish kings and the accession of Edward the Confessor heralded the final flourish of the Anglo-Saxon age. However, in 1066, an Anglo-Danish kingship was fleetingly restored when Harold II was crowned. He was the eldest son of Earl Godwin and his wife, Gytha. Harold's mother was the great-granddaughter of the one-time king of Denmark, Harold III.

◆ see House of Wessex

▲ ABOVE: Harthacnut

GUTHFRITH I (D. AD 895)

King of York (AD 883–95). Little is known about this Dane who was elected to be king by the Church leaders of the Viking area of Jorvik. It is possible that he had come to England as part of the 'Great Army' of the leader, Halfdan, but he may have arrived in York later on. Before Guthfrith, the people of York were subordinate to the kings of other regions, without a leader of their own, but towards the end of the ninth century, it was decided that they should pick one of their own to run the province. Guthfrith was already a Christian and this is likely to have swayed the election in his favour. Halfdan had driven out the monks of Durham; Guthfrith's reign saw their return. It was also marked by improved relations between the Vikings and the Angles. On his death, Guthfrith was buried in York Minster.

HALFDAN II (D. AD 910)

King of York (c. AD 902–10). Halfdan is belived to have been a joint ruler of the Viking kingdom of Jorvik (York), with Eowils, but little is really known of his reign, or indeed his status. There remains doubt about whether he was a king at all. However, what is clear is that this was a troubled time in Northumbria and in AD 909 Ethelflaed, the 'Lady of the Mercians', removed the relics of St Oswald from the area, for safekeeping. This was the period in which Edward the Elder attempted to bring the northern Danes under his control – a time characterised by invasion and battle.

◆ *see* Edward the Elder, Ethelflaed

RAGNALL I (D. AD 921)

King of York (AD 910–21). Ragnall was one of the many Vikings expelled from Dublin in AD 902 and immediately after this event he took to making border raids on Strathclyde and Scotland. In AD 910 he seized the kingdom of York and began extending its boundaries. In around AD 914 he declared himself king of Strathclyde, an area that he had continued to bombard with attacks since his time in York. He came into conflict with Ethelflaed, the Lady of the Mercians, in AD 917, but her death the following year proved fortuitous for Ragnall. Constantine II of Scotland then joined the fray, assembling a small army to march against Ragnall, but the Dane was successful once again.

On his return to York he discovered that various factions had arisen and there was opposition to his place as ruler. Undeterred, he reasserted his authority in this Danish kingdom. His luck eventually ran out in around AD 920 and he was forced to submit to Edward the Elder. He died in AD 921.

◆ *see* Ethelflaed, Edward the Elder, Constantine II

SIGTRYGR CAECH (D. AD 927)

King of York (AD 921–27); brother of Ragnall. Sigtrygr was one of the Vikings expelled from Dublin in AD 902 and joined Ragnall on his raids in Strathclyde and Scotland. He regained control of Dublin in AD 917 and ruled there until AD 921. With the death of Ragnall in that year, Sigtrygr decided to make a claim to his brother's kingdom of York. While Ragnall had acknowledged Edward the Elder as his overlord, Sigtrygr maintained his own kingship, but on the death of Edward and the succession of Athelstan he realised the support of Mercia for the Wessex king could pose problems and signed a treaty with him in AD 926. By the terms of this treaty the Dane converted to Christianity and married Athelstan's sister, Edith. It was not long before Sigtrygr reneged on his agreement, though. He did not live to face the consequences of this betrayal, dying in AD 927.

◆ *see* Athelstan, Edward the Elder, Ragnall II

ERIC BLOODAXE (D. AD 954)

King of York (intermittently AD 939–54). Eric Bloodaxe was the archetypal Viking warrior and possibly gained his name from the legendary slaughter he inflicted on members of his own family. Eric was the favourite son of Harald Finehair, the king of Norway, and he inherited the throne of this country from his father in AD 933, when the former abdicated. Eric's bloody reign resulted in his own deposition, though, and so he set off to see what other lands he could conquer. After spending some time on Orkney, where he established himelf as king, Eric seized the opportunity offered by the death of Edmund to lay claim to the Viking kingdom of York. He was assisted in this by the province's archbishop, Wulfstan, while the witan selected Edred as king. There followed a succession of battles between the Anglo-Saxon and Viking claimants to York and others threw in their lot as well, including the Viking Olaf Sihtricson. Eric was thrown out of York and Olaf permitted to rule there under the overlordship of Edred. The tables soon turned, however, and Eric was reinstated, prompting further retaliatory action from Edred. The scuffles continued until Eric was killed by soldiers waiting in an ambush. His wife and two of their sons escaped back to Orkney, where they continued to rule.

◆ see Edred

SVEIN FORKBEARD (D. 1014)

King of England (1013–14); first Danish king of England. The son of Denmark's sovereign, Harald III Bluetooth, Svein had replaced his father as king by AD 988. Soon establishing a reputation in northern Europe as an aggressive warrior king, he was a leading light in a massive attack launched on England in AD 994. Allied with the Norwegian, Olaf Tryggvason, that year the two Scandinavian leaders had sailed across the North Sea at the head of a fleet of 94 Viking longships. However, despite the size of their invasion force, they did not conquer the English kingdom of Ethelred II the Unready, settling instead for peace and a payment of £16,000.

Lesser raids followed, but in 1003, Svein Forkbeard masterminded a successful campaign, which was probably launched in retaliation for the St Brice's Day Massacre, the slaughter of Danes living in England which claimed many lives, including, it is said, Svein's sister, Gunhild.

Gunhild was also the name of his first wife. A fiery Polish woman, she became the mother of two sons, the eldest, Harald, succeeding his father as king of Denmark, the youngest, Cnut, succeeding Edmund II Ironside as England's ruler. Svein's second wife, Sigrid the Haughty, gave birth to a daughter, whose second husband was Duke Richard II of Normandy, the grandfather of William I the Conqueror.

In 1004 Svein Forkbeard sacked and set fire to Norwich. Gradually securing more and more English land with each passing year, in 1013 the

Danes invaded. Beginning their invasion in August 1013, they moved from Sandwich in Kent to Gainsborough in Lincolnshire. There, gaining the support of Northumbria, the Five Boroughs of the Midlands and other surrounding regions, Svein's forces moved south, and Oxford and Winchester surrendered without a fight. Then London was attacked.

◀ LEFT: Viking longship

The city stood firm and so the Danes headed west to overrun Wallingford in Oxfordshire and Bath. Then, with the eventual fall of London, Ethelred II fled. Acknowledged as England's new king in December 1013, Svein Forkbeard reigned just a few weeks. Dying on 3 February 1014 at his English base of Gainsborough, he was buried in Roskilde Cathedral in his native Denmark. England's first Danish king, he was succeeded by the man he had deposed, Ethelred II the Unready, but was survived by his son Cnut, who later succeeded Ethelred's own son, Edmund II Ironside.

◻ *see* Cnut, Edmund II

CNUT (C. AD 994–1035)

King of England (1016–35). The grandson of the Danish king Harald III ('Bluetooth'), Cnut was the second son born to King Svein and his first wife, Gunhild. Years later, as Svein sought to dethrone Ethelred II, the young prince fought at his father's side. Svein died after serving just six months as king of England. Cnut was about 20 years old at the time.

Ethelred had returned from exile to retake England's crown and Cnut once again began plotting his enemy's downfall. After bringing Northumbria back into Danish hands, Cnut began an advance on London in 1016. Ethelred's death brought the Danish challenger into direct conflict with the new king, Edmund II. Fighting for the right to rule, a series of skirmishes followed until the autumn of 1016 when fighting and fate combined to shape Cnut's destiny. At Ashingdon in Essex his men inflicted a heavy defeat on Edmund, who was forced to make substantial concessions to his conqueror. The sons of the two previous English monarchs then divided the country in two, with the Dane reigning over all English lands north of the Thames. It was not long, however, before Cnut was king of all England.

Ascending the throne following Edmund's death on 30 November 1016, Cnut's coronation was held two months later at St Paul's Cathedral, London. Brutally flexing his royal muscle, he ordered the murder of Eadric Streona, the turncoat Earl of Mercia, who had so frequently switched sides in the struggle between the Anglo-Saxons and the Danes. Also sacrificed was Eadwig, a brother of the former king.

In 1017, the year that he married Ethelred the Unready's widow, Emma, the English kingdom was divided up into the four earldoms of Northumbria, Mercia, East Anglia and Wessex, but as Cnut's empire expanded, to encompass Denmark (from 1019) and Norway (from 1028), changes in England were kept to a minimum and subsequently the country enjoyed a rare period of calm.

Cnut died at Shaftesbury, Dorset, on 12 November 1035 and was

interred at Winchester Cathedral. He was succeeded by a son from his marriage to Elgifu of Northampton, Harold I. When Harold I Harefoot died, the English crown passed briefly to that monarch's half-brother, Harthacnut, a son of Cnut and Emma.

◼ see Edmund II, Ethelred II

▲ *ABOVE. Watching the approach of Danish raiders from the English coast*

HAROLD I (C. 1016–40)

King of England (1037–40). The second son of Cnut and Elgifu of Northampton, in 1035 Harold succeeded his father as regent while Harthacnut remained in Denmark where he was king. Ruling England on behalf of his half-brother, Harthacnut, it was also agreed that Harold's stepmother, Queen Emma, would control Wessex. However, this arrangement lasted less than two years, Harold's cause helped considerably by Harthacnut's continued absence.

Acknowledged as king in 1037, his accession led to Emma's departure for Flanders, her flight probably hastened by the brutal treatment handed out the previous year to her son Alfred. The eldest of her two sons by Ethelred II the Unready, Alfred had travelled to see his mother in 1036, but had been taken prisoner, brutally blinded and left to die from his injuries.

Meanwhile, as Harold I assumed full control, Harthacnut sailed to meet his mother, Emma, at Bruges. Arriving there with his fleet late in 1039, still he made no move to claim the English throne. On 17 March 1040, the unmarried and childless Harold died at Oxford and Harthacnut succeeded unopposed. His half-brother's body was buried at St Clement Dane's Church in London, but legend has it that Harthacnut gave instructions for it to be dug up and thrown into a nearby marsh.

◆ *see* Cnut, Harthacnut

▲ *ABOVE: Harold I*

HARTHACNUT (C. 1019–42)

King of England (1040–42). The son of Cnut and his second wife, Emma, the widow of Ethelred II the Unready, he was still a boy when he became King of Denmark in 1028. Two years later his half-brother, Svein, ascended the throne of Norway, while in 1035 Cnut's death saw him recognised as his father's successor in England.

However, Harthacnut was preoccupied with the threat posed to Denmark by the new Norwegian ruler, King Magnus. As a result, his half-brother, Harold, gradually asserted control in England until finally proclaimed King Harold I in 1037. However, just as Harthacnut was poised to launch an invasion attempt, Harold's early death on 17 March 1040 gave Harthacnut a second chance to become the English monarch.

Sailing to England at the head of an impressively large fleet of 62 warships, on his arrival he was duly crowned at Canterbury Cathedral on 18 June 1040. Two summers later, though, Harthacnut was dead, his short reign clouded by the hostility and murders that followed the imposition of taxes intended to pay for the upkeep of the king's vast armada of ships.

Dying on 8 June 1042, the unpopular Anglo-Danish king was buried at Winchester and was succeeded by his half-brother, Edward the Confessor, the younger son of Queen Emma and Ethelred II the Unready.

◆ *see* Cnut, Edward the Confessor, Ethelred II

▶ *RIGHT: Harthacnut, son of Cnut*

HAROLD II (C. 1020–66)

King of England (1066). Born in 1020, Harold was the son of Godwin, Earl of Wessex, and Gytha, a great-granddaughter of King Harald Bluetooth of Denmark. One of several sons in a large and powerful English family, Harold was also the brother of Edith, who married Edward the Confessor in 1045. Gaining lands and titles, soon after his sister's marriage Earl Harold ruled over much of eastern England.

Falling from favour when his father and family were sent into exile by the king in 1051, Harold returned in 1052 intent on restoring his family's fortunes. It was part of a large force that converged on London and a pitched battle was averted when a hasty peace deal was agreed. The following year Harold's father's death saw him become Earl of Wessex; Berkshire and Somerset also coming under his rule. In 1055, Harold's brother, Tostig, was made Earl of Northumbria.

Harold consolidated his position as the leading English nobleman during the next decade, a period in which the question of who would succeed Edward the Confessor was often asked. There were several strong contenders including William, Duke of Normandy, and Edgar the Atheling, but when the old king died on 5 January 1066, he was succeeded by Earl Harold, who was crowned the following day at Westminster Abbey.

Aware from the outset that he would face challenges to his rule, he expected his brother, Tostig, to retaliate following his dismissal as Earl of Northumbria the previous year; the king of Norway Harald Hardrada was another likely opponent, as was William of Normandy. However, the first four months of his reign were peaceful. Tostig landed at Sandwich in Kent in May 1066, having earlier launched raids along England's south coast. However, as he sailed up the east coast his attacks petered out, but he would soon return. Meanwhile, Harald Hardrada was planning his attack and Duke William was recruiting more and more men to his invasion force.

In September 1066, Harald Hardrada landed on the East Yorkshire coast and marched his troops the short distance to York. An attack followed, but soon the city was forced to negotiate a peace treaty. A few days then passed before Harold II arrived in the north of England. At the head of his army, England's king attacked his Norwegian counterpart at Stamford Bridge, near York, on 25 October 1066. The fighting continued until Harald Hardrada, Tostig and many Norwegian warriors were dead. Harold had secured an important victory but there was little time to savour this success; news soon came through that a large Norman army had landed on England's south coast.

Immediately marching his battle-weary troops back to London, he stopped in London just long enough to recruit more men. In Sussex by 13 October 1066, the following morning Duke William struck the first blow of the Battle of Hastings. In the fighting that followed the king's brothers, Gyrth and Leofwine, were slain. Harold himself was fatally wounded by an enemy arrow. His men fought on, but by nightfall, William of Normandy had won a momentous victory.

His wife, Eldgyth, and his son, Harold, outlived the last Anglo-Danish king, who also left behind a large number of illegitimate children, whose mother, Edith Swan-Neck, reputedly buried the body of Harold II at Waltham Abbey in Essex.

◆ *see* Edward the Confessor, William I

NORMANS

NORMANDY, HOUSE OF

Reigning in England from 1066 to 1154, the House of Normandy originated not in northern France, but in Scandinavia. For it was from there that Rollo the Ganger sailed to pillage and plunder. The son of Rognvald of Moer and nephew of Sigurd the Mighty, Rollo, or Rolf, conquered Normandy. Later gaining acceptance by the French king, Charles the Simple, the Viking duchy of Normandy continued to maintain strong links with Danish rulers during the tenth and eleventh centuries and so the grandfather of William the Conqueror, Richard II of Normandy, married Svein Forkbeard's sister, Astrid.

However, the Norman dynasty also forged marriage alliances with other royal houses, for example, the marriage of William the Conqueror to

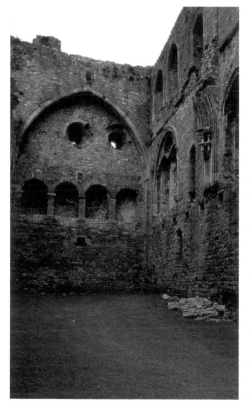

▲ ABOVE: O'Brien's Castle, County Galway

Matilda, the daughter of the Count of Flanders. There was also a strong English connection and it was this link that ultimately led to the Norman Conquest of England. For when Emma, the daughter of Richard I of Normandy, married first Ethelred II the Unready and then Cnut, the fortunes of England and Normandy became inextricably linked. And so it was that the mother of Edward the Confessor and the sister of William the Conqueror's grandfather gave Duke William a good claim to be Edward's successor.

Norman sources suggest that the duke was promised England's crown by both Edward and his eventual successor, Earl Harold of Wessex, but

when the Confessor died and was succeeded by Harold II, the Duke of Normandy was forced to claim the crown by force. Landing on England's south coast in September 1066, William won the Battle of Hastings in October and was crowned king on Christmas Day that year.

Within two years of his coronation the Norman Conquest was so well advanced that William could afford to return to his duchy on the other side of

◀ *LEFT: A Norman hunting scene*

the English Channel leaving his half-brother, Odo of Bayeux, to oversee his affairs in England. Meanwhile the Norman revolution continued. Castles and cathedrals were built and Norman customs were introduced. English clergymen were replaced by Normans and Norman nobles were granted land seized from the Anglo-Saxon nobility.

In fact William I effected such an overhaul of English society that, in the course of just two decades, it had been substantially and irrevocably altered, the nature of this change shown clearly by the Domesday Book. The Great Inquest or survey of English life was compiled 1086–87, and was intended to discover the ownership of land and livestock, and was collated in two volumes known as the Great and Little Domesday Books.

William I the Conqueror was succeeded by William II as the English king. He saw off the challenge from barons loyal to his brother, Robert, and defeated Gwynedd and the Scots, but fell out with St Anselm, the man he had appointed as Archbishop of Canterbury. William II Rufus was succeeded by his English-born brother, Henry I, who was another strong ruler. Also opposed by his brother, Duke Robert, he overcame this threat by capturing and imprisoning him and by taking possession of the duchy of Normandy. Known as Beauclerc, he continued the process of imposing the Crown's control.

However, like William II Rufus, Henry I did not leave a son to succeed him and so when King Stephen came to the throne civil war broke out with the king fighting to stave off the challenge of Henry's daughter, the Empress Matilda. Undefeated by the empress in war, he 'lost' the peace by agreeing to let Matilda's son, Henry of Anjou, succeed him. And so with Stephen's death in 1154, the House of Normandy gave way to the House of Anjou, Henry II becoming England's first Angevin or Plantagenet king.

◆ *see* Henry I, William I, William II

WILLIAM I (C. 1027–87)

King of England (1066–87); first Norman king. Born at Falaise in
Normandy in 1027 or 1028, William was the bastard son of Robert, Duke of
Normandy, and his mistress, Herleva. However, William's illegitimacy did
not prevent him becoming duke. Barely seven years old at the time of his
accession, his childhood years and his adolescence were fraught with
danger. All the young duke's chief protectors were killed as challengers
sought to overthrow William and his supporters in a duchy that was also
home to the future English king, Edward the Confessor. Successfully
negotiating the hazards of his early years, William then had to head off
challenges from fellow Normans, and he also fought against
neighbouring states.

In the years before the death of Edward the Confessor and the
accession of Harold II, Norman sources claim that Edward himself had
made William his heir. However, following the death of Edward the
Confessor on 5 January 1066, it was Harold II who was crowned. Duke
William did not launch an immediate attack on hearing the news of
Harold's coronation, but instead set about recruiting soldiers from
Normandy, Boulogne, Brittany and Italy. Then, having assembled an army
of 6–7,000 men, he sailed for England. Landing at Pevensey Bay on 28
September 1066, William and his troops had 16 days to prepare for
action, while the king's army came to the battle having just defeated
Harald Hardrada and Harold's brother, Tostig, at Stamford Bridge in
faraway Yorkshire.

At the Battle of Hastings the English forces resisted valiantly but
Harold II was killed and an important battle had been won, yet the war to
win a kingdom had only just begun. The major ports needed to be seized
and William's conquering army descended on Canterbury, London and
Winchester before the leading English earls, by then supporting the

claims of Edmund Ironside's grandson, Edgar the Atheling, finally capitulated. Acknowledged as king at Berkhamsted Castle in Hertfordshire in December, the Norman duke was crowned William I on Christmas Day 1066 at Westminster Abbey.

Still the new king continued to meet resistance as the first five years of his reign were relentlessly punctuated by rebellions. However, the Normans' response was decisive. Resistance forces led by folk heroes such as Hereward the Wake were defeated and land was seized and secured by implementing a vast programme of castle building, with Norman earls imported to replace native-born landowners. The English clergy too was similarly routed, churchmen being evicted from office and replaced by Normans, the newcomers including the king's half-brother, Odo of Bayeux, who as Earl of Kent came to rule over more English land than anyone except William the Conqueror.

After 1071 the king's own attentions turned back towards Normandy, where the dangers posed by France and Anjou were complicated by the defection of his eldest son, Robert, and by other intrigues, attacks and counter attacks. In 1087, riding into battle, as an attack was launched on Mantes, William's horse bolted. Suffering severe internal injuries, William survived some weeks before passing away on 9 September 1087 at a priory near Rouen. Then, in a grotesque postscript, his swollen corpse burst open as funeral attendants tried to force it into its final resting place at the Abbey of St. Stephen in Caen, Normandy. William I was survived by his wife, Matilda, the mother of his 10 children. Leaving his English crown to his second son, William II became king.

◆ see Edward the Confessor, William II

◄ *LEFT: William I*

WILLIAM II RUFUS (C. 1056/60–1100)

King of England (1087–1100). Born in Normandy sometime between 1056 and 1060, William Rufus was the fourth-born child of William, Duke of Normandy, and Matilda, daughter of the Count of Flanders. Little is known of his early life. Just a boy when his father triumphed at the Battle of Hastings, the early death of his elder brother, Richard, in 1075 then lifted young William one step up the royal ladder. Three years later his stock rose higher still when his eldest brother, Robert Curthose, betrayed the family by siding with enemy forces. William, though, stayed loyal to his father and was at the Conqueror's side in his last, dying days.

▲ ABOVE: William Rufus is slain by an arrow

Succeeding his father on 9 September 1087, William II was crowned at Westminster Abbey 17 days later. The second Norman king of England, he is usually referred to as William Rufus owing to his red hair or because of his ruddy complexion, but during his reign he was also known as William the Younger and William the Red.

With unrest rife in England in 1087, barons with estates in both Normandy and England sought to dethrone William II Rufus in favour of his elder brother, Robert, himself newly installed as the Duke of Normandy. The barons' revolt of 1088 foundered, though, their cause not helped by Duke Robert's decision not to join the fight. With this threat stubbed out, William's attentions switched from England to Normandy, just as Robert's attention switched to waging war in the Holy Land as part of the first crusade. So, in 1089, the elder brother pawned Normandy to the younger brother in exchange for 10,000 marks. Set on recapturing lost Norman territories, eventually William succeeded, while in England in 1095 his forces successfully put down an insurrection led by Robert Mowbray, Earl of Northumberland. Battleground triumphs were one thing, but winning over the English Church was quite another.

The king's attitude towards the Church was often hostile and self-serving, the justiciar (or chief justice) Ranulf Flambard proving to be a skilled, if cunning administrator, who oversaw the heavy taxation programme that transferred Church monies into the Crown's coffers. William was also slow to appoint abbots and bishops, although an appointment he did make in 1093 he soon regretted.

Choosing Anselm as the new Archbishop of Canterbury, king and cleric were frequently at loggerheads until finally the quarrelling came to an end in 1097 when Anselm left for Rome, two years after provoking the king by declaring that his first loyalty was to the pope. However, with Anselm in exile and his

▶ RIGHT: William II Rufus

Canterbury estates then in his royal possession, the king headed west in 1098. Marching to Wales, there he crushed a rebellion by Gruffudd ap Cynan of Gwynedd. This success in Wales mirrored his victory over the Scots five years before when Malcolm III had been killed in battle at Alnwick in Northumbria.

By 1100 William II Rufus was in full flow, his realms largely secure. Then on 2 August, his life ended. Out hunting that day in the New Forest, his death occurred in highly suspicious circumstances. The official line was that the king was killed by accident when struck by a wayward arrow loosed by Walter Tirel. A member of the royal hunting party, it was claimed that Tirel had fired at a stag as it burst into view, but hit the sovereign instead. Other versions of William's last moments deny that Tirel was in the New Forest that day. One man who definitely was in the vicinity at the time of the monarch's death was his younger brother, Henry, who raced to claim the crown soon after the fatal shooting.

HENRY I (1068–1135)

King of England (1100–35). Born at Selby, Yorkshire, in September 1068 Henry was the youngest son of William the Conqueror and Matilda. Given an excellent education, his intellectual prowess gave rise to the respectful nickname Beauclerc (meaning 'fine scholar'). He was only 13 or 14 years old at the time of his mother's death, who left her much-loved son her English land. However, when his father died in 1087 Henry was left a mountain of money, but his promised kingdoms went to his two elder brothers. Nineteen years old when his brother, William II, was crowned king of England, he spent the next 13 years fighting for or against William and his eldest brother, Robert, Duke of Normandy. Eventually, because of this, Henry was excluded from the line of succession to the English throne.

Henry was not deterred by this rebuff and on 2 August 1100 he struck.

In the south of England that day, by luck or design, he was ideally placed to take advantage of William Rufus's death while hunting in the New Forest. The moment he knew William was dead he hurried to Winchester, safe in the knowledge that his other brother, Robert, was still making his way back to Normandy after going on crusade in the Holy Land. Arriving in Winchester he took control of the treasury. Next heading for London, on 6 August 1100 he was crowned king at Westminster Abbey.

The first months of the new reign were busy ones. Three months after his coronation Henry I married Matilda (also known as Edith), the sister of the Scots' king, Edgar. He also arranged alliances with France and Flanders, which provided extra security in the likely event of an attack from his brother Robert. The following year that attack duly came, but all-out war was avoided as Duke Robert returned to Normandy with a settlement worth a sum equivalent to £2,000 a year. The truce did not last and victory at the Battle of Tinchebrai in 1106 led to the capture of Robert, and other powerful lords. Robert

◄ LEFT: Henry I

was subsequently kept under lock and key at Cardiff Castle, where he was doomed to remain until his death in 1134.

A dynamic, powerful figure, Henry I was reputed to be a king who ruled with a rod of iron. His intellect, drive and clear-headed approach to justice and the administration of his realm earned him the term the Lion of Justice. The judicial system was overhauled: severe punishments were issued and the death penalty was restored for crimes against property. His chief administrator, Roger, Bishop of Salisbury, who oversaw the collection of revenue by officials, extended the reach of royal taxation and legislation as never before. Taxation on this scale could not be levied without support, however, and so Henry ensured that loyalty to the crown by powerful magnates was appropriately rewarded.

The king's control was consolidated in other ways too. His many love affairs produced many illegitimate children. Yet even illegitimate daughters played a part in securing beneficial alliances and so Henry married off no fewer than eight daughters born out of wedlock. In stark contrast, his first marriage yielded just two children: Matilda and a son and heir, William. With the latter's birth in 1103 the succession issue seemed guaranteed, but a shipwreck in 1120 claimed the life of William.

He married again in 1122, but his second wife, Adela of Louvain, did not produce an heir. His options becoming increasingly limited, the king attempted to name his daughter as his successor. But the death of her husband, Henry V of Germany, in 1125, and her subsequent marriage to Geoffrey of Anjou made

◀ LEFT: King Stephen

that an unlikely prospect: most Norman and English earls were hostile to the Angevins. The king did somehow manage to win the barons round and Matilda was accepted as heir to the throne.

Henry I died in 1135 at St Denis-le-Fermont, near Rouen in Normandy. His body was brought back to England to be interred at Reading Abbey. The only English king to born and buried in England in the long period separating the reigns of Harold II and John, his 35-year reign was the longest since that of Ethelred the Unready more than a century before. Henry I was succeeded not by his daughter, Matilda, but by his nephew, Stephen.

◆ see Matilda, Stephen, William I, William II

STEPHEN (C. 1096–1154)

King of England (1135–54). Born in 1096 or 1097, Stephen was the youngest son of Adela, a sister of Henry I, while Stephen's father was Stephen, the Count of Blois and Chartres. However, when he died in 1102, the younger Stephen was raised by his mother. In time, though, the boy's future became more and more linked to the fate of Henry I, his uncle presenting Stephen with so much land that he became the second mightiest landowner in the kingdom. A powerful figure, he also profited from his marriage to Matilda, the only daughter of the Count of Boulogne.

Marrying in 1125, for the next 10 years Stephen remained loyal to Henry I, despite the king's problems regarding who would succeed him. Until 1120 the succession issue was settled, but then on 25 November that year Henry's son and heir was killed. Henry I chose his daughter, Matilda, as his successor. However, when the old king died on 1 December 1135, it was Stephen who seized the crown.

Initially content to lodge a peaceful objection to Stephen's accession, the Empress Matilda continued to enjoy considerable support for her claim, even if her case was weakened because she was a woman and because her husband, Geoffrey, Count of Anjou, was not well-liked. Yet, while his claim was weaker, Stephen's strike had been swift and assured. He had hurried from Boulogne to be first to state his case in London, but he also enjoyed the support of people in high places, not least his brother, Henry, Bishop of Winchester.

Crowned king on 26 December 1135, his St Stephen's Day coronation was staged at Westminster Abbey less than four weeks after Henry's death, his right to rule validated by Pope Innocent II. Also recognised as Duke of Normandy at this time, the first two years of King Stephen's reign passed very quietly, but then the peace was shattered as the monarch was attacked.

By the autumn of 1139 the early exchanges in the north and west of the kingdom and in Normandy had given way to a full-scale civil war in England, large numbers of men rallying around the flag of the Empress Matilda. Then came the first decisive battle when the enemy forces clashed at Lincoln in February 1141 and Matilda's army succeeded in capturing the king. Imprisoned in Bristol, Stephen was forced to look on helplessly as the empress, who had been hailed as the 'Lady of the English', planned her coronation.

Stephen was released in return for the Empress Matilda's half-brother, Robert of Gloucester. Free again, in 1142 the king laid siege to Oxford Castle with the empress trapped inside. However, a great opportunity was lost as she slipped away unnoticed, Matilda fleeing the castle dressed from head-to-toe in white so that she could blend in with the snowy landscape. Still the fighting continued in England, while across the English Channel the king suffered a serious defeat as Geoffrey of Anjou invaded Normandy in 1144. After this setback King Stephen stayed in England for the next 10 years, a decade dogged by the continuing civil war.

Following the death of his heir Eustace, however, in November 1153 the Treaty of Westminster stated that Stephen would rule for the rest of his days, while acknowledging that his successor would be the son of the Empress Matilda. Henry of Anjou did not have long to wait: less than a year later the king was dead. Passing away at Dover Castle on 25 October 1154, Stephen was buried at Faversham Abbey near Canterbury and was succeeded by Henry of Anjou who was duly crowned Henry II.

HOUSE OF PLANTAGENET

PLANTAGENET, HOUSE OF

The Plantagenets were England's ruling dynasty for more than 300 years; there were 14 kings in all spread across the different houses of Anjou (or Angevin), Plantagenet, Lancaster and York. Henry II, the first king of this dynasty, began his reign in 1154, while the last Plantagenet, the Yorkist monarch, Richard III, was killed in battle in 1485.

The name Plantagenet dates back to the time of Geoffrey of Anjou. The father of Henry II, this Angevin count was renowned for fastening to his

helmet a sprig of broom. The Latin name for this plant is Planta genista, while the French word for it is genêt: hence Plantagenet.

When Henry II became England's king he also ruled over a vast French empire, the reclaiming of which would become a priority for many of his successors. His son, Richard I the Lionheart, died trying to recover lands lost by his brother, John, while King John himself not only lost most of England's French possessions, but he was also forced to take flight when the French dauphin, Louis, invaded London. In the reign of Edward III the Hundred Years War with France began, the English winning and then losing vast

▲ ABOVE: Geoffrey Plantagenet, founder of the House of Plantagenet expanses of French territory. Later Henry V would emulate his greatest achievements, paving the way for his son and successor to be crowned king of France in 1431. Then the backlash began and by 1453 England was left clinging to its one possession: Calais.

The Plantagenet kings were also frequently engaged in fighting the Scots. Edward I was so successful north of the border that he earned the

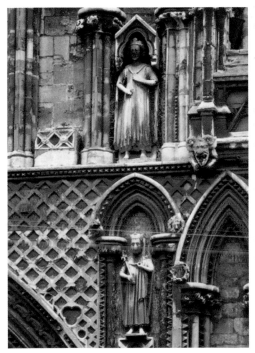

nickname the 'Hammer of the Scots', but Edward II was routed by Robert I the Bruce at Bannockburn in 1314. Edward I also campaigned in Wales, where he succeeded in establishing English control, chiefly by conquest and castle-building. King John also invaded Wales, but as Lord of Ireland he was far less successful than his father, Henry II, whose invasion force of 1171 began England's conquest of Ireland.

Civil war was an occupational hazard for

▲ *ABOVE: Lincoln Cathedral displaying Plantagenet figures*

medieval kings, while deposed kings and new ruling houses were another feature of the Plantagenet era. The first Angevin king, Henry II, came to power following years of civil strife and later had to contend with overly ambitious sons. Nevertheless the rebellion of 1173–74, which came soon after the martyrdom of Thomas Becket, did not mushroom into full-blown war. Then in the period overlapping the reigns of his son, John, and his grandson, Henry III, civil war was compounded by the presence in England of the French dauphin, Louis. Later still Henry III was challenged by his brother-in-law, Simon de Montfort, and then captured in 1264, before emerging triumphant in 1265.

Edward II was not so lucky. War broke out in 1323 with the king opposed by his queen, Isabelle, but after initially repelling his enemies, in 1327 he was caught, imprisoned, dethroned and done to death. Richard II was another monarch to antagonise England's barons and in 1399 this antagonism cost him his crown and probably his life too. Deposed by his own cousin, he died in prison soon afterwards, while the accession of Henry IV completed the rise to power of the house of Lancaster.

With Lancaster remaining the royal house as Henry V and his son, Henry VI, were crowned, the first blood in the Wars of the Roses was drawn by the house of York. Fighting the king's forces from 1455, Edward IV became the first Yorkist king six years later when he deposed Henry VI. The last Lancastrian ruler was briefly reinstated but, deposed a second time, in 1471 he was executed.

Edward IV established his dynasty on solid foundations, but when he died in 1483 the walls of the house of York came tumbling down. Firstly his son and heir, Edward V, became one of the Princes in the Tower as Richard, Duke of York (a brother of Edward IV), made his successful bid to become king. However, the reign of Richard III was as troubled as it was short. Finally and fatally attacked by the new Lancastrian leader, Henry Tudor, at Bosworth Field in 1485, the last Plantagenet king also earned the dubious distinction of being the last English king to die in battle.

Away from the battlefields, there were many advances in English common law during the years of the Plantagenet kings. John was confronted with the Magna Carta in 1215, this great charter holding the king to account for what his opponents saw as his abuses of power. In contrast, the rash of law-making in the reign of Edward I led to his admirers referring to the king as the 'English Justinian' (a reference to the sixth-century emperor of Constantinople who was famed for codifying Roman law).

The grandson of Edward I and his namesake, Edward III, emulated his grandfather's achievements in war, if not in the administration of his realm. However, he ruled for 50 years, his reign best remembered for the outbreak of the Hundred Years' War, but also for the Black Prince and the Black Death. The former was the name accorded the king's warrior son, Edward, whose deeds in battle during the Hundred Years' War were highly acclaimed. The latter was the name given to the plague epidemic that swept across England from 1348 killing over a million

Like famine, the 'great mortality' of plague was a recurring pestilence in the fourteenth century, but other aspects of life in England continued to evolve. English replaced French as the official language, while a one-time civil servant, Geoffrey Chaucer was still writing 'The Canterbury Tales', one of the great masterpieces of English literature at the time of his death in 1400. In the century that followed, William Caxton made his mark by introducing the first printing press to England, while in architecture there were changes as English Gothic was replaced from the 1350s by the Perpendicular style.

◆ *see* House of Lancaster, House of York

HENRY II (1133–89)

King of England (1154–89). The son of Geoffrey, Count of Anjou, and the Empress Matilda, the daughter of Henry I, Henry II was born at Le Mans in Anjou on 4 March 1133. Just two years old when his grandfather, Henry I, died, as a boy the younger Henry was caught up in the fight for the English crown that was fought by his mother and King Stephen. At 14 years of age he made his first attempt at deposing Stephen, yet a short time later he achieved his goal without bloodshed: the ageing king chose Henry as his heir on the understanding that his own son, William, would be allowed to retain his estates.

Following the death of Stephen on 25 October 1154, the crown passed unchallenged to Henry II. At the time of his accession he was also Count of Anjou, Duke of Normandy and Duke of Aquitaine. So, at the age of just 21, he began his reign as England's first Plantagenet (or Angevin) king at the head of a mighty empire.

One of his first tasks as king was to assert control over a realm that had been ravaged by civil war for much of his predecessor's reign. In addition, he set about capturing land that had earlier been lost to the Scots and the Welsh. More successful in the north, he regained Northumbria from Malcolm IV and later captured Malcolm's successor, William the Lion. Meanwhile, he sent

▲ *ABOVE: Henry II as featured in a manuscript*

forces into Wales in 1157, his men waging war there with the kings, Owain of Gwynedd and Rhys ap Gruffudd of Deheubarth.

Henry was also active in Ireland. Postponing a campaign he had planned in 1155, the year Pope Adrian IV had given his blessing for an attack on the heretic Irish Church, he did launch an attack in 1166. Then in 1171 a follow-up campaign ended with Irish kings acknowledging Henry II as Lord of Ireland. At home, the English heartland was untroubled by war until 1173, when the king's wife and three of his sons turned on their father forcing him to take up arms. Henry and his sons were reconciled in 1174, although Henry remained at daggers drawn with his queen and so after 1173 Eleanor of Aquitaine was often imprisoned.

The king's problems with his sons contrasted sharply with the very different problems of his three immediate predecessors. Not one of these men had been succeeded by a son, yet Henry II was cursed with a surfeit of male children. Marrying Eleanor of Aquitaine in May 1152, the couple's first son was born in 1153 just before Henry was crowned King of England. William did not survive infancy, but seven more legitimate children were born, including four sons. Dividing his territory between his sons, it was decided that Richard would be granted Aquitaine, Geoffrey would rule in Brittany, John would reign over Ireland, while the eldest boy, Henry, would inherit England, Anjou and Normandy. To this end Henry II arranged the unprecedented crowning of Prince Henry. The only incidence of an heir being crowned in the lifetime of a living English sovereign, it was this coronation that hastened Thomas Becket's fateful return from exile.

Once the best of friends, Henry had made Becket his Chancellor in 1155, elevating him to the position of Archbishop of Canterbury seven years later. However, the king and the archbishop later fell out. Leaving England for France in 1164, Becket returned home at the end of 1170. Days later he was dead. Perhaps the king complained about Becket, perhaps he did utter those famous words, 'Will no-one rid me of this turbulent priest?'. All that is certain is that four knights killed the archbishop on 29 December 1170. Becket's death deeply affected Henry II, who later did penance at Canterbury Cathedral, the very place where the martyred Becket had been slain.

In the years after Becket's murder, Henry was often forced on to the back foot. During the mid-1170s there was a period of stability, but when his sons reached maturity, so territorial disputes began. The situation was further clouded by the deaths of Henry the Young King in 1183 and Geoffrey in 1186, while the old king suffered further setbacks when both Richard and John again took sides against their father.

Known as Curtmantle because of the distinctive, Continental-style cloak he liked to wear, Henry II is widely recognised as one of England's greatest monarchs. Yet like his grandfather before him and his son and successor, Richard I, he spent years as an absentee ruler. Dying on 6 July 1189 at Chinon Castle in the heart of his Angevin territory, he was buried at Fontevraud Abbey and was succeeded by his son, Richard I.

💠 *see* John, Richard I, Stephen

RICHARD I (1157–99)

King of England (1189–99). Born at Beaumont Palace, Oxfordshire, on 8 September 1157, Richard was one of the eight children of Henry II and Queen Eleanor. He was the fourth-born child and so, until he was 15 years old, he was only second in line to the English throne. Before 1172 he was Duke of Aquitaine, the French region where his mother had grown up. Then, in the space of six eventful years, the course of the young duke's life was changed by two deaths in the royal family.

First to die was Henry the Young King, Richard's elder brother. His death

▶ *RIGHT: The coronation of Richard I*

on 11 June 1183 was followed by the death of Henry II on 6 July 1189. Previously hostile to his father, later he had made up with the old king and so, after returning from two years on crusade, Richard's coronation service occurred at Westminster Abbey on 3 September 1189, just a short time after his investiture as Duke of Normandy.

Typically, his stay in England was a short one. Soon returning to Normandy, he spent the next winter there before once again taking the Cross. Leaving for the Holy Land in July 1190, his journey to the Middle East took Richard I via Cyprus, where he met up again with Berengaria, the daughter of King Sancho VI of Navarre. Friends since childhood, Richard and Berengaria were married in Limassol and then travelled together throughout Richard's time on crusade.

Taking the Palestinian city of Acre in 1191, Richard the Lionheart went on to defeat the feared Saracen leader, Saladin, at Arsuf, near Jaffa, but fell short of capturing Jerusalem. With a truce agreed in September 1192, the English king and his queen then left the Holy Land. Berengaria headed for Italy, but Richard ventured across Europe only to fall foul of his enemy, Duke Leopold of Austria. Imprisoned by the duke in December 1192, Richard spent the next 13 months in a castle beside the River Danube.

Finally released from his faraway prison in February 1194, after a huge ransom of 100,000 marks had been paid, Richard I returned to the kingdom that he had left in the hands of William Longchamp. Appointed chancellor in 1189, Longchamp's main antagonist was the king's notorious younger brother, John, who forced Longchamp from office in 1191. However, on the king's return John was punished for seizing power in his absence and for giving up control of territories in France. Attempting to regain these lost lands, in May 1194 Richard I left England for the last time.

The warrior king largely succeeded in recovering French territories, while at the same time building castles such as the great stronghold known as Château-Gaillard. Continuing to carry the fight to his former friend and ally, the French king, Philip II, he was wounded by a crossbow bolt during a siege at Châlus. The injury was not life-threatening, but gangrene set in and on 6 April 1199 the great soldier died and was laid to rest at Fontevraud, although his heart was buried separately at Rouen. Survived by Berengaria, who is unique in being the only queen of England never to visit the country, Richard I was succeeded by his younger brother, John.

◪ see Henry II, John, House of Plantagenet

JOHN (1167–1216)

King of England (1199–1216). Born at Beaumont Palace in Oxfordshire on 24 December 1167, John was the eighth and youngest child born to Henry II and his wife, Eleanor, Duchess of Aquitaine. The first-born son, William, died

▶ RIGHT: King John

young, but Henry the Young King was crowned as his father's successor during the lifetime of Henry II, while older brothers Richard and Geoffrey were both ahead of John in the Angevin pecking order.

In 1186 his brother, Geoffrey, died. Then, in 1189, Henry II passed away and John's elder brother was crowned as Richard I. John himself was presented with large swathes of land, but with Richard away on crusade it was not long before he moved to seize power. Chasing William de Longchamp, the appointed justiciar (chief justice), from London in 1191, and with his brother fighting in the Holy Land, John was able to assert his control. However, when a large ransom was paid for the release of the imprisoned King Richard, the king returned to England early in 1194 and John was punished by having his castles and land seized.

The death of Richard I on 6 April 1199 saw John ascend the English throne without objection and the story was the same in Normandy, while in Aquitaine the new king's mother, Eleanor, ruled on her son's behalf. Only in Anjou, Maine and Touraine was there serious opposition to John's accession, the nobles there choosing as their ruler the 11-year-old Arthur of Brittany. The son of John's late brother, Geoffrey, young Arthur had been the natural heir in England, but Richard had opted for John. However, in 1200 Arthur was denied a second time by his uncle, John.

In August 1189, John had married the Countess of Gloucester, Isabella. The relationship lasted 10 years, but was annulled in 1200 on the grounds that, as husband and wife were second cousins, the couple were too closely related to be legally married. King John married a second bride: Isabella of Angoulême. However, in marrying this 12-year-old girl, England's monarch further upset the French king, who was already irate at the way John had brushed aside (and possibly killed) Arthur of Brittany. As a result, Philip II offered his support to Hugh X of Lusignan, the duke who had previously been betrothed to Isabella of Angoulême.

Fighting then broke out in 1203, and in 1204 Anjou and Normandy were taken by French forces. Forced to return to England, John inflicted massive taxation on a population already suffering the effects of rampant inflation. The clergy too was soon at odds with John, his objection to Stephen Langton's appointment as Archbishop of Canterbury sparking a crisis that led directly to the king's excommunication. However, by 1212 the threat of attack by France loomed large and so John sought papal protection, effectively regaining the support of Pope Innocent III in May 1213 by making England a pawn of the Vatican.

Before bowing down to the pope and returning to war with France, King John had marched into Wales to invade the kingdom of Llywelyn ap Iorwerth. The Gwynedd ruler, Llywelyn, had married John's illegitimate daughter, Joan, in 1205 and had then been able to count on his father-in-law's backing as he expanded his Welsh empire. But then, in 1211, the tables were turned as England's monarch attacked, forcing Llywelyn into submission.

Back in France in 1214, once there John was defeated at the Battle of Bouvines. He was also troubled at home at this time as, in May 1215 rebels stormed London. Then, as the net closed in on the increasingly despised king, on 15 June 1215 his enemies backed him into a corner, forcing him to put his seal on the Magna Carta at Runnymede, near Windsor.

The Magna Carta, or Great Charter, was a long list by England's leading barons and churchmen, which itemised 63 complaints and intended reforms. Yet even after John had reluctantly agreed to address the grievances listed in the Magna Carta, still the pressure continued to mount against him as the Dauphin Louis, the son of Philip II of France, sided with the rebels, marching into London in May 1216. Forced to take flight, just five months later King John was dead. Dying at Newark Castle in Nottinghamshire on 18 October 1216, 'Bad' King John was buried at Worcester Cathedral.

His eldest son and his successor was Henry III, while one daughter, Eleanor, later married Simon de Montfort and a second, Joan, wed Alexander II of Scotland.

◆ see Henry II, Henry III

HENRY III (1207–72)

King of England (1216–72). Born at Winchester on 1 October 1207, the eldest son of King John and his second wife, Isabella, Henry III succeeded his father when he was just nine years old. At the time of John's death in October 1216, much of eastern England was ruled over by Louis, the

Dauphin of France. So, with London under French control, Henry III was crowned in a hurried ceremony held on 28 October 1216 at Gloucester Cathedral, rather than Westminster Abbey. Yet from such unpromising beginnings a reign unfolded that was notable for the absence of power struggles like those that had tainted life under John.

More remarkable still was the speed with which the king's regents, William the Marshal and Hubert de Burgh, successfully won back the territories snatched by Louis of France. Decisive

▲ ABOVE: The coronation of Henry III

victories in battles at Lincoln and off Dover effectively defeated the dauphin during 1217, a year that saw the unrest among the barons further diminished when Henry III signed an amended version of the famous Magna Carta.

▲ *ABOVE: Henry and Philip of Spain embrace following the peace of Chateau Cambresis*

Later, the young king enjoyed a second coronation. Staged on 17 May 1220 at Westminster Abbey, the choice of this great church was an apt one for a king who later would devote so much time, love and money to religious buildings such as Edward the Confessor's abbey church. Assuming full control over his kingdom seven years after he had been crowned for the second time, his early years as sole ruler were quiet enough, at least on the home front.

When Henry III came of age the only French territory still held by the English Crown was the small province of Gascony. Yet, as England's dominions became ever fewer, so the influence of foreigners at the king's court grew, following the king's wedding in 1236. Marrying Eleanor of Provence, in time this marriage produced a large family including a son and heir, the future Edward I. In the short term, though, English barons came to resent the growing number of Frenchmen taken into the monarch's inner circle.

The barons fired a shot across Henry's bows in 1234 when their anger forced him to dismiss the Bishop of Winchester, Peter des Roches, and his foreign aides, so staving off the threat of insurrection. However, friction remained as the king floundered. An unworldly, pious figure, many of his domestic policies antagonised, while a foreign policy that limped from one capitulation to another was epitomised in 1254 by the king's failed attempt to gain Sicily for his son, Edmund.

In 1258, as the patience of England's magnates continued to be tested, Henry III was reined in. First came the Provisions of Oxford in October 1258; they were followed exactly one year later by the Provisions of Westminster. The concessions the monarch made included an agreement to convene parliament at least three times a year. In addition, Henry agreed that future kings' councils would comprise an even split of his choices and magnates' men. For the next few years an uneasy truce was kept, but then, with the rise to prominence of the king's own brother-in-law, Simon de Montfort, came the descent into war.

The first exchanges took place early in 1264. However, the decisive battle was fought on 4 August 1265 at Evesham, where royalist troops, commanded by Prince Edward, defeated and killed de Montfort. They also freed the king, who had been held captive by his enemies since the Battle of Lewes some 14 months previously. With Henry III restored to the throne, the last seven years of his reign proved uneventful.

Generally seen as a good man, but a poor king, who nonetheless wore England's crown for 56 years, he died on 16 November 1272 at Westminster. Buried in the abbey there, the great cathedral that Henry III himself had so lovingly rebuilt, he was succeeded by the eldest of his nine children, Edward I.

◆ *see* Edward I, Edward the Confessor, John

EDWARD I (1239–1307)

King of England (1272–1307). The eldest child of Henry III and Eleanor of Provence, Edward was born at Westminster, London, on 17 June 1239 and grew up at a time when England was relatively united. In October 1254 the 15-year-old prince married Eleanor of Castile. A decade then passed before Simon de Montfort and his supporters led a rebellion that was to see the emergence of a strong, new defender of the Plantagenet dynasty. A key figure at the Battle of Evesham in 1265, 'Lord' Edward, as he was then known, was the undisputed power behind the throne by the time he set off on crusade in 1270. He was away from England for four years, during which time he learned of his father's death (in 1272) and was wounded at Acre. He did not return to England immediately and it was not until 19 August 1274 that he and his wife Eleanor were crowned in a joint coronation ceremony held at Westminster Abbey.

It was not long before Edward proved himself to be a shrewd politician. Early in his reign he commissioned an in-depth review of his realm, which became the documents known as the Hundred Rolls. This was the most comprehensive summary of English life produced since the Domesday Book. The Hundred Rolls contained a mass of information, particularly about the distribution and ownership of land at the beginning of the reign. Also in the first years of his reign Edward introduced a number of statutes in parliament. Completing the judicial reforms of his father, in his long reign Edward I established the office of conservator of the peace (a forerunner of the modern Justice of the Peace) and created the Chancery Court, where aggrieved citizens could seek legal redress.

Set on taming over-mighty nobles at home, but ever eager to lead an army on foreign soil, the king soon had designs on Wales. In 1277 he marched on to Welsh soil and attacked the defiant Gwynedd king, Llywelyn ap Gruffudd, inflicting a heavy defeat. Five years later, however, the Welsh warriors struck back. The death of Llywelyn, the construction and revamping of castles in the north and west and new laws and administrative appointments confirmed English dominance and in two separate campaigns Edward I eventually overran the country.

Edward also mounted a series of campaigns to bring Scotland under his control. Beginning with the storming of Berwick in March 1296 and continuing on to victory at the Battle of Dunbar, the superiority of the English king's army forced the overthrow of John Balliol, the man Edward himself had placed on the Scottish throne just five years previously. In the Highlands and the northern territories resistance to the 'Hammer of the Scots' remained fierce, while to the south first William Wallace and then Robert the Bruce carried the fight to the English. Success for the Scots, notably at Stirling Bridge in 1297, was countered by English success the following year at the Battle of Falkirk. And so the war in Scotland rumbled on, continuing long after Edward's death in 1307.

Edward married twice. His first wife, Eleanor of Castile, was just a child at the time of the royal wedding in October 1254. She later became the mother of 15 of Edward's children and died in November 1290. Nine years later the king wed his second wife, Margaret, at Canterbury Cathedral. Forty years Edward's junior, in the last years of the old king's life the daughter of the French king, Philip III, gave birth to two sons and a daughter.

Edward passed away on 7 July 1307 at Burgh-on-the-Sands, near Carlisle. The old warrior king died while on his way to launch yet another attack on Scotland. Buried at Westminster Abbey, the English crown passed next to his eldest surviving son, Edward II.

🔹 *see* John Balliol, Edward II, Llewelyn ap Gruffudd, Robert I

▶ *RIGHT: Edward I*

179

EDWARD II (1284–1327)

King of England (1307–27). Edward II was born at Caernarfon on 24 April 1284; he was the thirteenth child born to Edward I and his first wife, Eleanor of Castile. With three of his older brothers dead, however, Edward was left as heir to the English throne at the age of only four months. He was formally invested with the title Prince of Wales at the age of 16, and seven years later, on 7 July 1307, the prince became king on the day his father died. He was crowned at Westminster Abbey on 25 February 1308 in a joint ceremony with his wife, Queen Isabella. The couple had wed in Boulogne a month before the coronation. The eldest daughter of the French king, Philip IV, but later known in England as the 'she-wolf of France', Isabella gave birth to two sons, including Edward III, and two daughters, one of them, Joan, who married David II of Scotland.

At the time of Edward II's accession royal policy was dominated by the struggle with the Scots. However, the new king lacked his father's enthusiasm, not to mention his aptitude for war, and quickly lost interest in

the Scottish campaign. He had indulged his friends while he was prince and continued to do so as king. Among these favourites none was more favoured than Piers Gaveston, with whom the king is reputed to have had a sexual relationship. But Gaveston's time in the king's inner circle was destined to be brief. Captured in Scarborough in 1312, he was found guilty of treason and summarily executed, much to the anguish of the king. Central to Gaveston's downfall was Thomas, Earl of Lancaster – a man who would play a central role in later events.

▶ *RIGHT: The Marriage of Edward II to Isabelle of France*

After the death of Gaveston, the king was forced to respond to the worsening situation in Scotland. Leading an army to Bannockburn in 1314, the king and his men suffered a devastating and ignominious defeat at the hands of Robert Bruce. In England too storm clouds were gathering as the king's cousin, Thomas of Lancaster, became still more powerful. In August 1321, an aggrieved group of nobles led by Lancaster marched on London. The king managed to draw the rebels' sting, but relief was only temporary: seven months later the two sides went to war.

The king took control in Wales and won the Battle of Boroughbridge in Yorkshire in March 1322. Lancaster was caught and executed one week after the conflict. Despite the swift and merciless punishment of the rebels opposition to Edward II remained. So, while the king's forces continued to engage Robert Bruce in Scotland, his English enemies regrouped behind Queen Isabella, her lover, Roger Mortimer, and this rebel couple's most valuable asset: the heir to the throne, Prince Edward. The rebels set sail from France in September 1326 and, on landing in England, they attracted enough support to force the king to head west.

Edward was captured on 16 November 1326 and, after his forced abdication the following January, he remained in prison until he was finally put to death on 21 September 1327. Edward II died at Berkeley Castle in Gloucestershire. Two months later, the body of the former sovereign was buried at Gloucester Abbey, the funeral shamelessly attended by his widow and his eldest son, who had been crowned Edward III nine months previously.

◆ see Edward I, Edward III, Robert I

▶ RIGHT: Seal of Edward II

EDWARD III (1312–77)

King of England (1327–77). Edward was the eldest son of Edward II and Isabella; he was born on 13 November 1312 at Windsor Castle. He was just 13 years old when his doomed father was captured by enemy forces led by his mother; as a result Edward was appointed Keeper of the Realm on 26 October 1326. Proclaimed king on 25 January 1327, he was crowned eight days later at Westminster Abbey. A year later he married his French bride, Philippa of Hainault, at York Minster.

Edward was quick to make his mark as monarch, and in 1330 the young king sanctioned the arrest of Roger Mortimer. Mortimer had been a leading figure in the downfall of Edward's father and also his mother's lover, thus his execution eliminated a potential rival to the throne. With this danger removed, attention turned towards the continuing problem posed by Scotland. Smarting from conceding sovereignty to the Scots just before Robert Bruce died leaving a minor as his heir, the English king was further stung by subsequent border raids. So, taking up arms, he laid siege to Berwick in 1332 and the next year he won a notable victory at the Battle of Halidon Hill.

▲ ABOVE: Victorian tile showing Philippa pleading with Edward III

He next turned his attention to France. In 1337 Edward III and his allies went to war against the French king, Philip IV. Among the early conflicts of the Hundred Years War, the naval Battle of Sluys in 1340 was won by the English. Then the English longbow archers loosed their deadly arrows at Crécy in 1346. A year later Calais was besieged and the French troops were dealt another crushing blow, at Poitiers in 1356. This victory tasted all the sweeter thanks to the capture of King John of France and so, with David II of Scotland a hostage in England, Edward III's winning hand contained not one, but two, kings. Further attacks on the French resulted in the Treaty of Brétigny in 1360, by which Edward III withdrew his claim to the French throne in exchange for Calais and Aquitaine, provinces that covered approximately one quarter of France.

Set on waging war abroad, the king had taxed his subjects to the hilt. Edward was a popular ruler whose foreign sorties had been well supported, yet there was a limit to the amount of money and service he could demand. Forced to back down between 1339 and 1343, Edward survived this minor crisis, but within a few years there came a more serious problem: plague. Reaching England in 1348, the Black Death spread relentlessly, wiping out around one third of the population.

The king's daughter, Joan, was one victim of the 'great mortality', but despite this sad loss Edward III's large family continued to grow. In an attempt to gain support while trying to overthrow his father, Edward's mother had agreed that he would marry Philippa of Hainault. He acquiesced to her wishes and the couple produced no fewer than 12 children. Such a large family secured the Plantagenet dynasty, as it enabled Edward III to arrange marriages to ensure much-needed support from magnates ambitious for power. Edward's eldest child, also christened Edward, was born in 1330 and became Prince of Wales in 1343. Known to history as the 'Black Prince' because of his armour, he was a warrior from a young age. He was only 16 years old when he took part in the Battle of Crécy, and it was the 26-year-old Black Prince who took all the accolades for the victory at Poitiers.

After 1360 events conspired against Edward III and the last 17 years of his long reign were punctuated with depressing losses and personal setbacks. The plague returned and the English hold on Aquitaine grew less secure. France clawed back so much territory that by 1374 England retained less French land than at any time since the outset of Edward's reign. The forlorn king was badly mauled by parliament in his last days.

There were personal tragedies too. Seven of his children had already died when the old king suffered two further losses. In August 1369 Queen Philippa died, then in June 1376 the sovereign mourned the death of his son and heir, Edward the Black Prince. Finally, the 64-year-old king, who had reigned for half a century, passed away. Dying at Sheen Palace on 21 June 1377, he was buried at Westminster Abbey. Edward III was succeeded by his grandson, Richard II.

◆ see Edward II, Richard II

RICHARD II (1367–1400)

King of England (1377–99). The second son of Edward the Black Prince and Joan of Kent, Richard II was born at Bordeaux on 6 January 1367. King at the age of 10, Richard II became the first minor to become king of England since Henry III had ascended the throne in 1216. Crowned at Westminster Abbey on 16 July 1377, the young monarch was then steered through the first decade of his reign by his mother and tutor, and by his uncle, John of Gaunt. In time, men such as Robert de Vere, Sir Michael de la Pole and the Earl of Arundel also exerted their influence at the royal court until Richard II came of age.

▶ *RIGHT: Richard II*

By then, though, the king had already made a favourable impression during the first major crisis of his reign. During the Peasants' Revolt, crowds of peasants from Essex and Kent marched on London. Fronted by Wat Tyler and John Ball, the chief cause of the revolt was the introduction of a steep new poll tax. The marchers laid waste to parts of the city, before coming face to face with the 14-year-old monarch. Richard II gave Wat Tyler an audience, but when scuffles broke out Tyler was killed. Then, as the mood became increasingly ugly, the young king rode out before the angry peasants defying them to take arms against him. But the mob had no grievance with the king, their slogan being 'With King Richard and the true-hearted commons', and so the Peasants' Revolt was brought to a peaceful conclusion.

However, Richard II did not have long to wait for the next crisis to arrive. Increasingly at odds with leading members of the nobility, he clashed with restless barons including his own uncle, the Duke of Gloucester. Themselves jostling for power and angered by the influence of the king's inner circle of ministers, the barons eventually brought about the impeachment of men such as de Vere and de la Pole, the 'Merciless Parliament' of 1388 further clipping the wings of the young king's men.

The next nine years saw calm return, though during this period Richard mourned the loss of his first wife. Marrying Anne of Bohemia, the daughter of the Holy Roman Emperor Charles IV, early in 1382, the royal couple enjoyed a happy, though childless marriage. But then Anne fell ill and died of the plague in 1394. Despite his attachment to his first wife, two years after her passing the king remarried. A daughter of the French king, Charles VI, Isabella was a child bride, who was still eight days short of her seventh birthday when she was married to Richard II at Calais on 1 November 1396.

However, this marriage was destined to end just three years later with the death of the king. The chief architect of Richard's fall was his cousin, Henry Bolingbroke. The son of John of Gaunt, he led the rebellion against the king while Richard II was back in Ireland. Taking advantage of the king's absence, his enemies launched their attempted coup. Carrying all before them, even the king's famed Cheshire archers backed off and so, when the king returned to England, he paid the price for the harsh line that he had adopted in previous years. Backed into a corner from which there would be no escape, the sovereign conceded defeat in Conwy in North Wales and was formally deposed on 29 September 1399

After the accession of Bolingbroke as Henry IV, the former king remained a prisoner at Pontefract Castle, where he died on 6 January 1400. Some suggested the king had a died a natural death, others claimed he had been murdered on Bolingbroke's orders, while a third rumour spread the fiction that the last monarch from the house of Anjou had escaped and would one day return to reclaim his crown.

But Richard II was dead. For many years his corpse was kept at the royal palace of King's Langley in Hertfordshire until 1411. Then, at last, the body was buried at Westminster Abbey, where it had been taken on the orders of Henry V, the son of the man who had succeeded Richard II some years earlier.

◈ see Edward III, Henry IV

HOUSE OF LANCASTER

LANCASTER, HOUSE OF

The House of Lancaster was, strictly speaking, a branch of the Plantagenet line. The Wars of the Roses between the houses of Lancaster and York have featured so large in the history of England, however, that the two have been accorded their own dynastic status. The House of Lancaster originated in 1267 when the younger son of Henry III, Edmund, was created Earl of Lancaster. The earldom was turned into a duchy for Henry of Grosmont and in this form it passed to John of Gaunt through his marriage to Grosmont's daughter, Blanche. The first Lancastrian king, Henry IV, was the son of John of Gaunt. When the Plantagenet king, Richard II, seized Lancastrian estates, Henry Bolingbroke fought back and put forward his own claim to the throne. He eventually overthrew Richard and settled down as king. As a usurper, Henry experienced many difficulties at the beginning of his reign from those who supported Richard, but Henry succeeded in holding on to his title.

It was his son, Henry V, who has become the most celebrated Lancastrian king. The epitome of everything a medieval warrior king should be, Henry had shown his mettle as a prince early on and the country rejoiced on his accession. His successes in France only served to enhance his reputation. Had he not died so young, the history of the English monarchy might have been very different, but he left a nine-month-old child as king in 1422 and this child, Henry VI, was to lose everything his father and grandfather had fought so hard for. The line ended with his overthrow by the Yorkist Edward IV.

HENRY IV (1366–1413)

King of England (1399–1413). The only child of John of Gaunt, son of Edward III and Blanche of Lancaster, Henry was born at Bolingbroke Castle, Lincolnshire, on 3 or 4 April 1366. A cousin of Richard II, in 1377 the

▲ ABOVE: Henry IV is presented with a book by Occleve

▶ RIGHT: Henry IV

12-year-old Henry attended the coronation of the king he would later depose. Three years later Henry married Mary de Bohun. His first wife and the mother of his seven children, she died in childbirth on 4 July 1394. By that time, Henry Bolingbroke had already flexed his muscles as one of England's most powerful nobles by opposing Richard II, even fighting and defeating the king's men in battle in 1387.

On 30 January 1398 Bolingbroke was accused of committing treason by Thomas Mowbray, Earl of Norfolk. As tensions mounted, a duel between the two nobles was arranged. However, before it could be staged, Richard II intervened to send both men into exile. Heading for France, Henry returned to England in July 1399 intent on taking back the estates of his late father, which the king had confiscated.

Once back on home soil he joined forces with the powerful Percy family and other northern barons. The rebels soon took control and, although Henry Bolingbroke's claim to the throne was weak, the Lancastrian armies were strong, and by the end of 1399 Henry had become king. Striking while Richard II was away in Ireland attempting to crush a revolt there, shortly after his return in August 1399 he was forced to surrender. On 29

September, Bolingbroke was recognised by parliament as King Henry IV.

Henry was crowned at Westminster Abbey on 13 October 1399 while Richard II still languished in prison. The new king had no time to settle into his new role, however. Opposition arose in the shape of the Welsh prince, Owain Glyndwr, who began a hostile campaign in Wales in 1400 that continued until 1415.

Meanwhile, Hotspur, one of the Percy family, had switched allegiance and now opposed the king. He was routed at Shrewsbury on 23 July 1403 by an army commanded by the king and his son, Prince Hal. Yet despite such battlefield victories opposition continued to mount behind leaders such as the Earl of Northumberland and two influential men of York: the duke and the archbishop. There were plots too, and France and Scotland were troublespots, while in 1411 even his son, Henry, Prince of Wales, was barred from the king's court.

Weighed down throughout his reign by an endless round of revolts and, it is claimed, wracked with guilt for the way in which he had come to be king, Henry spent his last years beleaguered and ill. He passed away on 20 March 1413 in the Jerusalem Chamber of Westminster Abbey. Henry IV was buried at Canterbury Cathedral.

🔹 *see* Henry V, Owain Glyndwr, Richard II

HENRY V (1387–1422)

King of England (1413–22). Born at Monmouth in September 1387, he was the second son of Henry Bolingbroke and his first wife, Mary de Bohun. Soon after his birth his father took to fighting the forces of Richard II at Radcot Bridge. Henry's mother died before he was seven years old; at the age of 12 his father became king and he gained the title, Prince of Wales. It was in Wales that he learned the tactics of war before entering the fray at the Battle of Shrewsbury in 1403, a conflict in which he lined up against his former guardian, Harry Hotspur. Helping his father win that battle, after leading the struggle in Wales against Owain Glyndwr, Prince Hal became an increasingly influential figure at the royal court.

In fact, with Henry IV a sick and troubled man, the younger man asserted himself to such an extent that there was much talk of the king abdicating or being overthrown. Forced into the background for a spell, on 20 March 1413 the king died and Henry V ascended the throne. Crowned at the age of 25, Henry was already an accomplished man-of-war. His first test came in 1414, when a revolt by a religious sect known as the Lollards was put down. Then, in the following year, nobles supporting Edmund Mortimer, Earl of March, were stopped in their tracks as they pressed the earl's claims to be king. A short time later Henry V set sail for France.

Reaching the northern coast, the English king stood poised on the threshold of greatness as he prepared, with the support of Burgundy, to recapture the lands lost in France during the last years of the Angevin kings. First to fall was Harfleur, which had resisted stubbornly despite being besieged for five weeks. In contrast, the Battle of Agincourt was won by Henry V in the course of one momentous day. After capturing Harfleur, the English force had marched through north-western Normandy before finally arriving in late October at Agincourt, where they came face to face with a vast French army. Weary and with a far smaller army, on 25 October 1415 Henry won a famous victory, losing less than 500 men while cutting down some 7,000 enemy soldiers.

Retaining the initiative Henry V returned to France in 1417 to begin the recapture of Normandy. Then, in 1419, the English seized Rouen, the city where the heart of Richard I had been buried more than two centuries earlier. All that then remained was for a peace deal, the Treaty of Troyes, to be ratified. With this treaty ratified in 1420, the peace between England

and France was sealed by the marriage of Henry to Catherine of Valois, daughter of the French king, Charles VI, who also confirmed Henry as his successor. Henry married Catherine at Troyes on 2 June 1420. Just 14 months later he was dead.

Struck down by dysentery in August 1422, he passed away at Vincennes in France. Buried at Westminster Abbey, Shakespeare's hero was survived by his young wife and succeeded by his baby son, Henry VI.

�« *see* Henry IV, Henry VI

HENRY VI (1421–71)

King of England (1422–61, 1470–71). The only child of Henry V and Catherine of Valois, daughter of the French king, Charles VI, Henry VI was born at Windsor Castle on 6 December 1421. King of England at the age of eight months, by the time Henry was nine months old he was the king of France. Still in the cradle at the time of his father's early death, initially the young Henry VI was looked after by his mother with responsibility for government placed in the hands of two men: his uncles, Humphrey, Duke of Gloucester, who became regent in England, and John, Duke of Bedford, who took charge in France. There, Bedford's troops continued to make headway, achieving notable victories at Cravant in 1423 and at Verneuil in 1424, while later English successes led to the coronation of Henry as king of France. Taking place at Notre Dame, Paris, in December 1431, this service came two years after his English coronation at Westminster Abbey on 5 or 6 November 1429. Yet even as Henry was crowned in France the backlash against his rule there had already begun. Inspired by Joan of Arc and aided by the defection to the French cause of Burgundy, France had started to reclaim lost territory.

Assuming the reins of power in 1437, Henry's approach to kingship was in keeping with his character: personally generous; politically naïve. Often dismissed as a bad king, Henry VI was a kindly, deeply Christian man, who dressed plainly. He was interested in the mind as well as the spirit and during the 1440s he founded both Eton College and King's College, Cambridge. It was also in this period that the king wed his queen, the 15-year-old Margaret of Anjou, in April 1445. The couple's solitary child was born in 1453. Christened Edward, the boy's birth came at a time when Henry VI suffered from his first bout of insanity and coincided with the fall of Gascony, Normandy having been lost in 1450. So, by 1453, England's only French territory was Calais.

The fall in fortunes across the Channel was mirrored at home. In 1450, a popular revolt in Kent led by John Cade followed soon after the murder of one of the king's favourites, William, Duke of Suffolk, and it was in this year that Richard, Duke of York, abandoned his post as Lieutenant of Ireland. In England only the king owned more land than the Duke of York, the man who would soon become a key figure in the war that erupted between the houses of Lancaster and York. Initially, Richard was appointed Protector until Henry VI had recovered from a bout of insanity, but three months later, in May 1455, the Battle of St Albans was fought, so beginning the Wars of the Roses. With victory going to the Yorkists, the Duke of York started his second term as Protector.

Although the fortunes of the two rival houses then ebbed and flowed, one constant was the cameo role of Henry VI, with the leading actors in this brutal drama being the Duke of York and the king's tenacious wife, Queen Margaret. Taking the fight to Duke Richard, in 1459 her forces defeated the Yorkist army at Ludlow in Shropshire. The respite was brief. In 1460, Margaret's army was soundly beaten at the Battle of Northampton and a short time later Duke Richard was formally appointed as Henry VI's rightful heir. The queen then attacked again, winning at Wakefield on 30 December 1460, the battle claiming the life of Richard, Duke of York.

Still the war raged and in March 1461 the Duke of York's son was proclaimed king. Edward IV was crowned in London and the capital remained set against Margaret and her mostly northern troops. Less than four weeks after his accession, Edward then won a vital, vicious battle at Towton. Margaret and her young son fled into exile, Henry VI staying behind only to be taken prisoner in 1465. Henry VI was restored to the throne in October 1470, but all the power then lay with men such as the 'Kingmaker', Richard, Earl of Warwick. Cutting a sad figure, Henry VI was doomed to reign but briefly second time around.

In 1471, Edward IV returned as king, sweeping aside the last

Lancastrian opposition, including King Henry's son, Edward, who was killed at the Battle of Tewkesbury on 4 May. Then, on 21 May at the Tower of London, Henry VI died, aged 49. In all probability executed by the new Yorkist regime. In death, as in the last years of life, there seemed to be no sanctuary for Henry VI and so the remains of the late king were buried first at Chertsey Abbey, then at St George's, Windsor. Later still, the coffin may have been taken for reburial at Westminster Abbey.

◆ *see* Henry V, Edward IV

▲ *ABOVE: Miniature from the Maresse code, Henry VI*

K. Henry ÿ 7.
mpson, & Dudley

HOUSE OF TUDOR/YORK

1483	Death of Edward IV
1483	The Princes in the Tower (one of whom was Edward V, son of Edward IV) are locked away and never seen alive again
1485	Richard III is killed at Bosworth Field.
1492	Christopher Columbus reached the West Indies
1494	Agreeing to divide the 'New World' between them Spain and Portugal signed the Treaty of Tordesillas
1509	Death of Henry VII
1513	Machiavelli writes The Prince
1517	Martin Luther nailed his theses to the door of the church of Wittenberg
1519	Ferdinand Magellan sets out to circumnavigate the globe
1521	Cortes the Conquistador conquers Mexico
1532	Francisco Pizarro conquers Peru
1533	Ivan the Terrible becomes Tsar of Russia
1536	Henry VIII breaks with Rome
1536	Act of Union in which England and Wales are formally linked
1543	Copernicus, the founding father of astronomy, dies
1547	Death of Henry VIII
1553	Death of Edward VI
1558	Death of Mary I
1564	The playwright and poet, William Shakespeare, is born; the painter and sculptor, Michelangelo, dies
1577	Sir Francis Drake begins his three-year-long round-the-world voyage
1582	The Gregorian or New Style Calendar is introduced.
1603	Death of Elizabeth I

▲ ABOVE: Edward IV

YORK, HOUSE OF

Like the House of Lancaster, the House of York was a branch of the Plantagenet family tree. The dynasty was founded by Richard, Duke of York. His claim to the throne came from Lionel, Duke of Clarence, from whom he was descended. Clarence was the third son of Edward III. York's challenge for the throne came up against the Lancastrian Henry VI, who was a descendant of the fourth son of Edward III. York thus claimed seniority of birth. It was this claim that sparked the famous Wars of the Roses between these rival Plantagenet branches. Although the Duke of York did not live to see his house established on the throne (he was killed at the Battle of Wakefield in 1460) his son eventually deposed the now insane Lancastrian Henry VI and seized the throne for himself and his heirs.

It was not to prove a successful or long-lasting dynasty. Edward's son was the target of the manipulations of his uncle, Edward's brother, Richard of Gloucester. When Edward IV died Edward V was travelling to London for his coronation when he was seized by Gloucester and sent, with his brother, to the Tower of London. A brief appearance later that year (1483) was the last anyone was to see of the Princes in the Tower, so

Edward V was never crowned. Gloucester took the throne as Richard III, but had no more luck than the nephew he had plotted against. The last Yorkist king was killed at the Battle of Bosworth Field in 1485, and a new line, the Tudors, was established.

▼ *BELOW: Princes in the Tower*

A 1597

PRINCESES·AND·DEFENDORS·OF·THE
TRVE·CATHOLICKE·FAYTHE

TUDOR, HOUSE OF

With deep-rooted Welsh origins this great English dynasty saw one of its monarchs take the title 'King of Ireland' before making way for the Scottish royal house of Stuart. Ruling in England from 1485 to 1603 the Tudors reigned at a time when the Renaissance and the Reformation were in full flow and explorers were discovering the New World.

◀ *LEFT: Henry VIII, Edward VI and Elizabeth I*

The first Tudor sovereign was Henry VII. Born in Wales, Henry Tudor (or Harri Tewdwr) was related to Welsh rebels such as Owain Glyndwr and great Welsh rulers such as Rhodri Mawr, while some family trees have even linked him to the legendary King Coel (whose name lives on in the nursery rhyme).

Henry VII's years in exile ended in 1485 with victory at Bosworth Field. Killing Richard III there, the Lancastrian leader was then crowned as the first Tudor monarch, his coronation effectively ending the Wars of the Roses. His marriage to Elizabeth, the daughter of Edward IV, symbolised the coming together of the two rival houses, while a symbol introduced at this time was the Tudor Rose, which combined the white Yorkist rose and the red Lancastrian rose to form a new design.

On the throne for nearly quarter of a century, Henry VII established the House of Tudor on firm foundations, foundations that survived the shaking they were given during the reign of Henry VIII. Probably the best-known of all English kings, the son of Henry VII married six wives, fathered three future monarchs, broke with Rome, dissolved the monasteries and was a catalyst for the English Reformation. He became the Defender of the Faith, Head of the English Church and King of Ireland, and he waged war on France and Scotland, while the chief ministers of his reign, More, Wolsey and Cromwell, were each named Thomas.

Reigning 38 years, Henry VIII was succeeded by his young son, Edward VI. A minor at the time of his accession, he was still only 15 years old when he died. However, although there was a brief succession struggle, Lady Jane Grey was Queen Jane for just nine days before the eldest daughter of Henry VIII took her place on England's throne. A Catholic queen, Mary I came to be known as 'Bloody Mary' as her short reign saw nearly 300 Protestants burned at the stake as heretics. Briefly reigning with her Spanish husband, Philip II, she overturned Protestant laws, re-aligned England with the pope in Rome and lost Calais, the last fragment of a once mighty English empire in France.

England's queen for just five years, Mary was succeeded by the youngest daughter of Henry VIII: Elizabeth I. Sovereign for 44 years and 69 years old at her death, no English monarch before her had ever lived to so great an age. Queen during an era of exploration and colonisation, Sir Walter Raleigh named the American state of Virginia after the Virgin Queen, while Sir Francis Drake became the first English mariner to circumnavigate the globe. Drake, of course, was also the man who singed the king of Spain's beard and helped to defeat the Spanish Armada.

But the reign of Good Queen Bess or Gloriana was not all sailing, plain or otherwise. She was excommunicated by the pope and so was vulnerable to Catholic plots, while Mary, Queen of Scots, posed a real or imagined threat. In exile in England for 20 years, eventually Mary, Elizabeth's cousin, was linked to the Babington Plot and was executed in 1587. Elizabeth I, though, lived on until 1603, when she, the last Tudor monarch, died and was succeeded by the son of Mary, Queen of Scots, the Stuart king, James VI of Scotland, who was crowned James I of England.

EDWARD IV (1442–83)

King of England (1462–70, 1471–83). Born in the French city of Rouen on 28 April 1442, Edward was the eldest son of Richard, Duke of York, and his wife, Cecily. At the time of Edward's birth, Henry VI was on the throne, but his gradual frailty opened the door of power to men such as the king's cousin, the Duke of York. York was twice appointed Protector of the Realm, when Henry VI was deemed unfit to rule. After participating in battles against Lancastrian troops loyal to Henry's wife, Queen Margaret,

◀ *LEFT: Edward IV*

Edward's father claimed the crown. Edward was finally acknowledged as heir to the throne in October 1460, but two months later the Duke of York and his younger son, Edmund, were killed at the Battle of Wakefield. The Yorkist cause was not to be denied, however, and on 28 June 1461 at Westminster Abbey the duke's son, Edward, who had fought alongside his father, was crowned Edward IV.

With Henry VI, Margaret and their son, Prince Edward, all still alive, however, the young king was heavily dependent on men such as his cousin Richard Neville, Earl of Warwick, and his younger brother, George, Duke of Clarence, for support and advice. His hold on the throne was tenuous and constantly under threat. These two men had proved to be loyal lieutenants during Edward's rise to power, but later they both turned to plotting against him. Despite the capture of the former king, Henry VI, in 1465, the house of Lancaster continued to fight against the Yorkists. Early progress by the Lancastrian rebels was not sustained and in early 1470 Warwick, Clarence and their supporters were driven into exile. Surprised, however, by a new rebellion in September, it was Edward's turn to flee the country. With the king in Burgundy, the Earl of Warwick assumed control and reinstated Henry VI as his puppet king.

Meanwhile Edward IV prepared to make his comeback. Persuading his brother-in-law, the Duke of Burgundy, to provide him with an army of 1,500 men, he returned to England. Triumphing in April 1471 at Barnet (where Warwick was killed), he then marched west to Tewkesbury where, on 4 May, the Yorkist king won a battle, took Queen Margaret captive and killed her son. The execution of the unfortunate Henry VI soon afterwards completed Edward IV's purge of the leading Lancastrians. Only Clarence remained at large; his treachery was forgiven until further schemings a few years later resulted in charges of treason. Sentenced to death, legend has it that Clarence was drowned in a butt of malmsey wine on 18 February 1478.

Restored as king in 1471, Edward IV was reunited with his wife, Elizabeth.

Whilst in sanctuary at Westminster Abbey she had given birth to the couple's first child. A widow, Elizabeth was already the mother of two sons when she had secretly married the future king in 1464. Six years later, the birth of the baby, Edward, provided the king with his eventual successor, while the arrival of a second son, Richard, in 1473 reinforced the foundations of the house of York.

▲ *ABOVE: Manuscript showing Edward IV*

With all threats to his throne abolished, Edward could turn his attention to the administrative matters of his kingdom. He introduced a measure of reform, kept parliament and the people more or less content by not levying too many taxes and oversaw a boom period in the wool and cloth trades. In foreign policy the emphasis was on building bridges, that is until July 1475, when Edward IV led a force of 10,000 men across the English Channel to wage war on the French king. Despite support from Burgundy, Edward negotiated the Treaty of Picquigny with the French king, Louis XI, who effectively paid off his English counterpart by offering him 75,000 crowns with a further annuity of 20,000 crowns.

After this rare sortie on foreign soil, the king's attempts at empire-building petered out. He had planned further raids on Scotland and France, but on 9 April 1483, at his palace at Westminster, Edward IV died of a fever. Just 40 years old at the time of his death, he was buried at St George's Chapel, Windsor, and was succeeded by his young son, Edward V

◆ see Edward V, Henry VI, Richard III

EDWARD V (1470–C. 1483)

King of England (1483); son of Edward IV. Edward V has gained his place in history through the dark dealings going on around him during this period rather than through any virtue of his own. As one of the 'Princes in the Tower', Edward never had the chance to prove himself. He succeeded his father at the age of 12, but the unfortunate child king was never crowned. He actually ascended the throne on 9 April 1483, but by 25 June 1483 he had been deposed. Sent to the Tower of London with his younger brother, Richard, neither boy was ever seen again in public. Killed by persons unknown, Edward V was succeeded by his 'wicked uncle' Richard III.

◀ LEFT: Edward V

Although many theories have been proposed about the fate of the princes, none has yet been proved and the fact remains that we will probably never know. In 1678 the bones of two young boys were discovered is a secret hole in a wall in the Tower of London. It is likely that these were the remains of Edward V and his brother Richard. The reigning monarch at the time, Charles II, ordered that these bones be interred at Westminster Abbey.

◨ see Edward IV, Richard III

HENRY VII (1457–1509)

King of England (1485–1509). Born at Pembroke Castle, Wales, on 27 or 28 January 1457, Henry VII was the only child of Edmund Tudor, Earl of Richmond, and Margaret Beaufort, daughter of the Duke of Somerset. A child of the Wars of the Roses, which he would later bring to an end, Henry's birth occurred three months after the death of his Lancastrian father. Spending his early years in Wales, Henry was 14 years old when his uncle, Jasper Tudor, was defeated at Mortimer Cross. Just months later Edward IV became king and his return to power in 1471 was the signal for young Henry Tudor, the new head of the house of Lancaster, to hurry into a long exile abroad.

Heading for France, for the next 14 years he lived in Brittany. Continuing to plot the downfall of the house of York, in December 1483 at Rennes Cathedral Henry pledged to marry Elizabeth, the eldest daughter of Edward IV, whose brother, Richard III, had become England's king a short time before. Then, in the summer of 1485 he sailed to Milford Haven in South Wales. From there he moved across Wales and east into England, gathering support as he went until he reached the small Leicestershire town of Market Bosworth. There fighting and defeating an army commanded by Richard III himself, on 22 August 1485 Richard's death in battle and Henry's victory saw him proclaimed King Henry VII.

Crowned at Westminster Abbey on 30 October 1485, he was back at the abbey less than three months later when he fulfilled his promise to marry Elizabeth of York. However, the marriage of two of the leading members of the Lancastrian and Yorkist factions could not prevent the revolts that were a feature of the first years of the new reign.

▶ *RIGHT: Henry VII before the altar*

A nephew of Richard III, the young Earl of Warwick had been imprisoned in the Tower of London after Bosworth Field, yet in 1487 the imposter, Lambert Simnel, pretended to be Warwick and was hailed as Edward VI. Defeat at the Battle of Stoke in 1487 ended Simnel's time in the spotlight, but his place as pretender to the throne was then filled by Perkin Warbeck. Impersonating the younger of the two 'Princes in the Tower', he was hailed as Richard IV. However, when Warbeck and the real Earl of Warwick were executed the likelihood of Henry VII being deposed began to fade.

At last able to concentrate fully on ruling over his kingdom, Henry's attempt at invading France ended in 1492 with the Tudor king winning a lucrative peace settlement via the Treaty of Etaples. Domestically too his policies proved profitable, the king accumulating great wealth and power. Transforming his financial fortunes, during his reign customs' taxation increased by 100 per cent and income from crown lands also doubled as a hefty debt became a vast surplus, while the workings of the Royal Council and its offshoots proved highly effective in governing a peaceful realm.

◀ *LEFT: Henry VII with Empeson and Dudley*

The father of seven children, in 1501 Henry saw his son and heir, Arthur, wed Catherine, the daughter of Ferdinand and Isabella of Aragon. Then, in 1503, his eldest daughter, Margaret, married James IV of Scotland. However, while the sudden death of Prince Arthur in 1502 was a personal tragedy and created a dynastic problem, there was a silver lining of sorts as Arthur's widow was married to the king's third child, by then King Henry VIII.

Outliving his wife, Elizabeth, who had died in 1503, Henry VII spent his last years quietly. Passing away on 21 April 1509 at Richmond, where a grand palace had been built for him, Henry VII was buried at Westminster Abbey and was succeeded as king by his son, Henry VIII.

see Henry VIII, Richard III

HENRY VIII (1491–1547)

King of England (1509–47). The second son of Henry VII and the former Elizabeth of York, Henry was born at Greenwich Palace on 28 June 1491. At the time of his birth his father had been monarch for nearly six years and had already sired a son and heir. This child was Arthur, Prince of Wales. Later married to Catherine of Aragon, just five months after their wedding in April 1502 Arthur was dead. From that time on the life of Henry, Duke of York would never be the same again. His

▲ *ABOVE: Henry VIII with Anne of Cleves*

▲ *ABOVE: Henry VIII*

brother's death left him as heir to the throne and seven years later, the young prince became Henry VIII.

Succeeding his father on 21 April 1509, he was crowned at Westminster Abbey on 24 June – just 13 days after he had married Arthur's 23-year-old widow, Catherine of Aragon. The first of the six wives of Henry VIII, she was five years older than her second husband. Destined to lead a sad and unfulfilled life, her marriage to Henry was dogged by miscarriages and infant deaths with only one child, the future Mary I, surviving. Cast aside by her second husband, their marriage was eventually dissolved in 1533.

Having convinced himself that his marriage to his brother's widow was contrary to divine law, Henry eventually wed his second wife, Anne Boleyn. The younger sister of one of the king's former mistresses, she was a high-spirited woman who knew her own mind. Marrying the king in 1533, she gave birth to a daughter, later Elizabeth I, but was soon found guilty of adultery, divorced and then beheaded in May 1536.

Jane Seymour was the king's third wife. This daughter of a Wiltshire knight became England's queen the day after the execution of Anne Boleyn. Queen Jane gave birth to a son, the future Edward VI, in 1537, but died just 12 days later. Marrying again in January 1540, Henry's fourth wife was Anne of Cleves. However, the king soon divorced the 'Flanders mare' and in July 1540 wed his fifth wife. Attractive, but flighty, Catherine Howard was destined to fall as the sovereign's second had fallen: found guilty of adultery, she was executed in February 1542.

Last of all came Catherine Parr. A widow twice over, this educated woman became wife number six in 1543. A caring stepmother to Henry's three children, she outlived her third husband, dying in 1548.

Notoriously fickle concerning his many wives, Henry VIII also favoured and then dispensed with three chief ministers. Sir Thomas More was canny enough to know that Henry VIII would readily sacrifice him. Lord Chancellor for three years from 1529, More was executed, having been found guilty of committing high treason. Earlier, Thomas Wolsey had filled the role of Lord Chancellor. A much disliked figure, the powerful and immensely wealthy Cardinal Archbishop of York had tried to gain the pope's consent for an annulment of Henry's marriage to

Catherine of Aragon. However, by 1529 Wolsey was a spent force. Cast aside, by 1530 he was dead.

Yet, just as the butcher's son, Wolsey, fell, so Thomas Cromwell rose. The king's chief minister from 1534, his reforming influence was well to the fore as the monasteries were dissolved. But then, in 1540, he was sacrificed and, like More before him, was sentenced to death and beheaded. Earlier, Acts that Cromwell had steered through parliament enshrined in law the English sovereign's position as Supreme Head of the Church of England, thereby sweeping away the country's long-standing loyalty to the pope. In an age of faith this was revolution indeed. Pope Leo

▲ *ABOVE: Henry VIII with Cranmer and Cromwell*

X had awarded Henry VIII the title Fidei Defensor ('Defender of the Faith') in 1521, yet the break with Rome was all but sealed by 1536.

That same year the Tudor monarch had continued his attack on the English Church. A survey of the nation's religious houses had revealed many abuses and so a full-scale dissolution was ordered. Confiscating the estates and vast wealth of the monasteries, most of which had owed their ultimate allegiance to the pope, by 1539 Henry VIII had legally ransacked around 560 religious houses. Henry sold most of the lands he seized but a few remained in royal hands, some of these existing today as London's major parks.

An ambitious, virile and wealthy ruler, in 1509 Henry had been eager to prove himself as a warrior king winning glory and territory in foreign lands. In league with Spain and Venice in 1512, he had waged war against France, with the king himself leading his forces in 1513. That same year the Earl of Surrey won a victory over the Scots at Flodden, killing the Scottish king, James V. However, this was a rare battlefield success for Henry. The wars with France were costly failures, while the war with Spain, declared in 1528, never started. Not returning to this trail until the last years of his life, Henry VIII then spent vast sums pursuing wars with Scotland and France.

In 1536 Henry had sent troops to the north of England where a rebellion, known as the Pilgrimage of Grace, was brought to a brutal end. Elsewhere in the British Isles, the Welsh and Irish were suppressed more by decree than by bloodshed. The Act of Union of 1536 had formally linked England and Wales, while Henry VIII was acknowledged as king of Ireland by the Irish parliament in 1541 and by the English parliament in 1542.

Dying on 28 January 1547 at Whitehall, Henry was buried at St George's Chapel, Windsor, and was succeeded by his nine-year-old son, Edward VI.

◆ *see* Edward VI, Elizabeth I, Henry VII, Mary I

EDWARD VI (1537–53)

King of England (1547–53). Edward was the first and only child born to Henry's third wife, Jane Seymour. Married in 1536, Queen Jane gave birth to the next king of England on 12 October 1537. Henry VIII was delighted

▲ *ABOVE: Latimer preaching to Edward VI at Paul's cross, 1458*

and ordered celebrations on a grand scale, but joy at the birth of a son and heir was soon diminished by Jane Seymour's death at Hampton Court, 12 days after the arrival of baby Edward. A motherless child, during the next nine years his father remarried three times and the young prince and his older half-sisters, the future queens, Mary and Elizabeth, only enjoyed a more settled home life when Henry wed his sixth wife, Catherine Parr.

Ascending the throne on 28 January 1547, in the first months after the death of Henry VIII, Edward VI was guided by his uncle, Edward Seymour, Duke of Somerset. Appointed Lord Protector of the Realm, Somerset began by fighting in Scotland, where he won the Battle of Pinkie on 10 September 1547, but his fortunes soon declined as unrest grew. France declared war on England, while at home a population hit by religious upheaval, rising inflation and radical changes to land enclosure laws vented their anger by rioting and rebellions such as that led by Robert Kett in July 1549. Three months later Somerset's time as Protector was ended by a coup mounted by John Dudley, Earl of Warwick, later Duke of Northumberland. Somerset was imprisoned and then released, but he was later found guilty of treason and beheaded.

As heads rolled, the English Reformation, which had begun during the reign of Henry VIII, continued to take effect, overseen by Thomas Cranmer, who had become Archbishop of Canterbury during the reign of Henry VIII. In 1552 Edward VI became terminally ill. Struck down in the winter of 1552–53 by pneumonia (or possibly tuberculosis), the 15-year old king died at Greenwich Palace on 6 July 1553. Buried in Westminster Abbey, he was briefly succeeded by the daughter-in-law of the Earl of Northumberland, Lady Jane Grey.

◆ see Elizabeth I, Lady Jane Grey, Henry VIII, Mary I

RICHARD III (1452–85)

King of England (1483–85).
The eleventh child and
eighth son of Richard, Duke
of York, and his wife, Cicely,
Richard III was born at
Fotheringhay Castle in
Northamptonshire on 2
October 1452. Just three
years old when the Wars of
the Roses broke out
between the houses of
Lancaster and York, his
father was a leading light
of the Yorkist cause and
had twice been Protector of
the Realm before his death
in 1460.

After Richard's elder brother
had snatched the crown to
become Edward IV, he
distinguished himself as a
military man and as the
governor of territories in Wales
and the north of England.

▲ *ABOVE: Richard III and Queen Anne*

Accompanying Edward IV into exile in 1470 following the restoration of
Henry VI, when the Yorkists staged their successful fightback in 1471
Richard was in the forefront in the victorious battles at Barnet,
Hertfordshire, and at Tewkesbury, Gloucestershire.

Honoured with the title, Duke of Gloucester, in 1461, some 22 years later Richard assumed the role of Protector shortly after the death of Edward IV on 9 April 1483. The uncle of his brother's appointed successor, Edward V, a whirlwind series of events saw Richard, Duke of Gloucester, crowned Richard III in under three months. The heir to the throne was the former sovereign's 12-year-old son, but the unfortunate boy was to be king for less than three months.

Riding to London with Edward V in his clutches, opponents were rounded up and executed, the younger brother of Edward V, the nine-year-old Richard, was taken from his refuge at Westminster Abbey, and then the marriage of Edward IV to Queen Elizabeth was declared illegal. Proclaimed king on 26 June 1483, just 10 days later the coup of Richard III was complete when he was crowned at Westminster Abbey.

King for little more than two years, at Bosworth Field in Leicestershire he became the last English monarch to die in battle. So ended a brief reign that had begun with his nephews, Edward V and Richard, imprisoned in the Tower of London. From such unpromising beginnings his reign staggered from one problem or calamity to another, and always there was the threat of insurrection. The dark shadow of the Lancastrian leader, Henry Tudor, loomed large, while the Duke of Buckingham paid with his life for

▶ *RIGHT: Richard III*

221

plotting against Richard III. On a personal level too the short period from 1483 on was a traumatic one with the deaths of his son and heir, Edward, in 1484 and his wife, Anne, the younger daughter of Warwick the Kingmaker, whom Richard had married in 1472.

Killed on 2 August 1485 at the Battle of Bosworth Field by Henry Tudor's troops, his Lancastrian conqueror won the battle and was crowned Henry VII. Meanwhile, the body of Richard III was buried at Greyfriars Abbey, Leicester, but was later dug up and thrown into the River Soar.

◆ *see* Edward IV, Edward V, Henry VII

GREY, LADY JANE (1537–53)

Queen of England (1553). A distant cousin of Edward VI, Lady Jane Grey briefly succeeded him. She was proclaimed queen on 10 July 1553, but was deposed and imprisoned by Mary I on 19 July. The protégée and later daughter-in-law of John Dudley, Duke of Northumberland, like Northumberland and her husband, Lord Guildford Dudley, England's 'Nine-Day Queen' was executed.

John Dudley, formerly the Earl of Warwick, but from 1551 Duke of Northumberland, the son of Henry VII's one-time finance minister, had been a notable army commander, but by the time of Edward VI's minority he had emerged as a leading political

▶ *RIGHT: Lady Jane Grey*

figure. Replacing the disgraced Edward Seymour, Duke of Somerset, he soon won the confidence of Edward VI. Then, in 1553, with the king in the grip of the illness that was to kill him, the ambitious, sometimes ferocious duke began to promote the cause of Jane Grey, who had become his daughter-in-law when marrying his son, Lord Guildford Dudley, on 21 May 1553.

Dudley won the support of the dying king for his Protestant protégée and with it the approval of 26 peers of the realm. So, under the cover of securing English Protestantism, Dudley's bloodless coup was successful and on 10 July 1553, four days after Edward VI had died, the 15-year-old Lady Jane Grey was hailed by her supporters as Queen Jane.

▲ *ABOVE: Tower of London; The young Lady Jane*

223

As Jane entered the capital, however, the supporters of Princess Mary were preparing to strike. Then, just a few days later, Mary rode to London in the company of her half-sister, Elizabeth, to assume her rightful place as sovereign and to end the brief reign of Lady Jane Grey.

Retribution was inevitable and followed soon enough. Dudley was arrested, charged and executed. Imprisoned in the Tower of London for seven months after her arrest, Lady Jane Grey was executed on 12 February 1554. Taken to Tower Green, she was beheaded just a few hours after she had bid a poignant farewell to her husband, Lord Guildford Dudley, before he had placed his head on the executioner's block. A short and sad chapter in the story of English royalty ended with the joint burial of the ill-starred couple at the Tower's Chapel Royal of St Peter-ad-Vincula.

◆ *see* Edward VI, Mary I

MARY I (1516–58)

Queen of England (1553–58). Born at Greenwich Palace in London on 18 February 1516, Mary was the daughter of Henry VIII and his first wife, Catherine of Aragon. Mary had been made 'Princess of Wales' in 1525, but at the age of 17 she was rendered illegitimate when her parents' marriage was formally annulled. In 1533 Mary's half-sister, Elizabeth, was born. In 1537, the king's legitimate family was completed with the birth of a son, Edward, by his third wife, Jane Seymour.

Ten years later, on 20 February 1547, the bastardised daughter of Henry VIII looked on from the sidelines as her half-brother was crowned Edward VI. A Catholic in an increasingly Protestant land, her woes were multiplied when Lady Jane Grey was hailed as Edward's successor when the young king died on 6 July 1553. Mary was in East Anglia when 'Queen Jane' was proclaimed on 10 July. Nine days later Mary rode to London to seize the Crown so recently worn by her late half-brother. Gaining control

▼ *BELOW: Mary Tudor*

with little difficulty, the leader of the coup, John Dudley, Duke of Northumberland, and others were rounded up and summarily executed, and Lady Jane Grey was imprisoned. Mary ascended the throne on 19 July and was crowned 10 weeks later, on 1 October 1553, at Westminster Abbey.

No sooner had she become queen, however, then she was betrothed to the Spanish king, Philip II, a widower and a devout Catholic. A special occasion for the queen, the royal wedding of 25 July 1554 inflamed religious tensions and provoked hostility among English nationals, who disliked the idea of their monarch being married to a foreign prince. Opposition was so intense that four rebellions were planned in 1554, although only the one fronted by Sir Thomas Wyatt posed a serious danger to Mary before it was put down. However, before long the queen's marriage was over in all but name as Philip II abandoned his English wife and returned to the Low Countries.

Despite the difficulties she faced at the start of her reign, Mary I wasted no time in undoing the Protestant legislation that had been put in place during the previous two reigns. She soon returned England to the papal fold, overturning the anti-Catholic laws introduced by her father and half-brother. In addition three former statutes relating to heresy were reintroduced, while in 1556 the papal legate, Cardinal Reginald Pole, became the new Archbishop of Canterbury.

By the time Pole was appointed, the latest religious upheaval to afflict England had already claimed the lives of many Protestants. The first 'heretics' had been burned to death at Smithfield in London in February 1555, but many more would die in the months that followed these. The leading bishops, Hugh Latimer and Nicholas Ridley, died at the stake in 1555, while a later victim was Thomas Cranmer, the former Archbishop of Canterbury, who had introduced the revolutionary English Prayer Book in 1552 and overseen the annulment of the marriage of Mary's parents.

As the purge of leading Protestants continued, so Mary's enemies waged a propaganda war against the queen and Archbishop Pole. Then, Mary herself went on the warpath. Forming a military alliance with her husband, in 1557 she declared war on the French monarch, Henri II. The first French campaigns went well enough, but then Calais was lost. A major port, Calais was the last remaining outpost of England's once mighty empire in France. It too was recaptured by the French in January 1558 and 10 months later Mary I was dead.

The queen died at St James's Palace, London, on 17 November 1558. The first female sovereign to rule in England was buried at Westminster Abbey and was succeeded by the second queen to reign alone: her half-sister, Elizabeth I.

◆ *see* Edward VI, Elizabeth I, Henry VIII, Lady Jane Grey

ELIZABETH I (1533–1603)

Queen of England (1558–1603). Born at Greenwich Palace on 7 September 1533, the early life of the daughter of Henry VIII and Anne Boleyn was often clouded by disappointment and loss. Imprisoned in the Tower of London a short time when she was suspected of being involved in a rebellion led by Sir Thomas Wyatt, on 15 November 1558 the death of Mary I saw Elizabeth ascend the throne.

Crowned at Westminster Abbey on 15 January 1559, she came to power at a difficult time, her accession following an 11-year period in which a regency, a nine-day queen and the religious turmoil of Mary's brief reign had undermined the Tudor dynasty. In the early years of her reign threats came from every angle. Mary, Queen of Scots, was a potential challenger and Lady Margaret Douglas (like Mary Stuart a descendant of Margaret Tudor) and relatives of Jane Grey (herself a descendant of Henry VIII's youngest sister, Mary) were others. Then, in late 1562, Elizabeth suffered a near-fatal attack of smallpox. Made head of the Church of England just three years earlier, her subsequent excommunication by Pope Pius V made an assassination attempt on the Protestant queen all the more likely. Inevitably there were plots. A highly ambitious one fronted by Roberto Ridolfi was uncovered in 1571, while the Babington Plot was foiled by agents working for the Principal Secretary of State, Sir Francis Walsingham. Finally, there was the major threat posed by Philip II of Spain.

The former husband of Mary I, the Spanish king became a sworn enemy of the English queen. Yet earlier Philip had seen Elizabeth as a potential wife. He was not alone in thinking this; many pressed their suit, yet none were chosen as the 'Virgin Queen' remained a spinster to the end of her life.

Once rejected by England's queen, Philip II of Spain returned to his native country, determined to wreak revenge on the queen and restore the country to its Catholic status. In 1587 the Catholic Mary, Queen of Scots, had been executed after a long period of imprisonment and Sir Francis Drake had led a raid on Cadiz singeing 'the King of Spain's beard' as he did so. These events spurred Philip to action and in 1588 he ordered the galleons of the Spanish Armada to set sail for England. What happened next soon passed into English legend and made a national hero of Drake. Approaching the enemy ships anchored off Calais in the dead of night, the English fleet unleashed a collection of fire ships. Lashed together and filled with explosives these flaming vessels caused the Armada to panic. A battle then ensued and the remaining Spanish ships were forced to sail north towards Scotland taking the threat of invasion with them.

Judged by some to have mixed strong rule with a laissez-faire approach verging on indecisiveness, Elizabeth managed to outlast potential usurpers, ruling over England at a time when Drake, Shakespeare and Raleigh were some of her illustrious subjects. So it was that the death of the last Tudor monarch was viewed by many as the end of the golden Elizabethan age. Living to a greater age, 69, than all of her many royal predecessors, she also enjoyed the longest reign of any English monarch since the days of Edward III. Dying at Richmond Palace on 24 March 1603, Elizabeth I was buried at Westminster Abbey and was succeeded by James I.

see Edward VI, Henry VIII, James VI, Mary I, Mary Queen of Scots

HOUSE OF STUART

STUART, HOUSE OF

The ruling house for most of the seventeenth century, the first Stuart monarch to reign on both sides of Hadrian's Wall was the son of Mary, Queen of Scots. James VI of Scotland, in England in 1603 he succeeded Elizabeth I and was crowned James I.

This historic union of the crowns of two countries that had frequently been sworn enemies came about when England's last Tudor sovereign died without producing an heir. Because of this James VI of Scotland, who was the great-great-grandson of Henry VII, ascended the English throne,

having sat on the Scottish throne for 35 years.

He had endured an eventful reign in Scotland and his time in England began in a similar vein with the uncovering in 1605 of the Gunpowder Plot. Allegedly a Catholic plot to blow up parliament, the Protestant James was well used to ruling over a land where religious tensions ran high, and he would experience more of the

▲ ABOVE: William III with Anne, her husband, George, and son, William same during his reign in England with Protestant settlers being 'planted' in Ireland and the Pilgrim Fathers setting sail for a new life in New England. James's reign also witnessed the publication of the Authorized Version of the Bible.

In the reign of Charles I tensions between Protestants and Nonconformists continued, but a still greater problem proved to be the friction between the king and parliament. This friction ultimately resulted in a civil war pitting Royalists (or Cavaliers) against Parliamentarians (or Roundheads). Lasting seven years, this conflict ended dramatically in 1649 with the execution of Charles I and the creation of a republic that remained in place until 1660.

During this 11-year Interregnum the king-in-waiting was the exiled Charles II. The son of Charles I, he was finally restored in 1660. The reign that followed was one of contrasts.

The king fathered no legitimate children, but sired a number of illegitimate sons and daughters and, while he was acknowledged as a charming personality with 'the common touch', Charles II often clashed with parliament. In addition the Restoration period was dogged by religious differences. Various Acts relating to faith and public life were passed, the Test Act of 1673 barring Catholics and other Nonconformists from holding political office.

▶ RIGHT: *Charles I on scaffold in Whitehall*

Despite this ban, Charles was succeeded by his Catholic brother, James II, who was known as James VII in Scotland. King for less than four years, his short reign began with rebellions, but with these soon crushed, James sought to lift many of the restrictions then placed on Nonconformists. However, when he introduced two Declarations of Indulgence in 1687 and 1688, he found himself set on a path that led directly to his own deposition.

The fate of the doomed king was sealed when his wife, Mary, gave birth to a son, James, in the summer of 1688. Six months later James was a king without a crown, his successors his own daughter, Mary, and her husband, William of Orange. Years earlier William had fought on the Netherlands side in the Third Anglo-Dutch War, but in 1689 he was crowned jointly with his wife.

The first couple to reign in the British Isles since Mary I and Philip II of Spain had ruled over England for a short time during the 1550s, William III (but William II in Scotland) and Mary II were joint monarchs until the latter's death in 1694. William then ruled alone for the last eight years of his life, one of the more significant pieces of legislation passed during his short reign being the Act of Settlement of 1701, which determined that the head of the House of Hanover would be crowned if Queen Anne should die without a natural heir.

William was succeeded in 1702 by his sister-in-law. Anne was the younger sister of Mary II, her 12 years as monarch dominated by the War of Spanish Succession and the victories at Blenheim and Ramillies, while at home the two main political parties to emerge were the Whigs and the Tories. Anne's reign also witnessed the passing of the Act of Union in 1707. Formally uniting the kingdoms of England and Scotland, this Act led to the dissolution of the Scottish parliament. Seven years later Queen Anne died and was succeeded by the first Hanoverian sovereign, George I.

JAMES VI (JAMES I OF ENGLAND) (1566–1625)

King of Scotland (1567–1625) and king of England and Ireland (1603–25). The sixth successive Stuart monarch to ascend the Scottish throne as a minor, he was the only child resulting from the short-lived marriage of Mary, Queen of Scots, and her second husband, Henry, Lord Darnley. Born at Edinburgh Castle on 19 June 1566 and baptised Charles James, long before his second birthday his father had been killed and his mother deposed and he had been crowned.

He was carried north to Stirling for his coronation on 29 July 1567, and for the first 14 years of James's reign as king of Scotland the Earl of Morton acted as regent. Despite the earl's protection the life of the young monarch was fraught with danger as was made all too clear in 1581: the regent's execution was followed in 1582 by the Raid of Ruthven, which saw a Protestant group kidnap the king. Soon escaping from captivity, James Stuart took up the reins of power at the age of 17. In 1587 he learned of the beheading of his mother, Mary, Queen of Scots, following years in exile in England, while in 1600 a plot to kill him was uncovered.

▲ ABOVE: Royal heraldry of James I

235

In the last hours of her life the English queen, Elizabeth I, named James VI of Scotland as her successor, and on her death on 24 March 1603, Scotland's Stuart king ascended the English throne. Uniting the crowns of England and Scotland, on 25 July 1603 the king of the Scots was crowned King James I of England and Ireland at Westminster Abbey.

Crowned with him that day was his wife, Anne. The daughter of Frederick II of Denmark and Norway, she had married James in 1589 and was, by the time of her coronation in England, the mother of six of the eight children she was to produce. The eldest child was Henry, a boy of whom much was expected, but the 18-year-old prince died in 1612 to leave his brother, Charles, as son and heir. Of the other children, only Elizabeth reached maturity, the second-born child later marrying Frederick V, Elector Palatine of the Rhine and King of Bohemia. An important marriage for the future of the British monarchy, Elizabeth's daughter would become the mother of the future George I.

James began his reign in England by ending the long-running war with Spain. At home all was not well and the continuing conflict over religion threatened to come to a head as Puritans pressed for the total abolition of Catholic rituals in church services.

On 5 November 1605 the notorious Gunpowder Plot was foiled. Guy Fawkes has become the best-known conspirator and under him a band of Catholic extremists had planned to kill James while he attended the state opening of parliament, by exploding 30 barrels of gunpowder secreted in the cellars of the parliament building. Although the Gunpowder Plot proved to be the last serious attempt at insurrection during his reign, religious discord remained, even though, like Elizabeth I before him, the king generally adopted a conciliatory position between the ideological extremes. This policy took solid form when the Authorized Version of the Bible, also known as the King James Bible, was published in 1611, but was not forced upon worshippers.

Outliving his queen, who had passed away in 1619, James I died on 27 March 1625 at Theobalds Park in Hertfordshire. He was buried at Westminster Abbey, where the following February his son was crowned Charles I.

◆ see Charles I, Elizabeth I, Mary Queen of Scots

CHARLES I (1600–49)

King of England (1625–49). Charles was born on 19 November 1600 at Dunfermline in Scotland, the second son of James I (VI of Scotland). He became heir to the thrones of England and Scotland when his elder brother, Henry, died of smallpox in 1612. Then, on 27 March 1625, James I died. England's second Stuart monarch was crowned in England at Westminster Abbey on 2 February 1626, but was not crowned king of the Scots until 18 June 1633. He married Henrietta Maria, the sister of the French monarch, Louis XIII, two months after his accession. The royal couple had a large family with six children reaching adulthood. The eldest of these was the prince who became Charles II. Another son was crowned James II and a daughter, Mary, was mother to William III.

The young monarch declared war on Spain in an attempt to regain lands the Spanish had taken from the Elector Palatine of the Rhine, the husband of Charles's sister, Elizabeth. Marriage to a French princess did not prevent Charles I from going to war with France as well, in 1626. However, from 1625 to 1630 campaigns foundered badly as parliament withheld its support. The king retaliated by ruling from March 1629 to the

▲ ABOVE: A Miniature of Charles I by M. Snelling

spring of 1640 without once summoning parliament, a period that became known as the 'Eleven Years' Tyranny'. The question of faith could not be so easily ignored, especially in Scotland, where the imposed introduction of a new prayer book sparked a controversy that, in turn, led to all-out war.

Defeated by the Scots in the campaign that became known as the Bishops' Wars of 1639 and 1640, in the latter year Charles twice recalled parliament in an effort to gain funds for his campaigns. Having been overlooked for 11 years, parliament was unwilling to concede to the king's demands and pressed for a change. A band of dissenters objected to what they believed were the pro-Catholic leanings of the king and the Archbishop of Canterbury, William Laud, but the main demand was that parliament never again be dismissed without its own consent. Attacked on all sides, the king agreed to meet some of parliament's demands, but remained rigidly opposed to others. Dissension became more pronounced and rebellious factions formed. On 4 January 1642, during a visit to the House of Commons, Charles tried to arrest five leading members of these factions, including John Pym. This only served to further antagonise members of the Commons.

Relations between monarch and Commons continued to deteriorate until, on 22 August 1642, Charles I raised his standard at Nottingham to signal the start of the English Civil War. On 23 October, at Edgehill in Warwickshire, neither Royalists nor Parliamentarians were able to secure victory, but in 1643 the king won a battle at Newbury. Then parliament turned the screw, its forces grinding out a key victory on 2 July 1644 at the Battle of Marston Moor in Yorkshire and triumphing again the following year at Naseby in Northamptonshire. From then on, there was no stopping the Roundheads, the well-drilled New Model Army under Sir Thomas Fairfax, pressing home their superiority over Cavalier troops.

Finally abandoning the fight, Charles attempted to curry favour with the Scottish army occupying North-East England, but instead the so-called Covenanter army passed him into parliament's custody. Throughout 1647, Fairfax and Oliver Cromwell negotiated with the defeated king, but in 1648 the Royalists launched another wave of attacks, which ended in August that year with the rout of Charles's Scottish army at Preston. With victory secured, Charles I was put on trial. A believer to the end in the divine right of kings, he refused to acknowledge the legitimacy of the court. Condemned to death by the massed ranks of judges at Westminster Hall, the 'Martyr King' was executed at Whitehall on 30 January 1649 and was buried without ceremony at St George's Chapel, Windsor.

◆ *see* Charles II, Interregnum, James I, House of Stuart

INTERREGNUM (1649–60)

When Charles I was beheaded on 30 January 1649, his dramatic death marked not only the end of the Stuart king's life, but also the end of the English Civil War. What came next was an extraordinary period in British history. The way to a brave, new, republican world was cleared by Pride's Purge: an interregnum lasting 12 years. Overseen by Colonel Thomas Pride in December 1648, his purge forcibly expelled all members of parliament then in favour of holding further talks with the defeated king, Charles I. Within weeks of this purge the king had been tried and executed and a republican parliament had assumed power. Known as the Rump Parliament, this body of MPs governed for four years (1649–53), a period in which parliamentary forces under the leadership of Oliver Cromwell were brutally successful in Ireland and in Scotland.

A leading Roundhead figure during the civil war, in 1649 Cromwell and his army showed no mercy in conquering Ireland, overwhelming

Drogheda and Wexford, and massacring many innocent people in the process. Next Cromwell defeated supporters of Charles II, the son of Charles I, first routing a Scottish force at Dunbar in September 1650, then overpowering the Royalist army at Worcester in September 1651.

Two years later Oliver Cromwell enjoyed still more success as he

dissolved the Rump Parliament and replaced it with what was known as the Nominated Assembly or the Barebones Parliament. However, this was a short-lived body, its more extreme members bringing about a change of direction, which saw Cromwell appointed Lord Protector as part of the new-style administration outlined in a paper entitled the 'Institute of Government'.

The Protectorate formed in the last days of 1653 lasted for six years in all. A period of foreign war, the first Anglo-Dutch conflict (1652–54), ended with little gained by either side, so war was declared on Spain in 1655.

◄ LEFT: Oliver Cromwell

241

That same year a Royalist group made a failed attempt to re-establish the monarchy, while two years later Cromwell rejected the proposal contained in the 'Humble Petition and Advice' for him to become king. Meanwhile, reflecting the military flavour of the times, the Major Generals exercised great power, these commanders effectively ruling as lords in the 11 zones into which England was then divided.

Then, on 3 September 1658, the Puritan soldier–statesman, Oliver Cromwell, died. He was succeeded by his son, Richard Cromwell, who was Lord Protector for just eight months. Dissolving parliament in April 1659, the following month the younger Cromwell was deposed. The Rump Parliament and the revived Commonwealth then governed for a further 13 months until May 1660, when the king-in-exile, Charles II, returned to London to begin his reign in earnest.

◆ see Charles I, Charles II

CHARLES II (1630–85)

King of England (1660–85); son and heir of Charles I. Charles II succeeded his executed father in 1649, but did not rule until 1660. Born at St James's Palace in London on 29 May 1630, the second son born to Charles I and Henrietta Maria enjoyed an untroubled childhood until he was 12 years old. Then, in 1642, the English Civil War commenced. Whisked from his privileged surroundings, the heir to the throne accompanied his father on his early adventures before being sent abroad. Having reached Holland, from there he led a fleet of warships against the Parliamentarians. After his father's execution and the creation of a republic, Charles allied with the Scots in an attempt to restore the monarchy, but was defeated at the Battle of Worcester.

Fleeing from this rout, Charles was hunted down by Roundhead soldiers, at one time eluding capture at Boscobel, Worcestershire, by

◀ LEFT: Regal Heraldry of Charles II

hiding in an oak tree. He continued to mount further small-scale attacks, but it was not until the death of the Lord Protector, Oliver Cromwell, and the subsequent resignation of Cromwell's son, Richard, that Charles was invited back to England in 1660 and eventually crowned king on his thirtieth birthday.

Restoring the Stuart line, the new sovereign did not have things all his own way, with religious concerns rising to the fore during his reign. The Popish Plot loomed large in 1678, due to Titus Oates and others feeding rumours that a pro-Catholic group intended to murder the Protestant Charles and install as king his Catholic brother, James. Next came the Exclusion Crisis (1679–81), with arguments raging for and against the idea that James Stuart, as a Catholic, should be barred from succeeding. In addition, two Test Acts curtailed the influence on public life of practising Catholics. As for foreign policy, this was dominated by the wars with the Dutch. The first of these naval conflicts coincided with two domestic disasters: the Great Plague, which ravaged the population with a final outbreak in 1665, and the Great Fire of London which took hold during the hot summer of 1666.

In 1662 Charles II had married Catherine of Braganza, the daughter of John IV of Portugal. However, although the marriage endured, it did not produce any children. In contrast the sovereign's extra-marital liaisons saw various mistresses give birth to 13 or more illegitimate children. Of all the king's affairs, the best-known by far was the one he enjoyed with Nell Gwynne. Doted on by the king to the end of his life, the orange-seller-turned-actress outlived her lover, Charles II, who died on 6 February 1685 at Whitehall Palace, London, and was buried at Westminster Abbey. After his death the Stuart line was carried on by his younger brother, James II.

◆ *see* Charles I, Interregnum, James II, House of Stuart

JAMES VII (JAMES II OF ENGLAND) (1633–1701)

King of Great Britain (1685–88). Born at St James's Palace, London, on 14 October 1633, he was the fourth child born to Charles I and Queen Henrietta Maria. James enjoyed only a few settled years of childhood, then in 1642 the English Civil War broke out. Created Duke of York the following year, the next phase of the young prince's life was dominated by war as his father's Royalist forces fought the Parliamentarians in a series of battles. In 1646 Charles I was forced to abandon his Oxford headquarters and James was taken prisoner.

An invaluable hostage, in 1648 the future king escaped from Parliament's grasp and was spirited out of the country disguised as a girl. Next heading for Holland, which was home to his elder sister Mary, later he was joined there by his elder brother Charles. This period of exile then lasted until the Restoration was confirmed by the coronation of James's brother as King Charles II.

Two aspects of the future king's private life had been the talk of society. One topic was his concealed marriage, the second was James's interest in Roman Catholicism. A public wedding was then arranged for 3

▶ RIGHT: *The Duke of Monmouth pleads for his life before James II*

September 1660, James's marriage to Anne Hyde later producing eight children, the two surviving beyond infancy becoming the Stuart queens, Mary II and Anne. Then, after the death of his first wife in March 1671, James married Mary of Modena, the daughter of an Italian duke, who became the mother of six children, including a boy, also James, whose birth would hasten the overthrow of his father.

Succeeding Charles II on 6 February 1685, on 23 April he was crowned king at Westminster Abbey. Monarch for less than four years, as James VII of Scotland and Britain's James II he ruffled feathers with his often dismissive attitude and his commitment to the Catholic faith. He was also the subject of two attempted overthrows just months after his coronation. The Marquees of Argyll led a force against him in Scotland, while in southern England the Duke of Monmouth commanded another band of rebels.

Yet both these insurrections were crushed, with Monmouth and his men defeated at the Battle of Sedgemoor in July 1685. A brief lull then followed before further tensions provoked James to dismiss parliament

◄ LEFT: The flight of James II after the Battle of the Boyne

on 20 November 1685. Then came two Declarations of Independence, which relaxed restrictions placed on Catholics and other religious Nonconformists. However, these attempts to force through change were destined to founder during 1688.

The first significant event was the birth that summer of a son and heir to James II. There were allegations that the baby had not been born to Queen Mary, but had been smuggled into her bedchamber. With these rumours still circulating, just three weeks after the birth of Prince James came the acquittal of seven bishops, who had been put on trial by the king charged with seditious libel. Then, with acrimony in the air, an invitation was sent out to William of Orange pleading with him to replace James II.

The monarch's son-in-law, through marriage to the king's eldest daughter, Mary Stuart, he took up the invitation, landing on English soil on 5 November 1688. Next marching from Devon towards London, the size of his army and the volume of support for William saw the Glorious Revolution succeed with ease as James fled. Caught while making his escape, he was soon allowed to slip away to France, where he arrived on Christmas Day 1688.

In January 1689 England's parliament formally declared that James II had abdicated, a short time later proclaiming the accession of William and Mary. Meanwhile James plotted his return to power. Still recognised as king in Ireland, on 1 July 1690 he led an army into action at the Battle of the Boyne, but was defeated there by William's troops. On 6 September 1701, the ex-king died at his Parisian home. Buried at the Church of the English Benedictines in Paris, later his remains were reburied at Saint-Germain-en-Laye.

◘ see Charles I, Charles II, William III

MARY II (1662–94)

Queen of England (1689–94). Born at St James's Palace in London on 30 April 1662, Mary was the eldest daughter of the future James II (VII of Scotland) and his first wife, Anne Hyde. Mary was one of eight children born to the couple. She grew up at a time when the monarchy had only just been restored.

Suffering the loss of her mother when she was still only 10 years old, two years later her father remarried. At the age of 15, Mary herself was married. She took as her husband her much older cousin, William of Orange. At the time the marriage was arranged Mary had been dismayed at the thought of marrying the son of her aunt, Mary, but the wedding duly took place in London in November 1677.

After the wedding Mary made her home in the Netherlands, but then, in April 1685, Mary's father was

▶ *RIGHT: A waxwork Queen Mary II*

▼ BELOW: William III and Mary listen to the Bill of Rights

crowned king. Both the new monarch's daughters were staunch Protestants, yet James was a Roman Catholic, his faith and his personality immediately setting him on a collision course with parliament. Consequently, in his short reign, problem followed problem until the day when the king's second wife gave birth to a son. Also called James, his birth jeopardised the chances of Mary's succession as well as threatening to transform the royal House of Stuart into a Catholic dynasty. Such a prospect galvanised Whigs and Tories alike and so Mary's husband, William of Orange, was invited to sail to England to depose and succeed Mary's father, James II.

William III and Mary II were proclaimed king and queen. Named as joint sovereigns on 13 February 1689, they were crowned together at Westminster Abbey on 11 April. Although they agreed to rule together from the start, in reality William ruled alone, with Mary deputising for the king during his periods abroad.

Mary was queen for just five years, but during her reign English forces were active in Ireland, France and Scotland. Immediately faced with the threat posed by James II and his French allies, William and Mary declared war on France in May 1689. However, there were also foes to be fought in Scotland. Officially recognised as king and queen of the Scots in April 1689, William and Mary continued to be opposed by Jacobites such as John 'Bonnie Dundee' Graham. A loyal supporter of James VII and II, Graham was killed in action in July 1689 as the fighting men of the Scottish Highlands fought royal forces in Perthshire. The year 1689 also saw James besiege Londonderry, but in July 1690 he was decisively beaten in Ireland when losing the Battle of the Boyne.

However, while the old king sailed back to France, the Highlands of Scotland continued to resist the call to recognise William and Mary as monarchs in Scotland. Ordered to do so by New Year's Day 1692, most clans met the deadline.

Meanwhile, in England, Mary's reign saw important pieces of legislation emerge. The Toleration Act of 1689 gave citizens greater religious freedom, while the same year's Mutiny Bill banned the reigning monarch from maintaining a standing army without parliamentary consent. Then came an Act committing the monarch to calling parliament at least every three years, while at the same time limiting the life of a parliament to three years. Known as the Triennial Act, this became law in 1694, a year that ended with Mary's death.

Dying at Kensington Palace, London, on 28 December 1694, she was buried at Westminster Abbey. Her widowed husband then ruled alone, until his death in 1702 brought to the throne Mary's sister, Anne.

see Anne, James II, William III

WILLIAM III (1650–1702)

Grandson of Charles I and nephew of Charles II and James II, better known as William of Orange. He was married to Mary II, the couple reigning jointly from 1689 following the abdication of Mary's father, James II, in 1689. Swept to power by the Glorious Revolution of 1688, after

his wife's death in 1694 William III reigned alone, and as the war with France ended, James II died and the Act of Settlement was passed. The last Stuart king, William, was succeeded by his sister-in-law, Queen Anne.

Born in The Hague, Holland, on 4 November 1650, he was the only son of William, Prince of Orange, and Mary, who was the sister of Charles II and James II. The young Prince of Orange and Count of Nassau never knew his father, who had died shortly before his son's birth, and so young William was brought up by his mother.

◀ LEFT: William III

251

▲ ABOVE: *Insignia of William III*

Soon drawn to military matters, the serious-minded prince proved himself to be a capable officer, rising to the rank of captain general of the Dutch forces. Then locked in battle with the English in the Third Anglo-Dutch War, which ended in February 1674 with the signing of the Treaty of Westminster, two years earlier, at the age of 21, he had succeeded his father as Stadhouder or chief military commander.

William's star continued to rise as he made a successful marriage to Mary, the eldest daughter of the future James II. The couple's wedding ceremony took place in November 1677 at St James's Palace in London. Then, on 11 April 1689, William and Mary returned to the English capital, this time to be crowned jointly as king and queen. Four years earlier Charles II had died without a legitimate son and heir and had been succeeded by Mary's father, James II. However, the reign of the Catholic king was doomed to end with the Glorious Revolution.

Proclaimed king on 13 February 1689, that same day Mary was proclaimed queen. Also crowned together, their joint coronation took place on 11 April 1689 at Westminster Abbey. Earlier it had been decided that William III and Mary II would rule jointly, William declining to be his wife's 'gentleman usher'. Effectively, though, it was the king who played the leading role, the queen deputising in her husband's absence, but otherwise staying in the background until her death.

A king alone from 1694, the first significant event of William's kingship was the peace treaty agreed in 1697. Long at war with France, where the former king James II was still living, the Treaty of Ryswick brought to an end a period in which William III's soldiers had battled with Jacobite and French troops at the Battle of the Boyne in Ireland (in 1690) and in Flanders too.

Another notable year was 1701. A major alliance was formed that year with Austria and Holland, while at home the Act of Settlement determined a Protestant succession. Passed in the year of James II's death, this legislation guaranteed the accession of the head of the House of Hanover in the likely event of William's successor, Anne, not producing an heir.

The younger sister of the king's late wife, Queen Anne duly succeeded William III the following spring. Dying on 8 March 1702 at Kensington Palace, from injuries he had sustained when the horse he was riding stumbled on a molehill, William of Orange was buried at Westminster Abbey.

ANNE (1665–1714)

Queen of Great Britain (1702–14). Anne was the second daughter of the then Duke of York and his first wife, Anne Hyde. She was born at St James's Palace, London, on 6 February 1665. As a child her father, James, was a leading figure at the court of his brother, Charles II. Still an infant when featured in Peter Lely's well-known portrait of James's family, Anne was just six years old when her mother died, but she soon gained a stepmother in Mary of Modena, her father's second wife. At the age of 18 Anne wed the Danish prince, George, and two years later, on her twentieth birthday, her father began his reign as king. It was not long, though, before his Catholic sympathies forced his abdication and exile and a war began between the king and his son-in-law, William of Orange, husband of Anne's elder sister, Mary. When the Glorious Revolution occurred in 1689, Anne agreed to allow William to rule alone if Mary should die first without producing an heir; in return she received £50,000 a year and the exclusive use of the Cockpit, a London mansion that stood on what is now Downing Street.

Anne was desperate for a family and, most importantly, an heir. She fell pregnant at least 18 times, but tragically only one child survived infancy:

William, Duke of Gloucester. With his death in 1700, at the age of 11, hope of the continuance of the Stuart line also died.

Mary II had died in 1794 and William had continued to serve as king as agreed. His death in 1702 led to Anne's accession as queen. Crowned at Westminster Abbey on 23 April 1702, the ailing monarch was carried to and from her coronation in a sedan chair. Two weeks later, the first shots were fired in a war with France, a nation then supporting the 'Old Pretender', James Edward Stuart. Continuing until 1713 and costing around £150 million, the War of the Spanish Succession saw John Churchill, Duke of Marlborough, the husband of the queen's long-time friend, Sarah Churchill, win great victories at Blenheim (1704), Ramillies (1706) and Oudenaarde (1708).

At home a notable facet of Anne's short reign was the growing influence of the Whigs and the Tories in parliament and the rivalry of these political parties was mirrored by the improved standing of parliament and the holding of regular general elections.

The major event for which Anne's reign is remembered, though, is the Act of Union. This was the formal creation of the United Kingdom of Great Britain: two realms united politically. Placed in the statute books on 6 March 1707, the Act of Union of England and Scotland disbanded the Scottish parliament, although it left unchanged Scotland's legal and ecclesiastical systems. The Act also changed the sovereign's title and Anne became Queen of Great Britain and Ireland.

A passionate Protestant and a diligent queen, Anne frequently suffered from ill health. She died at Kensington Palace in London on 1 August 1714 and was buried at Westminster Abbey.

◆ *see* House of Hanover, House of Stuart

◀ *LEFT: Anne presents the plans of Blenheim to the Duke of Marlborough*

HOUSE OF HANOVER

HANOVER, HOUSE OF (1714–1901)

The ruling British dynasty from the moment George I succeeded his cousin, Queen Anne, right up to the death of the sixth and last Hanoverian monarch, Victoria.

▲ *ABOVE: George III*

George I ascended the throne on 1 August 1714, just a few weeks after the death of his mother, Sophia, the Electress of Hanover. Until her death, she had been the likely successor to the last Stuart sovereign, Anne, Sophia having filled that role since 1701 when the Act of Settlement passed by the English parliament ensured that there would be a Protestant monarch after Anne's death. The Act declared that if Anne died leaving no legitimate heir to the throne, then the head of the House of Hanover would succeed her, because Sophia and her son, George, were direct descendants of James VI and I.

A Stuart king, James's eldest daughter, Elizabeth, had married Frederick, the Elector Palatine of the Rhine, in 1613. Later, the couple became the parents of a large family that included a daughter, Sophia, who in time married the Elector of Hanover and gave birth to the son who was later crowned George I.

The great-grandson of James I, like his Stuart ancestor the first Hanoverian monarch arrived in England as a middle-aged man, one who had ruled in a very different political environment. George I also had to face the Jacobite threat that had troubled the later Stuart monarchs, but his prickly relationship with his eldest son and heir proved to be a hereditary Hanoverian problem.

When George I died he was succeeded by his eldest son, George II. Born in Hanover, he became the last British monarch to lead an army into battle, while his brother, the Duke of Cumberland, brutally cut down Bonnie Prince Charlie's Jacobites at Culloden. Frederick, the eldest son of George II, was a thorn in the king's side, but he died before his father, who was later succeeded by Frederick's son, George III.

The first Hanoverian sovereign to be born in Britain, no British king before George III ever lived to so great an age or reigned for so long. A lover of music, books and agriculture, Farmer George was a committed king, who was greatly depressed when the American War of Independence was lost in 1783.

Later the outbreak of the French Revolution led to Britain waging war on the new republic of France. Beginning in 1793 and ending in 1802, the peace was short-lived as in 1803 the Napoleonic Wars commenced. These lasted 12 years in all, yet by the time the efforts of Nelson, Wellington and others had defeated Napoleon Bonaparte, George III had been overtaken by insanity.

His son, George, was appointed Prince Regent in 1811, a position he held until his father's death in 1820, when he

▲ *ABOVE: The Brighton Pavilion, a Hanoverian splendour*

ascended the throne as George IV. A playboy, who had frittered away a fortune, the fourth Hanoverian king was an unpopular figure, whose 10-year reign ended with his death in 1830.

George IV's younger brother, William IV, was already 64 years old when he became king. A naval man, like his elder brother he died without producing a legitimate heir and was therefore succeeded by his niece, Victoria.

Queen for 63 years, Victoria reigned at a time when Britain was galvanised by the Industrial Revolution. The Victorian era was also the age of empire: Britain's colonies at this time in her history stretched over one quarter of the world's land mass. Married to Prince Albert, after his early death the queen shunned public life for many years, but later re-emerged to be proclaimed Empress of India.

A mother of many children, who married spouses from far and near, Queen Victoria died in 1901, precisely 200 years after the English parliament had passed the Act of Settlement, the very Act that had paved the way for the accession of the first Hanoverian sovereign. The last monarch of the House of Hanover, Victoria was succeeded by her eldest son, Edward VII, the only British monarch to reign as a member of the House of Saxe-Coburg-Gotha.

GEORGE I (1660–1727)

King of Great Britain (1714–27). Born at Leineschloss in Hanover, Germany, on 7 June 1660, George was the eldest son of the man who eventually became the Elector of Hanover and his wife, Sophia. Sophia's mother was the eldest daughter of James I of Scotland. However, this connection with the British royal family would have meant little to the young George Louis. Growing up on his family's estates, he eventually left Hanover to fight in foreign wars. It was while in England in 1680 that he met Anne, his second cousin and eventual royal predecessor. The meeting was not a success, however, and all thoughts of a possible marriage match were promptly forgotten.

When George married in November 1682 it was to another cousin, Sophia Dorothea. She gave birth to a boy, called George, and a girl, also called Sophia Dorothea, but in all other respects the marriage was a failure. Both partners embarked on affairs and in 1694 Sophia's lover, Count Philip von Königsmark, was killed. Sophia was then dealt another crushing blow as her embittered husband divorced her and sent her to a castle, where she spent more than three decades under virtual house arrest, forbidden either to see her children or to remarry.

Four years later the death of George's father saw him become the new Elector of Hanover, while in 1701 the English parliament passed the Act of Settlement. This Act established George's mother as heiress presumptive. However, her death just weeks before that of Anne robbed Electress Sophia of the chance to be addressed as Queen of Great Britain and Ireland and, with her passing, right of accession was transferred to her son, George.

Ascending the throne on 1 August 1714, George I was 54 years old when he became the United Kingdom's first Hanoverian monarch. Unable to speak more than a few words of English, his coronation service – which took place on 20 October 1714 at Westminster Abbey – was conducted in Latin. George was similarly handicapped during discussions with his ministers, although his son acted as a translator in the early years. The relationship between the two Georges was a stormy one, however.

The king's tempestuous relationship with his eldest child was a personal problem, but the threat posed by the Jacobites in the first months of the king's reign was a national one. Gathered around the flag of the 'Old Pretender', James Edward Stuart, the son of the last Stuart king, James II, the Jacobites had seized and then retained control of much of Scotland by 1715. Forced to act, the king's men defeated the Stuart army at Sheriffmuir. With the threat of invasion averted the attention of the royal family turned again to the worsening feud between George I and his son, the Prince of Wales.

In 1716 the king set off for Hanover, but not before drastically reducing the authority of the prince. The following year the rift deepened still further as the king came down hard on the younger George following a violent disagreement with his father's chamberlain. Placing the prince under house arrest, George I took his son's children from him and had him banished from St James's Palace. Typically, the Prince of Wales responded by setting up home at Leicester House, where a rival court soon attracted men such as the politician, Robert Walpole.

Meanwhile, a national crisis erupted in 1720 with the bursting of the South Sea Bubble. So called because of the fall of the South Sea Company, this finance firm had been set up in 1711. Persuading rich and poor alike to part with their money, huge profits were promised, but in 1720 the company went under. Bankruptcies resulted and vengeance was in the air among investors, much of it directed at a government that had backed the scheme in exchange for funds to clear the national debt. As the crisis deepened, George I was called back from yet another stay in

Hanover and Robert Walpole, the new First Lord of the Treasury and Chancellor of the Exchequer, set about repairing the damage done to the government.

The crisis proved to be the last major event of George's reign. He died at Osnabrück in Hanover on 22 June 1727. Buried at his home town church, he was succeeded by his son, George II.

⬥ *see* George II, James I

GEORGE II (1683–1760)

King of Great Britain (1727–60). The son of George I and his wife, Sophia Dorothea, George Augustus was born at Herrenhausen, Hanover, on 30 October 1683. Three-and-a-half years later, George Augustus gained a sister, Sophia, who later became the wife of the king of Prussia. Of greater impact on the young George was the imprisonment of his mother by his father on suspicion of adultery. This ensured that her two children would be placed in the care of their grandmother, Sophia, Electress of Hanover.

In 1701, the British Act of Settlement ceded the right of accession to the House of Hanover and gave George British citizenship.

With his father's accession in 1714, George, was bestowed the traditional title of Prince of Wales. Uprooting from Hanover, the 30-year-old prince attended his father's coronation and settled at St James's Palace with his wife, Caroline, and their first four children. Able to speak English the younger George acted as a translator for his father at early meetings of the Privy Council.

▲ *ABOVE: George II*

Such co-operation between king and prince was short-lived and the reign of George I was frequently punctuated by the two men's squabbles. On 22 June 1727 the king died and was succeeded by the Prince of Wales, whose joint coronation with his wife, Caroline of Ansbach, took place four months later, on 11 October, at Westminster Abbey.

By then 43 years of age, George II had fathered nine children, although two had died young. The oldest of the survivors was Frederick Louis, who inherited the title of Prince of Wales. The new monarch's chief minister at the time of his accession was Robert Walpole. War with Spain in the early part of George's kingship ended in 1729 with the signing of a peace treaty and so, for a time, Britain was not distracted by armed conflict.

However, just as the first years of the reign were peaceful ones, the last 21 years were studded with conflicts, not all of which were fought abroad. By 1739, Britain was at war with Spain again. This time it was the so-called War of Jenkins' Ear, which resulted from an incident at sea in which a Captain Jenkins had an ear cut off. France too was an enemy, the Anglo-French conflict creating royal history in 1742 as George II became the last British sovereign to lead his subjects into battle. He was victorious at Dettingen, but the War of Austrian Succession lasted six more years until peace was confirmed in 1748 by the Treaty of Aix-la-Chapelle.

With the return of the Jacobite threat in the 1740s, the king's troops were once again forced to fight on home soil. No longer led by the Old Pretender, the new leader of the Stuart faction was the charismatic Bonnie Prince Charlie. Initially successful, the Young Pretender's forces marched from Scotland as far south as Derby before the latest Jacobite opposition was crushed in bloody fashion on 15 April 1746 at Culloden Moor near Inverness..

In 1755, Britain waged war on France once more and so for the last five years of George II's life, Britain would be engaged in various conflicts around the globe. The early results of this newly aggressive approach were poor, but later outstanding generals such as Robert Clive and James Wolfe won great victories. Clive of India triumphed at Plassey in 1757, while Wolfe's defeat of the French at Quebec two years later secured possession of Canada for Britain. This momentous victory proved to be the last major event of George II's reign.

Outliving both his wife, Caroline of Ansbach, and his eldest son, the king died at Kensington Palace on 25 October 1760, just five days short of what would have been his 77th birthday. Buried at Westminster Abbey he was, at his insistence, laid to rest alongside his beloved Caroline, their coffins touching and with the adjacent sides removed. George II was succeeded by his grandson, George III.

◆ *see* George I, George III

GEORGE III (1738–1820)

King of Great Britain (1760–1820). The first Hanoverian king to be born in England, George William Frederick was the son of Frederick, Prince of Wales, and his wife, Augusta. The couple's second child, he was born at Norfolk House in London on 4 June 1738 at a time when his father, Frederick, was not on speaking terms with his grandfather George II. George was one of nine children fathered by the Prince of Wales and when he died in January 1751 the 12-year-old George succeeded him as heir to the throne, becoming king on 25 October 1760, the day that George II died.

Crowned George III at Westminster Abbey on 22 September 1761, two weeks earlier he had married a little-known princess, Charlotte of Mecklenburg-Strelitz. A year later the couple had their first child, the future George IV. Other offspring were born at regular intervals thereafter: Queen Charlotte eventually gave birth to 15 children, among them the future William IV.

For several years after his accession, George III relied greatly on personal favourites to represent him in the minefield of politics. Initially, his shield was the prime minister, John Stuart, Earl of Bute, while later Lord North spent 12 years as premier. Both were subjected to virulent attacks at the hands of politicians and satirists alike, but neither of these Conservative prime ministers was at the helm when Britain was forced to come to terms with a humiliating defeat in 1783, for that was the year in which the American Revolution finally reached its end with the irrevocable loss of the distant colonies. Lord North had been in charge from the outbreak of hostilities in 1775 until 1782, a seven-year period in

◀ *LEFT: New Yorkers pull down the statue of George III*

which the signing of the Declaration of Independence in 1776 had been followed by major military defeats at Saratoga (1777) and Yorktown (1781).

With the American colonies lost, William Pitt the Younger took over as prime minister. The French Revolution began in 1789, Britain declared war on France in 1793 and the conflict lasted until 1802. One year earlier the Act of Union had formally joined England and Ireland. In 1803 Britain returned to the fight against the French emperor, Napoleon Bonaparte, and two years later, with Horatio Nelson at the helm of the Victory, Britain routed the French fleet at Trafalgar.

Yet, while politicans such as Pitt attempted to shape Britain's destiny during such eventful times, George III slipped away from the centre of the political stage. Afflicted by porphyria from 1764, recurring bouts of the illness took their toll on his health and on 11 February 1811 the king's powers were transferred to the Prince Regent, George's eldest son, George, Prince of Wales.

Previously a man who had taken the business of kingship seriously, George III had developed such a passion for agriculture that he had become known as Farmer George. He had a similar passion for music and had patronised the arts and sciences, while his impressive collection of books was central to the later foundation of the British Library. But after 1811 the king's deteriorating health reduced the old king to a shadow of his former self.

The royal family mourned the death of George III at Windsor Castle on 29 January 1820. He was buried at St George's Chapel, Windsor. Eighty-one years old when he died, George III was succeeded by his eldest son, the Prince Regent, who was later crowned George IV.

◆ *see* George II, George IV

GEORGE IV (1762–1830)

King of Great Britain (1820–30); Regent (1811–20). Born at St James's Palace on 12 August 1762, the eldest son of George III and Queen Charlotte, George's early promise soon evaporated when the Prince of Wales reached the age of maturity. A constant source of frustration to his father, his debts continued to mount up. Pressing for more money in 1783, the prince's request was turned down, but four years later his financial affairs were discussed again by parliament. This time, it was agreed that £10,000 would be provided by the king, while parliament would clear his debts and would cover the considerable cost involved in finishing the heir to the throne's new home, Carlton House. Still the extravagant spending continued and by 1811, the year that marked the start of George's spell as Prince Regent, his total debts amounted to the enormous sum of £500,000.

The son of a king who had been a faithful husband to his wife and an often doting father to 15 children, George IV was very different to George III. Falling for his first older

▲ ABOVE: Thoughts on Matrimony. George IV considers potential marriage partners

woman when he was still a youth, his love life took him from affair to affair. Then, in 1785, he secretly married Maria Fitzherbert, a woman who had already been married twice before. However, the marriage was declared invalid as George had not sought or been given permission to marry. Ten years later, though, he was legally married to Caroline of Brunswick. A first cousin of George, she met her future husband in the spring of 1795. A few days later the couple were wed, but the marriage of convenience intended to help repay the prince's mountain of debts produced just one child, Charlotte, and very little else except separation and bitterness.

Appointed Prince Regent on 5 February 1811, the early years of George's regency were dominated by the closing chapters of the Napoleonic Wars, which culminated in Wellington's famous victory at Waterloo in 1815. However, basking in this reflected glory did not improve the regent's popularity in the country at large and George was the target of an assassination plot in 1817, a year also marred by the death of his daughter, Charlotte.

▶ RIGHT: The Lord of Misrule, Wellington and George IV

Finally ascending the throne following his father's death on 29 January 1820, the coronation of George IV on 19 July 1821 was a typically lavish and spectacular event. It was also one touched with farce, the new king's estranged wife vainly attempting to enter Westminster Abbey in order to be crowned queen. It was almost her final public appearance as she died just three weeks after the coronation ceremony. Caroline of Brunswick, however, had enjoyed one last victory over her husband. Appearing before the House of Lords to defend herself against charges of adultery and scandalous behaviour, eventually in November 1820 the government spiked what was known as the Bill of Pains and Penalties. This very public defeat for George IV prompted celebrations across London that lasted for three whole days.

The king later embarked on a series of royal tours that took in Ireland, a country devastated by famine in 1821–23, Hanover and Scotland. Meanwhile, in England the short reign of George IV was notable for the legalisation of unions and the opening of the pioneering Stockton to Darlington railway line (both in 1825), while four years later an Act was introduced that removed many of the centuries-old restrictions on the civil rights of Roman Catholics. As a result, from 1829 Catholic citizens could at last hold some public offices. This was the last major piece of legislation passed during the king's lifetime. George IV died on 26 June 1830 aged 67. He was succeeded by his younger brother, William IV.

◆ *see* George III, William IV

WILLIAM IV (1765–1837)

King of Great Britain (1830–37). The third son of George III and Queen Charlotte, Prince William Henry was born on 21 August 1765 at Buckingham House. The first royal baby to be born at the mansion later remodelled and renamed Buckingham Palace, he grew up in the shadow of his older brothers, George and Frederick. At that stage in his life there seemed little likelihood of William ever becoming king and so, when he was 14 years of age, he started out on a career in the navy.

Beginning his life at sea as an ordinary seaman, during the next few years he rose steadily through the ranks. Commander of the Andromeda by 1787, two years later William was made Duke of Clarence. Then 24 years old, his elevated status allowed him to take his seat in the House of Lords. Soon retiring from the navy, it was then that he fell in love with an actress whose stage name was Dorothy Jordan. Before long an affair developed that was to last 20 years and produce 10 children.

In time, though, William decided to marry. However, his bride was not Mrs Jordan, but Adelaide of Saxe-Meiningen. Fifty-three years old when he wed Adelaide in July 1818, she was then a 25-year-old princess. Yet despite the difference in age and background, the marriage was a success, although three pregnancies failed to produce a child that lived more than three months.

Just eight months before King William's royal wedding, there occurred

▲ ABOVE: *Coronation of William IV*

the first of three deaths that were to alter the Hanoverian line of succession drastically. The 21-year-old daughter of William's older brother, George, Princess Charlotte died in November 1817. A full decade then passed before the death of Frederick, Duke of York. An older brother of William, his death was followed three years later by that of his other brother, George III, the latter's death seeing William become the fifth and last Hanoverian king.

Ascending the throne on 26 June 1830, William, Duke of Clarence, wanted to be crowned Henry IX, but was persuaded to reign as William IV. Crowned at a joint coronation service with Queen Adelaide on 8 September 1831, later the new monarch's adventurous approach proved popular, but he clashed frequently with politicians and parliament alike.

King for less than seven years, William's reign was notable for the high turnover of prime ministers. The grand old Duke of Wellington had completed a brief term of office in 1830, then came Earl Grey. He lasted for four years before Robert Peel took over, while in 1835 he was followed by the king's personal choice of premier: Viscount Melbourne.

Despite the turmoil at the top of the political ladder, there were several important Acts passed. The Reform Act of 1832 opened out the election process to more voters, while the Factory Act made it illegal for children under the age of nine to be employed and restricted the number of hours that older children could work. Passed in 1833, that year also saw another major change take place in the British Empire when slavery was finally abolished. The 1830s was also a boom time for the economy and for the up-and-coming form of transport: the railways.

The last Hanoverian king, William IV, died on 20 June 1837 at Windsor Castle and was buried at St George's Chapel at Windsor. Survived by his young queen, he was succeeded by an even younger woman, his niece, Queen Victoria.

VICTORIA (1819–1901)

Queen of Great Britain (1837–1901). Alexandrina Victoria was the only child of Edward, Duke of Kent and Victoria of Saxe-Coburg. Born at Kensington Palace on 24 May 1819, she was only a few months old when her father died in 1820. That same year also saw the passing of her grandfather, George III, and the accession of Victoria's uncle, George IV.

Ten years later another uncle, William IV, ascended the throne. Already 64 years old he had fathered four children in the first years of his marriage, but none had survived. So it was that he was eventually succeeded by his 18-year-old niece, Victoria. Ascending the throne on 20 June 1837, Victoria was not crowned until the following summer, her coronation at Westminster

Abbey taking place on 28 June 1838. Unmarried at that time, a short time later she would marry the love of her life, Prince Albert.

Victoria and Albert had met at Windsor in 1836, but when their paths crossed three years later they fell in love and before long the 20-year-olds were engaged to be married. The younger son of the Duke and Duchess of Saxe-Coburg and Gotha, Albert was a first cousin of Victoria as his father and her mother were brother and sister. Married in London on 10 February 1840, before her marriage the young Queen Victoria had been heavily dependent on the advice and support of her prime minister, Lord Melbourne, and her trusted uncle, Prince Leopold of Belgium. Yet, while their influence remained strong, increasingly her husband, Prince Albert, became her main adviser.

Inevitably, some politicians questioned the role of the newly arrived German prince, but it was not too long before he was accepted as a force for good and, in June 1857, he was given the title of Prince Consort. By then the father of five girls and four boys, his death in December 1861 so depressed Queen Victoria that for years she lived a semi-reclusive existence.

When her beloved husband passed away in December 1861, Victoria had already been on the throne for 24 years, yet she was to continue as queen for another 39 years, so making her reign the longest ever enjoyed by a British monarch. In personal and dynastic terms, the reign saw many of the queen's children marry spouses from European royal families, including those of Germany, Russia and Prussia, but she also lived so long that she outlived her daughter, Alice, and sons, Alfred and Leopold.

The Victorian era was also the age of the British Empire. With colonies all over the globe, during the queen's long reign Britain's empire incorporated territories as far apart as Africa, Australia and Canada. India was another cherished colony, and in 1876 Victoria was given the title of

Empress of India. Twenty years earlier, the first major war of the queen's reign had come to an end. Beginning in 1854, Britain and France had fought against Russia in the Crimean War, a conflict best known for the Charge of the Light Brigade at Balaclava near Sevastopol and the care and compassion of the nursing heroine Florence Nightingale.

Years later, British soldiers were active in Sudan, but in 1884 General Gordon and his men died in Khartoum at the end of a siege lasting 10 months. However, this was not the end of Britain's military involvements during Victoria's reign as in 1899 the Boer War began in southern Africa.

Closer to home Ireland suffered a terrible potato famine in the years 1845–48, while in the last decades of the nineteenth century Irish Home Rule was the subject of parliamentary bills in 1886 and 1893. On the British mainland, the Industrial Revolution witnessed the advent of iron and steel, canals and railways, while the first 'horseless carriages' (cars) powered by internal combustion engines appeared. Primary education became compulsory in 1870 and there were concentrated attempts by reformers to improve sanitation and hygiene. An age of plenty for some, many Victorians lived tough lives in acute poverty and there were workhouses at the heart of the great British Empire.

Changing times, often turbulent ones, in the Victorian era even the woman who gave the period its name was a target for extremists. The subject of seven assassination attempts, the queen survived each and every one to live to the age of 81. Dying in her bed at Osborne House on the Isle of Wight, she was buried beside Prince Albert at Frogmore, Windsor, and was succeeded by her eldest son, Albert, who was crowned Edward VII.

◐ *see* Edward VII, William IV

▶ *RIGHT: Victoria and family at Osborne House*

HOUSE OF SAXE-COBURG-GOTHA

SAXE-COBURG-GOTHA, HOUSE OF

Often seen as the last of the Hanoverian monarchs, Edward VII was actually Britain's first and only Saxe-Coburg-Gotha sovereign. Sometimes described as the House of Wettin, this royal house took its unwieldy title from the German duchy of the same name.

Edward VII was descended from this line on his father's side, Prince Albert having been the son of Duke Ernest I of Saxe-Coburg and Gotha. A long-lived dynasty with the branches of its family tree growing from tenth-century roots, during the last years of

◄ *LEFT: Edward VII*

the nineteenth century Edward VII's younger brother, Alfred, was duke until his death in 1900.

King for just nine years, Edward VII began his reign following the death of his mother, Queen Victoria, in 1901. Like her he gave his name to the period in which he reigned, the Edwardian age coming to be viewed by many as a golden late summer before the storms of World War I killed millions and destroyed the old order.

However, the monarch himself played little part in shaping Britain's destiny in the first decade of the twentieth century. A time when Britain was busy forming alliances with Japan, France and Russia, at home the Labour Party was born and the Liberals were reborn, returning to power after 10 years in opposition.

After the death of Edward VII in 1910, the royal family retained the name of Saxe-Coburg-Gotha until 1917. Then, with World War I still raging, Edward's son and successor, George V, renamed his dynasty the House of Windsor.

◄ *LEFT: Maria Clementina Carolina of Orleans, Princess of Saxe-Coburg-Gotha*

EDWARD VII (1841–1910)

King of Great Britain (1901–10). Albert Edward was born at Buckingham Palace on 9 November 1841. The eldest son of Queen Victoria and Prince Albert, he was followed into the royal nursery by three brothers and four sisters. He was a spirited, friendly boy, known to his family as 'Bertie'. On reaching maturity the Prince of Wales began to make his way in the world, embarking on a tour of North America. Back in Britain he moved into a new home, enjoyed a stint at university and went to Ireland for military training. He was 20 years old when his father, Prince Albert,

▶ RIGHT: Edward VII

died in December 1861. Two years later the Prince of Wales married his Danish bride, Princess Alexandra. After their wedding the young couple moved into Marlborough House, a London mansion that became the birthplace of four of the six children born between 1864 and 1871. Alexandra devoted her time to raising her children and charity work. She stood by her husband despite his well-publicised affairs that caused one wit to comment that he 'preferred men to books, and women to either'.

Edward spent most of his life waiting in the wings, and he was 59 when he ascended the throne on 22 January 1901. Crowned Edward VII at Westminster Abbey on 9 August 1902, the new king proved to be a capable monarch. Edward was particularly interested in the military and was a strong francophile; some commentators believe that he was instrumental in arranging the Entente Cordiale, the unofficial alliance forged by Britain and France in 1904.

When not engaged on royal duties, the popular king continued to enjoy the good life, not least horse racing, 'the sport of kings'. Edward's horse, Minoru, won the Epsom Derby in 1906. That same year the Liberals returned to power, while the Labour Party won its first seats in the Commons. Under the leadership of Prime Minister Campbell-Bannerman, the Liberal government placed a strong emphasis on social reform introducing free school meals, old-age pensions and labour exchanges.

Meanwhile, the king's health steadily deteriorated and on 6 May 1910 he died at Buckingham Palace. Edward VII was buried at St George's Chapel, Windsor. Survived by his wife, Queen Alexandra, he was succeeded by his eldest surviving son, George V.

◆ *see* Queen Victoria, George V

LONG MAY THEY

HOUSE OF WINDSOR

1912	China becomes a republic
1914	Assassination of Archduke, Franz Ferdinand triggers the outbreak of World War I
1918	The signing of the Armistice signals the defeat of Germany and ends World War I
1919	First direct transatlantic flight is completed
1921	The Irish Free State is established; Albert Einstein is awarded the Nobel physics prize
1924	Death of Vladimir Ilyich Ulyanov Lenin
1929	The Wall Street Crash
1930	Death of D.H. Lawrence and Sir Arthur Conan Doyle
1933	Adolf Hitler appointed German chancellor
1936	The Spanish Civil War breaks out
1936	Death of George V
1936	Edward VIII crowned; abdicates same year
1939	World War II begins
1940	Battle of Britain
1945	World War II, United Nations formed
1952	Death of George VI
1952	Coronation of Elizabeth II
1961	Yuri Gagarin is the first man in space
1963	John F. Kennedy is assassinated
1965	Death of Sir Winston Churchill
1969	Neil Armstrong: first man on the moon
1982	The Falklands War breaks out
1997	Death of Diana, Princess of Wales
1998	Good Friday Agreement signed
2002	Death of Elizabeth, the Queen Mother

WINDSOR, HOUSE OF

The present-day dynasty came into being on 17 July 1917. Previously known as the House of Saxe-Coburg-Gotha (or Wettin), during World War I this Germanic title became a source of embarrassment for the reigning monarch, George V. A cousin of the German emperor, Wilhelm II, in 1917 King George opted to change his family's name to Windsor. The Kaiser was not amused, but in Britain the decision to call the royal house after its best-known castle proved popular.

As the first Windsor monarch George V reigned for 26 eventful, often traumatic, years. However, as crowned head of a parliamentary democracy, the king played a back-seat role as prime ministers such as

▲ *ABOVE: Windsor Castle; The Duke and Duchess of Windsor*

Asquith (Liberal), Baldwin (Conservative) and MacDonald (the first Labour premier) wrestled with the problems presented by World War I, Irish independence, the women's suffrage movement, the General Strike and the Great Depression.

Then, in 1936, came the year of the three kings. In January George V died and was succeeded by his eldest son, Edward VIII. However, he reigned only 11 months, the second Windsor monarch abdicating in December 1936. Faced with the choice of marrying the woman he wished to wed, the twice-married Wallis Simpson, or remaining a bachelor king, Edward VIII put love before duty. Later marrying Mrs Simpson, as Duke of Windsor the former king then faded into the background as his brother stepped into the foreground.

Like his father, George V, the second son of a king, George VI had not expected to be crowned king himself, but crowned he was, together with his wife, Queen Elizabeth. Then, just as George V had become monarch of a nation fighting a world war, so George VI reigned as Britain became embroiled in World War II.

Staying in England throughout the 1939–45 conflict, the king, queen and their two young daughters, Elizabeth and Margaret, soon came to be seen as symbols of the British resolve to win through. An even more potent symbol was the wartime prime minister, Winston Churchill, the man whose leadership and speeches rallied people to the cause during the darkest days before, during and after the evacuation of Dunkirk, the Battle of Britain and the Blitz.

A one-time Liberal MP who had defected to the Conservatives, Churchill and his party were defeated in the first post-war election in 1945. However, there was still life in the old politician and he returned to power in 1951, the year before George VI passed away. The late king was succeeded by his eldest daughter, Elizabeth II, who was just 25 years old at the time of her accession in February 1952. Later coming to be known simply as 'The Queen', the fourth Windsor sovereign had married Prince Philip, Duke of Edinburgh, in 1947, and came to the throne as the mother of two children, Charles and Anne.

Crowned in 1953, the beginning of the second Elizabethan age also marked the start of a new chapter in the life of the widow of George VI. Taking the title of Queen Elizabeth the Queen Mother, her popularity then increased with each passing decade until in 2000 she reached another personal landmark. Celebrating her 100th birthday that year, the Queen Mother could then look back on a century that began with one long-reigning queen on the throne and ended with another, her daughter Elizabeth II, poised to enter her sixth decade as sovereign.

As monarch for half a century the Queen has reigned at a time when her role, like that of the United Kingdom, has been forced to change. No longer at the hub of an empire, Britain has allied itself with its NATO partners and then with the European Community, while at home government has been devolved in Scotland, Wales and, after three decades of the 'Troubles', in Northern Ireland.

Meanwhile, the House of Windsor has been the subject of many attacks from politicians, media and public alike. Yet, for the most part, the Queen herself has remained an admired figure, retaining a respect not given to many members of the royal family. Celebrating her Golden Jubilee in February 2002, on her many royal tours Elizabeth II has travelled further and to more countries than any previous British monarch. A passionate believer in the Commonwealth and a hard-working, if conservative monarch, she is a grandmother and the mother of four children: Anne, Andrew, Edward and her son and heir, Charles.

Invested with the title Prince of Wales in 1969, like his great-great-grandfather, Edward VII, the future Charles III has spent years as a king-in-waiting. The father of two sons by his ill-fated marriage to Princess Diana, who was killed in a car crash in 1997, Charles's eldest son, William, is second-in-line to the throne.

GEORGE V (1865–1936)

King of Great Britain (1910–36). Born at Marlborough House, London, on 3 June 1865, George Frederick Ernest Albert was the second son of Edward, Prince of Wales, and his wife, Alexandra. A grandson of Queen Victoria, George spent most of his childhood on the royal estate of Sandringham, which had been bought by the royal family in 1862. When he was 15 years old, George and his older brother, Albert (Eddie to his family), became naval cadets at Dartmouth in Devon. Before long the two young royals had fully adjusted to their new life. His life aboard Britannia fostered a love of the sea in George that never left the man who would come to be known as the 'Sailor King'. However, after rising to the rank of commander, he became ill with typhoid. He recovered, but when Albert died of pneumonia in 1892, George was forced to abandon his naval career.

In 1893 his life changed again when he married his late brother's fiancée, Princess Mary of Teck. The Duke of York, as he then was, soon became father to a large family of five boys and a girl. The first two sons became the twentieth-century kings Edward VIII and George VI, while daughter, Mary, eventually became known as the Princess Royal. Of the other sons, Henry was made Duke of Gloucester and George, the Duke of Kent, and John died while still in his teens.

George had been 35 years old when his father had ascended the throne in 1901. George succeeded Edward VII nine years later on 6 May 1910. Recognised now as the first monarch of the house of Windsor, George V began his reign as the second king of the Saxe-Coburg-Gotha dynasty. The change of name occurred in 1917, just as World War I was about to drag on into a fourth year, and was prompted by a fierce public loathing for all things German. George V's decision to adopt the very English name of Windsor for his royal house did not impress the king's cousin, the German ruler, Kaiser Wilhelm, but did endear the monarchy to the British people.

▲ ABOVE: George V with Mary and their children

George V reigned for 26 years, yet even after the peace treaty known as the Armistice was signed on the eleventh hour of the eleventh day of the eleventh month of 1918, the memory of the 'Great War' cast a long shadow over the decades that followed. Breaking out in 1914, this 'war to end all wars' killed and maimed millions of soldiers, the war-dead including the British tommies who laid down their lives in bloody battles such as the Somme (1916), Passchendaele (1917) and the Marne (1914 and 1918). Yet the 1914–18 war was not the only conflict of the period. In Dublin the Easter Rising of 1916 sparked a nationalist revolt in Ireland that continued to preoccupy politicians and fighting men before, during and after World War I until finally the Irish Free State (comprising 26 southern counties) was created in January 1922.

The immediate post-war years were politically momentous, as the suffragette movement campaigned for equal rights for women. Lady Astor became the first female MP in 1919. Then in 1920 women over the age of 21 were allowed to vote. Four years earlier, the general election of 1924 had led to the formation of Britain's first Labour government under Ramsay MacDonald. A short-lived administration, after just 10 months the Labour Party was swept from office. However, the return of Stanley Baldwin's Conservatives could not prevent the General Strike of May 1926. Then came the widespread misery of the Thirties. Brought on by the worldwide economic recession that followed the Wall Street Crash of 1929, by 1932 some three million British citizens were out of work. The Great Depression eventually lifted, but by then George V was dead.

Bluff and ruddy-faced, but well-liked during a period when revolution toppled the monarchies of other European powers, George V was a jocular man given to occasional volcanic explosions. He enjoyed living the life of a country aristocrat, while two abiding interests were sailing and stamp collecting. Dying at Sandringham on 20 January 1936, the first

Windsor sovereign was buried at St George's Chapel, Windsor, and was succeeded by his eldest son, Edward VIII.

see Edward VIII, Edward III

EDWARD VIII (1894–1972)

King of Great Britain (1936). Born at White Lodge, Richmond Park, on 23 June 1894, the first child of the then Duke and Duchess of York was christened Edward Albert Christian George Andrew Patrick David. The last four names are, of course, those of the patron saints of the countries that make up the United Kingdom, and it was by the last of these, David, that he was known to his family. Gaining four brothers and a sister before he was 11 years old, as a boy he spent much of his time on the Sandringham estate, where York Cottage was home. Educated by private tutors before enroling at naval college, after a short time at sea the prince went to Oxford University. From there he moved on to a life in the Officers' Training Corps. Then came the horrors of World War I. Pressing for active involvement Edward became an army officer and served throughout the 'Great War' of 1914–18 and for a year beyond.

With his military service at an end, the 25-year-old, unmarried prince set out on the next phase of his life as heir to the throne. Slight and dapper, Edward had an easy charm and soon became popular as he travelled from country to country as a royal ambassador. Relations were less easy with his father, as the king viewed with disdain his eldest son's liking for parties and the company of married women such as Wallis Simpson, who the prince first met in 1930.

Raised in Baltimore by her widowed mother, in 1916 Wallis Warfield (as she then was) married her first husband, a naval officer. This marriage

▶ RIGHT: Edward VIII

lasted until December 1927 and the following summer she married her second husband, Ernest Simpson. Transferring to London, it was there that she met the Prince of Wales. Then the heir to the throne, on 20 January 1936 George V died and the prince succeeded his father as Edward VIII.

Edward was six years old when his great-grandmother, Queen Victoria, died and he ascended the throne at the age of 39. In government circles there were many who admired the personable approach of the new sovereign, but there were also men who had serious reservations about a man so obviously besotted with Wallis Simpson, a married woman and divorcée. In the course of the next 10 months, the king's personal life increasingly became a public issue. At the beginning of November 1936, Edward VIII attended the state opening of parliament for the first and only time: the storm clouds were gathering over his choice of partner. British magazines and newspapers had consistently turned a blind eye to the king's love affair, but by late 1936 their approach seemed set to change, especially as Mrs Simpson had just been granted a decree nisi.

Before long a series of discussions took place behind the scenes as politicians tried to prevent the constitutional crisis that would follow the marriage of a British sovereign to a twice-divorced woman. The king made his position very clear and informed the prime minister, Stanley Baldwin, that he was determined to marry Wallis Simpson. The crisis had begun. Baldwin and his advisers investigated various possibilities. One option open to Edward was to enter into a marriage that gave his wife no royal title, property or rights of succession, and would disqualify any children from acceding to the throne. But the idea of a morganatic marriage had to be abandoned and the Irish government even went so far as to state that such a marriage would mean that Edward VIII would no longer be recognised in Ireland as the British sovereign.

With the king standing his ground, alternatives were scarce. Then, on 10 December 1936, the king put his name to a document that began with the words, 'I, Edward the Eighth, of Great Britain, Ireland, and the British Dominions beyond the Seas, King, Emperor of India, do hereby declare My irrevocable determination to renounce the Throne for Myself and for My descendants...'.

After signing this Instrument of Abdication, the second Windsor king spoke to the nation in a radio broadcast, and then he was gone. Travelling by car to Portsmouth, from there he sailed into a long exile abroad.

Succeeded by his younger brother, who became George VI, the 42-year-old former sovereign was created Duke of Windsor in March 1937. Three months later the duke married his duchess, Wallis Simpson. The subject of allegations that he was a Fascist sympathiser, he spent the war years as governor and commander-in-chief of the Bahamas (1940–45). Later settling in Paris, the duke died there on 28 May 1972, but was buried at Frogmore, Windsor. Survived by the duchess, she lived on in the French capital until her death on 24 April 1986.

◆ see George V, George VI

GEORGE VI (1895–1952)

King of Great Britain (1936–52). Born Albert Frederick Arthur George on 14 December 1895, his birthplace was the family home of York Cottage on the Sandringham estate in Norfolk. The son of George V and his wife, Mary, when Albert was born his great-grandmother, Victoria, was still queen. However, by the time he was 14 years old, his father was king and he was second-in-line to the throne. Called Bertie on the Sandringham estate where he passed much of his young life, he was a sickly boy, who was also afflicted with a stammer.

Following his elder brother, Edward, to the naval colleges at Osborne and Dartmouth, George was not a gifted student, preferring instead to play the fool and sports such as cricket. Indeed, it is said, he once achieved an unlikely hat trick when, with three successive deliveries,

LONG MAY THEY REIGN

he bagged the wickets of three British sovereigns: Edward VII, George V and Edward VIII.

However, by 1913 white flannels had been cast off in favour of a naval uniform as the future king enrolled as a midshipman. When World War I broke out in August 1914, George played his part, seeing front-line service at the Battle of Jutland in 1916. By then a sub-lieutenant, later the prince transferred to the Royal Naval Air Reserve before becoming a pilot in 1918 with the newly formed Royal Army Flying Corps (later renamed the Royal Air Force).

▲ ABOVE: The Crescent of George VI

With World War I finally at an end, George once again followed a path taken earlier by his brother, Edward, by spending a year as a university student. Becoming Duke of York in 1920, it was in that same year that he renewed acquaintances with his future wife, a woman who would later come to be synonymous with the best of British royalty. Then known as Lady Elizabeth Bowes-Lyon, in the second half of the twentieth century the world would know her simply as the Queen Mother. The young couple were married in 1923, their first child, Elizabeth (later Elizabeth II), arriving in April 1926, and their second, Margaret, in August 1930.

Content with a place in the shadows, the duke went about his royal duties diligently and without fuss. A devoted family man, a move to Royal Lodge at Windsor saw George develop an interest in gardening.

◄ LEFT: The Coronation song book

In 1936, however, such simple pleasures were forced to take second place as the monarchy lurched from one crisis to another. The turbulent year for the Windsors began with the death of the duke's father, George V, and ended with his own accession as George VI. For a shy man, who disliked public speaking, such a sudden elevation came as a huge shock. However, once his elder brother, Edward VIII, had decided to abdicate on 10 December 1936, George was forced to adjust. He did not make the transition any more easily than his father, who had also acceded as a second son, but he persevered to become a popular king. Crowned in a joint coronation ceremony with his wife, the new Queen Elizabeth, the service on 12 May 1937 was covered by the BBC. Formed just 12 years before, it broadcast a special wireless (radio) programme to honour the occasion.

Then, at the close of the 1930s, a decade that had begun with mass unemployment, ended with more misery: the outbreak of World War II. This time there was to be no mainstream role for George. However, he did make many trips to visit front-line troops stationed abroad and the king and queen together visited London's East End to see the damage caused by enemy bombs – Luftwaffe bombs also struck Buckingham Palace in 1940. At the beginning of the war plans had been made to send the royal family to a safe country such as Canada, but neither George VI nor Queen Elizabeth would hear of such a thing and so the Windsors stayed, emerging from the conflict more popular than ever before and a symbol of national resolve.

With war finally at an end, in November 1947 Buckingham Palace was the setting for a celebration: the wedding reception of Princess Elizabeth and the Duke of Edinburgh. Meanwhile, the Labour government of Clement Attlee introduced a radical programme of social reforms that included the formation of the National Health Service and the nationalisation of coal mines, railways, electricity and gas services. For the king, though, the immediate post-war years were a mixed bag; he became a grandfather following the births of Princess Elizabeth's first children, Charles and Anne, but was dogged by recurring illness.

On 6 February 1952 aged 56, he passed away in his sleep at Sandringham. Buried at St George's Chapel, Windsor, he was succeeded by his eldest daughter, who was later crowned Elizabeth II, while the late king's widow soon came to be known the world over as Queen Elizabeth the Queen Mother.

■ *see* Edward VIII, Elizabeth II, Queen Elizabeth the Queen Mother

ELIZABETH, THE QUEEN MOTHER (1900–2002)

The wife of George VI. Born in London on 4 August 1900, the ninth child of Claude and Cecilia Bowes-Lyon was named Elizabeth Angela Marguerite. Descended on her father's side from Scottish royalty and on her mother's side from the Duke of Wellington, when Elizabeth was three years old Claude Bowes-Lyon became the 14th Earl of Strathmore and Kinghorne.

Spending her childhood at the family home in Hertfordshire and at Glamis Castle in Angus, Scotland, she spent most of World War I at Glamis, where she

▲ *ABOVE: The engagement portrait of Elizabeth Bowes-Lyon*

helped care for the wounded soliders who were brought there. Eighteen years old at the end of the 'Great War', in which one brother had been killed and three wounded, less than five years after the Armistice was agreed, Lady Elizabeth married Prince Albert, the second son of George V.

Soon given the title 'the Duchess of York', she gave birth to a baby girl, Elizabeth, in April 1926. Then, in August 1930, the Duke and Duchess celebrated the arrival of their second daughter, Margaret. However, the Yorks did not have long to enjoy a quiet family life as in December 1936 Edward VIII abdicated, to be succeeded by his younger brother, Albert, Duke of York.

With Albert taking the title George VI, the duchess became Queen Elizabeth the Queen Consort. Crowned jointly with her husband at Westminster Abbey on 12 May 1937, just two years were to pass before the outbreak of World War II. Immediately, there was much talk of evacuating the royal family, but the Queen Consort's reply was unequivocal: 'The

princesses could never leave without me and I could never leave without the king and, of course, the king will never leave.' Seemingly an easy decision to make, it also proved to be a popular one.

Attending the wedding of Princess Elizabeth and Prince Philip, Duke of Edinburgh, in November 1947, just over four years later the Queen Consort was hit hard by the death of George VI on 6 February 1952. A widow at the age of 51, later she carved out a new role for herself as Queen Elizabeth the Queen Mother.

▲ *ABOVE: The Queen Mother and previous queens*

A great-grandmother, who lived through all but seven months of the twentieth century, the ever popular 'Queen Mum' celebrated her 100th birthday in 2000. Living a long life that has encompassed two World Wars and the reigns of six different sovereigns, she was a baby during the last days of Queen Victoria and a child during the reign of Edward VII. Later, of course, she became the daughter-in-law of George V, the sister-in-law of Edward VIII, the wife of George VI and the mother of Elizabeth II.

◆ *see* Elizabeth II, George VI

ELIZABETH II (B. 1926)

Queen of Great Britain (since 1952). Born on 21 April 1926 at 17 Bruton Street, London, the first child of the Duke and Duchess of York was not expected to become queen. At the time of her birth her 69-year-old grandfather, George V, had been king for 15 years while waiting in the wings was his son and heir Edward, Prince of Wales. Next in line in 1926 was Elizabeth's father, Edward's younger brother, Albert. Ten years later, the situation would remain unchanged, but in the meantime 'Lilibet', as Elizabeth was known to her family, was joined in the royal nursery by a sister, Margaret, who was born on 21 August 1930. Enjoying a relatively normal childhood, in 1936 the lives of the two sisters changed dramatically.

The year of three kings, 1936, began much the same as any other. On 20 January, however, George V died. Succeeded by his eldest son, Edward VIII, on 10 December 1936 the new king

▶ *RIGHT: Elizabeth and Margaret*

▲ ABOVE: *The Queen and the Duke of Edinburgh arrive at Ascot*

abdicated so that he could be free to marry the twice-divorced Wallis Simpson. Elizabeth's father stepped into his shoes and Elizabeth found herself heiress apparent.

Crowned as George VI, her father's 16-year reign was dominated by World War II (1939–45), which shook the world to its foundation and changed so much (including the public's opinion of the monarchy). Refusing to leave Britain during the conflict, the popularity of the royal family at this time was further increased by Elizabeth's stint as an officer in the Auxiliary Territorial Service.

The wedding of Princess Elizabeth and Prince Philip in November 1947 helped lift the gloom of post-war Britain. Enjoying the next four years as a married princess, she became queen following the death of George VI on 6 February 1952. By then the mother of Charles (born 14 November 1948) and Anne (15 August 1950), both children attended the queen's coronation at Westminster Abbey on 2 June 1953. A short time later,

Elizabeth II embarked on the first of the many royal tours that were to become such a feature of her reign this round of trips and 'walkabouts' make her the most travelled British monarch of all time.

However, popular though these early excursions proved to be, they took place in an era when the sun had long since set on the old British Empire. Such a contraction of power, coinciding with an increased boldness in society, inevitably led to questions being asked about 'The Establishment' and to doubts being expressed about the place in a twentieth-century democracy of a royal family, a family viewed by many during the 1960s as being out of touch with everyday life.

By the middle of that decade, the queen had become the mother of four children: Charles, Anne, Andrew (born 19 February 1960) and Edward (10 March 1964). A hard-working sovereign, whose professionalism was rarely doubted, Elizabeth II had long been reluctant to allow the media to intrude on the private life of her very public family. Nevertheless, aware of changing attitudes, she grasped the nettle and sanctioned the making of a 1969 BBC documentary simply called 'The Royal Family'.

Eight years later, the Windsors were once again under the spotlight as the Silver Jubilee celebrations showed the great affection many British people felt for the queen. A mass of street parties also gave a foretaste of the scenes that would accompany the wedding of Prince Charles and Lady Diana Spencer in 1981.

▶ RIGHT: The Queen at the naming of HMS Ocean

305

Since then Elizabeth II has weathered several storms, the most recent coming in the wake of the death of Diana, Princess of Wales, in 1997. However, the queen, like the Queen Mother, retains a degree of popular respect accorded few other members of the royal family. A woman of great wealth and instantly recognised all around the world, Elizabeth II celebrated her Golden Jubilee on 6 February 2002. Enjoying the longest reign since that of Queen Victoria, only two English/British monarchs have reigned longer: Henry III (56 years) and George III (59 years). The fourth British sovereign of the House of Windsor, the queen's heir is her eldest son, Charles, Prince of Wales.

� *see* Prince Charles, Queen Elizabeth the Queen Mother, George II, House of Windsor

CHARLES, PRINCE (B. 1948)

The eldest son of Elizabeth II and Prince Philip, Charles Philip Arthur George Windsor was born at Buckingham Palace on 14 November 1948. At that time, his mother was heiress apparent to the throne, but in February 1952 George VI died in his sleep and the princess became queen. Crowned at Westminster Abbey, Elizabeth's coronation was attended by her own heir, the four-year-old Charles, while an even younger onlooker was the prince's two-year-old sister, Anne.

Charles was the first Windsor child to break with a long-held tradition of being taught by personal tutors and instead the prince was sent away to school at Hill House, Cheam, and then to Gordonstoun, where years earlier his father had been a pupil. The first heir to the throne ever to go to school, on leaving Gordonstoun, a brief stay at a school in the Australian outback known as Timbertop was followed by the prince enrolling as an undergraduate at Trinity College, Cambridge.

While still at university, Charles was given the title of Prince of Wales in an investiture ceremony staged at Caernarfon Castle on 1 July 1969. The investiture ceremony coincided with the screening of a television documentary entitled 'The Royal Family'. Innovative then, the BBC's cameras recorded the Windsors away from the pomp, circumstance and majesty of royal engagements.

After his investiture and his graduation the new Prince of Wales embarked on a life in the Royal Navy. Then, with the success of the Queen's Silver Jubilee celebrations of 1977 still fresh in the memory, the Windsors' standing in the affections of the British public rose higher still when the engagement of Prince Charles to Lady Diana Spencer was announced. The couple were married on 29 July 1981 in what became known as a 'fairy-tale' wedding, amid the splendour of St Paul's Cathedral, with thousands lining the streets to watch

▲ ABOVE: Charles, the current Prince of Wales, speaks to Chelsea pensioners the wedding procession and millions more watching from afar via their television sets. Eleven months later, on 21 June 1982, the Princess of Wales gave birth to Charles's son and heir, William; a second son, Henry, always referred to as Harry, was born on 15 September 1984.

For the next 13 years images of Diana adorned newspapers and magazines, while the world's television companies covered her every move. She was the darling of the media. Welcome or not, media coverage of a royal figure, fêted as one of the world's most attractive women, became as relentless as it was intrusive, not least when rumours concerning the Wales's troubled marriage were confirmed in 1992 by the announcement of a legal separation, one that would eventually lead to a full divorce four years later. Stories about the private lives of the prince and the princess then made news as much as their official engagements or their charity work.

In August 1997 Diana, Princess of Wales (as she became known after her divorce from Charles), was killed in a car crash in Paris. Her death

evoked an unprecedented response from the public that was as remarkable as it was unparalleled, the outpourings of grief reaching their zenith on 6 September, the day of her funeral. This difficult time for the Prince of Wales was made tougher still by the furore stirred up by the tabloid newspapers – a furore that engulfed the

◀ LEFT: The crown of Prince Charles

Windsors following the death of Diana. However, the perception of a royal family out of touch with the popular mood was not a new one, any more than the difficulties of living life as heir to the throne were new to Charles.

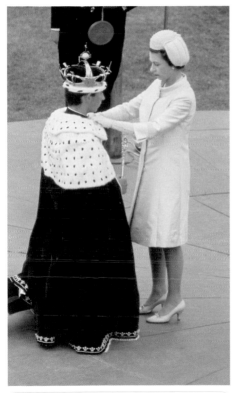

▲ *ABOVE: Investiture of Prince of Wales*

First-in-line to ascend the throne for most of his life, the Prince of Wales has had to adjust and then re-adjust to a life in the wings. He has not been the first Prince of Wales to live in the shadow of a long-reigning monarch, but he has been the first to do so in an era when the focus on the monarchy and its future has been particularly intense. Now in his fifties, Prince Charles continues to attend to the unending round of official duties that are part and parcel of being a leading royal figure, although like other royals he also has his own pet projects, one of which is the Prince's Trust.

◼ *see* Elizabeth II, House of Windsor

Chronology

AD 61   Death of Boudicca, queen of the Iceni

AD 871   Alfred the Great becomes king of Wessex

AD 899   Death of Alfred the Great

AD 939   Edmund I becomes king of England

AD 942   Malcolm I becomes king of the Scots

AD 955   Edwy becomes king of England

AD 975   Edward the Martyr becomes king of England

AD 978   Ethelred the Unready becomes king of England

1013   Sweyn Forkbeard is acknowledged king of England

1016   Edmund II ascends the throne of England

1034   Duncan I becomes king of Scotland

1035   Harold I becomes king of England

1042   Edward the Confessor becomes king of England

1058   Malcolm III becomes king of Scotland

1093   Donald III seizes the throne of Scotland; Duncan II briefly usurps the throne

1100   Henry I becomes king of England

1107   Alexander I becomes king of Scotland

1124   David I becomes king of Scotland

1153   Malcolm IV becomes king of Scotland

1154   Henry II becomes king of England

1190   Alleged tomb of King Arthur discovered at Glastonbury Abbey

1199   John becomes king of England

1216   Henry III becomes king of England

1272   Edward I becomes king of England

1307   Edward II becomes king of England

1312   Nobles murder Edward II's favourite Piers Gaveston

1327   Edward III becomes king of England

1329   David II becomes king of Scotland

1376   Death of Edward, the Black Prince

1399   Henry IV becomes king of England

1406   James I becomes king of Scotland

1413   Henry V becomes king of England

1422	Henry VI becomes king of England	**1649**	Charles I is executed and the country becomes a commonwealth under the leadership of Oliver Cromwell
1461	Edward IV becomes king of England		
1470	Edward IV is deposed and Henry VI restored to the throne	**1660**	Charles II is restored to the throne
1471	Henry VI is once again replaced by Edward IV	**1685**	James II becomes king of England
1483	Edward V is taken to the Tower of London to await his coronation; it never takes place, Richard III assumes the throne	**1689**	Constitutional monarchy introduced with the accession of William and Mary
1485	Henry Tudor becomes Henry VII	**1701**	Act of Settlement ensures the succession of the Electors of Hanover
1509	Henry VIII marries Catherine of Aragon	**1702**	Anne becomes queen of England
1513	James V becomes king of Scotland	**1714**	George I becomes king of England
1536	Anne Boleyn is executed at the Tower of London	**1727**	George II becomes king of England
1542	Mary becomes Queen of Scots	**1795**	The future George IV marries Princess Caroline of Brunswick
1547	Edward VI becomes king following the death of Henry VIII		
1553	Mary I becomes queen of England	**1861**	Death of Prince Albert
		1876	Queen Victoria is created Empress of India
1558	Elizabeth I becomes queen of England	**1901**	Edward VII becomes king
1565	Mary, Queen of Scots marries Lord Darnley	**1936**	Edward VIII abdicates
		1948	Birth of Prince Charles
1567	James VI becomes king of Scotland	**1952**	Elizabeth II becomes queen of England
1603	James VI of Scotland becomes James I of England	**1979**	Earl Mountbatten murdered by the IRA
1625	Charles I becomes king of England	**1981**	Marriage of Prince Charles and Lady Diana Spencer
		1997	Diana, Princess of Wales, is killed in a car crash in Paris
		2002	Queen Mother dies

GLOSSARY

ABDICATION The renunciation of the throne, usually voluntarily but sometimes enforced, by the reigning monarch. The most famous abdication occurred in 1936, when Edward VIII gave up the throne so he could marry the twice-divorced Wallis Simpson.

ABSOLUTE MONARCHY Rule by a monarch in which they wield absolute authority, without reliance on government or parliament for approval of decision-making.

ANGLES Name given to one of the great Germanic tribal groups (with the Saxons and Jutes) who invaded and settled in the British Isles from the seventh to ninth centuries. The Angles claimed the kingdoms of East Anglia, Mercia and Northumbria.

ANGLO-SAXONS Name given to the descendants of the Jutes, Angles and Saxons who invaded the British Isles between the fifth and seventh centuries. They were finally overthrown by the Normans in 1066.

BEAKER PEOPLE Some of the earliest settlers in the British Isles, from about 1900 BC. Beaker folk were essentially warriors and were the first to make regular use of metals in tools.

BRETWALDA Saxon word meaning 'overlord'. The Bretwalda came into existence in AD 825 after centuries of in-fighting between the Angle, Saxon and Jute settlers in Britain, when the kingdoms fell under the overlordship of Wessex.

BURHS Network of fortified towns ordered by Alfred the Great to protect his people, goods and livestock against invasion from the Vikings. The suffix 'borough' to a place name indicates an area that was once an Anglo-Saxon burh.

CELTS Ancient settlers of the British Isles who migrated there from mainland Europe. The Celts were eventually marginalized by the conquering Romans and later invaders.

CLIENT-KING Ruler of a province or kingdom, normally Welsh or Irish, who acknowledged an overlord elsewhere. Although the client-king was nominally in charge of their region, effective power was asserted by the more dominant monarch.

COMMONWEALTH Name first applied to the republican parliamentary protectorate under the leadership of Oliver Cromwell in the mid-seventeenth century. The term is now also used to describe the association

formed since World War II comprised of now-independent ex-British colonies.

CONSTITUTIONAL MONARCHY Method of rule by which the powers of the monarchy are subject to parliamentary control. Introduced in 1689, constitutional monarchy limited the monarch's rights to wage war, and curtailed his or her power of veto and choice of when to dissolve parliament.

COUNTER-REFORMATION Sixteenth-century movement instigated by the Catholic Church as a reaction to the Protestant Reformation. Key amongst its methods was the European Inquisition and the development of the Jesuit Order.

CRUSADES Series of wars from the eleventh to thirteenth centuries, originally to recover territories lost to Muslim control in the Holy Land, but later gaining imperialist foundations.

DANEGELD Money raised by taxation and paid by the English in exchange for peace with the Danes during the tenth and eleventh centuries.

DANELAW Area of north-east England settled by the Danes in the eleventh century in which they were entitled to live by their own laws, customs and language. It was formed as part of an agreement to secure peace and prevent further invasion and infiltration on Anglo-Saxon territory.

DIVINE RIGHT OF KINGS Belief that the monarch is God's representative on Earth and is therefore not subject to the laws or will of any man, being answerable only to God. Charles I's staunch belief in his Divine Right led to the English Civil War and eventually his execution.

DRUIDS Celtic priests and one of the most respected positions in the Celtic social hierarchy. Druidism involved belief in spirits of the Earth and centred their rituals around the sacred oak. The practice of Druidism was eventually obliterated by the Romans.

EISTEDDFODS Welsh tradition in which poets meet and recite verses to one another, established in the twelfth century by Rhys ap Gruffudd.

ELEVEN YEARS' TYRANNY Name given to the period 1629–40 during which Charles I refused to convene parliament and ruled without their advice.

ENGLISH CIVIL WAR Series of battles (1642–48) between the royalist supporters of Charles I and republicans under the leadership of Oliver Cromwell, later Lord Protector of England. The Civil War was caused by Charles's refusal to convene parliament and rule with their guidance for a period of 11 years.

GLORIOUS REVOLUTION Name given to the overthrow of the Catholic James II and the establishment of his Protestant daughter Mary II and her husband William of Orange (William III) on the throne of England in 1689.

HEIR APPARENT Eldest son of a reigning monarch, with a right to the throne senior to all others. The Heir Apparent is certain to succeed the throne unless they predecease the reigning monarch or are disinherited.

HEIR PRESUMPTIVE A near relation (daughter, brother, sister, cousin) of the reigning monarch who is presumed to be the heir to the throne until a child is born to the monarch and supersedes them.

JACOBITES Followers initially of the overthrown James II, and later also applied to supporters of his descendants, who wished to restore the usurped king and the Stuart line to the throne.

JUTES Name given to one of the great Germanic tribal groups (with the Angles and Saxons) who invaded and settled in the British Isles between the seventh and ninth centuries. The Jutes claimed the kingdoms of Kent and South Hampshire.

MAGNA CARTA 'Great Charter' – agreement sealed at Runnymede on 15 June 1215 between the king, John, and his barons, who objected to the king's foreign policies and what they saw as the tyrannical nature of his reign. Copies of the original document

can still be found in Salisbury and Lincoln Cathedrals and the British Library.

NEW MODEL ARMY Army created by Oliver Cromwell and commanded by Thomas Fairfax during the English Civil War, and maintained throughout the Commonwealth, to help him establish the Puritan 'Society of Saints'. The New Model Army wielded significant power during this period.

ORDER OF THE GARTER Highest order of English knighthood, established by Edward III in 1344. Its motto is 'shame to be him who thinks evil of it'.

PICTS Scottish tribes who inhabited Britain prior to the arrival of the Celts. The Picts and the Scottish Celts joined forces in the mid-ninth century. The name means 'painted people'.

PRETENDERS Name given to those who assume the identity of a royal figure in order the claim the throne, normally under the control of an opposing faction in order to overthrow the reigning monarch.

PRIMOGENITURE The right to succession of the eldest son of the reigning monarch or the right to inherit all his father's property and titles. In early times, kings were often elected rather than having automatic rights of succession, although they were normally selected from among members of the royal family.

PRINCESS ROYAL An honorific title conferred on the eldest daughter of the reigning monarch. Princess Anne is the current Princess Royal.

PRESBYTERIANISM Strict Puritan branch of Protestantism which emerged in the sixteenth century, notably in Scotland, and eliminated many traditional Catholic rituals in church services.

PROTESTANTISM Christian denomination which emerged in the early sixteenth century as a 'protest' against corruption in the Catholic Church. Henry VIII used this to break with the Church of Rome and establish the Church of England, while in Scotland extreme forms of Protestantism such as Calvinism were adopted.

PUPPET-KING Derogatory term given to a monarch who reigns but does not rule and who is under the control of a stronger character. Richard Neville, Earl of Warwick controlled the weak Henry VI after he suffered bouts of insanity.

REFORMATION Sixteenth-century European movement to instigate reforms in the Catholic Church, resulting in Protestantism and its denominations. In England, Henry VIII established the Church of England.

REGENT Figure elected to rule the country in the absence of a monarch who is at majority age or who is deemed unfit to rule. The most famous regency period in the UK was between 1811–20,

when Prince George (later George IV) ruled in place of George III.

RENAISSANCE Intellectual and artistic movement across Europe, beginning in the fourteenth century and spanning some 300 years. The Renaissance ('rebirth') saw a revival of interest in the arts, science and exploration.

RESTORATION Name given to the re-establishment of the monarchy in England. Charles II was restored the throne in 1660 after 11 years of government as a republic under Oliver Cromwell.

REPUBLICANISM Belief in a system in which the head of state is not a monarch. England's only period of republic was after the English Civil War when Oliver Cromwell was the head of state, taking the title 'Lord Protector'.

SAXONS Inhabitants of the German state of Saxony, applied loosely to one of the great tribal groups (with the Angles and Jutes) who invaded Britain in the fifth and sixth centuries. The kingdoms of the West, South and East Saxons gave rise to the territorial divisions or counties of Wessex, Sussex and Essex.

STONE OF SCONE Also known as the Coronation Stone and the Stone of Destiny; the stone upon which Scottish kings were crowned at Scone. The stone was seized by Edward I and kept in the coronation chair at Westminster Abbey. It was returned to Scotland in 1996.

TANISTRY Method of electing the next monarch from within the

ranks of the royal family, rather than being nominated by the reigning monarch.

TORIES Political party, forerunner of the modern Conservative Party, and advocating Conservative values. The Tories were traditionally supported by the upper classes and were the main opponents of the Whigs.

VIKINGS Warriors, traders and settlers from Scandinavia with fearsome reputations for plundering and pillaging the lands they invaded. The Vikings first made coastal attacks on England in the ninth century and established settlements in the country, most notably at York.

WARS OF THE ROSES Dynastic civil wars (1455–85) over claims to the throne between two branches of the Plantagenet line, the House of Lancaster and the House of York. The wars were ended when Richard III was killed at the Battle of Bosworth Field by Henry Tudor.

WHIGS Political party, forerunner of the Liberal Party and main political opponents of the Tories. The Whigs had their heyday in the eighteenth century.

WITAN Anglo-Saxon council, established in the ninth century and seen as the precursor to modern parliament. The Witan gave advice to the king on matters of state and checked and balanced the power of the monarch. It also proceeded with government business during times when there were no kings.

BIBLIOGRAPHY

Arnold, C.J., *An Archeology of the early Anglo-Saxon Kingdoms*, Routledge, London, 1998

Ashley, Maurice, *Charles I and Oliver Cromwell*, Methuen Publishing Co, 1987

Ashley, Mike, *Mammoth Book of Kings and Queens*, Constable Robinson, 1999

Baumgartner, Frederic, *Henry II*, Kendall/Hunt, 1996

Brooks, Edward Charles, *Life of St. Ethelbert, King and Martyr*, 779AD-749AD, 1995

Brooman, Josh, *Bloody Mary: Cruel Queen or Good Catholic?*, Longman, 1998

Bruce, John (ed.), *Charles I in 1646, Letters of King Charles the first to Queen Henrietta Maria*, 1984

Bruce, Mary Louise, *The Usurper King: Henry of Bollingbroke 1366-99*, The Rubicon Press, 1998

Bryant, Arthur, *King Charles II*, House of Stratus, 2000

Campbell, Marion, *Alexander III, King of Scots*, House of Lochlar, 1999

Carlton, Charles, *State, Sovereigns and Society in Early Modern England: Essays in honour of A.J. Slavin*, St Martins Press, 1998

Cecil Wingfield-Stratford, Esme, *Charles, King of England, 1600-1637*, Greenwood Press

Coward, Barry, *Oliver Cromwell*, Longman Publishing, 1991

Delderfield, Eric, *Kings and Queens of England and Great Britain*, David & Charles, 1998

Douglas, Mary and Humphreys, Graham (Illustrator), *Collins Fact Books: Kings and Queens of Britain*, Collins, 1999

Elton, Sir Geoffrey, *England under the Tudors*, Routledge, 1991

Erickson, Carolly, *Her Little Majesty; the life of Queen Victoria*, Robson Books Ltd, 1999

Lyton, Robert William, *Court, Household and Itinery of King Henry II*, Golms Verlag, 1974

Fraser, Antonia (ed.), *The Lives of the Kings & Queens of England*, Weidenfeld and Nicholson, London, 1993

Fraser, Antonia, *Mary Queen of Scots*, Arrow, 1989

Fraser, Antonia, *King Charles II*, Arrow, 1993

Gardiner, Judith, *The History Today Who's Who in British History*, Collins and Brown, London, 2000

George, Margaret, *Mary Queen of Scotland and the Isles*, Pan, 1993

Goodman, A., *The Wars of the Roses, Military Activity and English Society, 1452-1497*, London, 1981

Grant, Neil, *Collins Gem of Kings and Queens*, HarperCollins, 1999

Gregg, Pauline, *King Charles I*, Phoenix Press, 2000

Griffiths, R.A., *The Reign of King Henry VI*, Sutton Publishing, 1997

Guy, John, *Charles I and Oliver Cromwell*, Ticktock Publishing, 1998

Haigh, Christopher, *English Reformations: Religion, Politics & Society under the Tudors*, Clarendon Press, 1993

Hawkins, Michael, *Politics and administration of Tudor and Stuart England*, Harvester P Microform Publishing, 1980

Hefin, Mathias, *Wales and Britain in the Early Medieval World c 1000-c 1500*, London, 1996

Hennessy, James-Pope, *Queen Mary*, Phoenix Press, 2000

Hibbert, Christopher, *Queen Victoria*, Harper Collins, 2000

Hibbert, Christopher, *Queen Victoria in her Letters and Journals*, Sutton Publishing, 2000

Higham, N.J. & Hill, David (eds.), *Edward the Elder, 899-924*, Routledge, 2001

Holmes, Richard, *The English Civil War*, Peter Young, 2000

HRH Queen Victoria, *Queen Victoria's Highland Journals*, Hamlyn, 1997

Lace, William W, *The Little Princes in the Tower (Mysterious Deaths)*, Lucent Books, 1997

Lasky, Kathryn, *Elizabeth I: Red Rose of the House of Tudor, England, 1544, (The Royal Diaries)*, Scholastic, 1999

Lewis, Jayne Elizabeth (ed.), *The Trial of Mary Queen of Scots*, Palgrave, 1998

Loades, David, *Mary Tudor: a Life*, Blackwell Publishers, 1992

Loades, David, *Power in Tudor England*, Palgrave, 1996

Luke, Mary, *The Nine days Queen*, Buccaneer Books Inc, 1994

Macinnes, Alan, *Clanship, commerce and the House of Stuart, 1603 – 1788*, Tuckwell Press, 1996

MacCulloch, Diarmaid, *The Boy King: Edward VI and the Protestant Reformation*, St Martins Press, 2001

Melchior, Giorgio (ed.), *King Edward VI and the Protestant Reformation*, Cambridge Uni Press

Morillo, S., *Warfare Under the Anglo-Norman Kings, 1066-1135*, Woodbridge, 1994

Morrow, Ann, *Without Equal, The Queen Mother*, House of Stratus, 2000

Munich, Adrienne, *Queen Victoria's Secrets*, Columbia University Press, 1998

Newman, P. A. *A Companion to the English Civil Wars*, Oxford, 1990

Owen, Morfydd, Charles-Edwards, Thomas, and Russell, Paul (eds.), *The Welsh King and his court*, 1990

Partridge, Robert B., *"O Horrible Murder": the Trial, Execution and Burial of King Charles I*, The Rubicon Press, 1998

Pimlott, Robert B., *A Biography of Elizabeth II*, 1998

Potts, D.M. and W.T.W., *Queen Victoria's Gene*, Sutton Publishing, 1999

Reanell, Tony, *Last days of Glory: the death of Queen Victoria*, Penguin Books, 2001

Ross, Josephine, *Kings and Queens of Britain*, London, 1982

Smout, T.C., *A History of the Scottish Peoples*, London, 1969

Steele, James, *Queen Mary*, Phaidon Press, 2001

Thurley, Simon, *The Royal Palaces of Tudor England*, Yale University Press, 1993

Warren, W.L. and Green, Judith, A., *Henry II*, Yale University Press, 2000

Wormald, Jenny, *Mary Queen of Scots*

Zeepvat, Charlotte, *Queen Victoria's family*, 2001

ACKNOWLEDGEMENTS

AUTHORS

PROFESSOR DAVID LOADES (Introduction) David Loades is
one of the leading historians of the Tudor and Stuart periods.
He is Research Professor at the University of Sheffield and
has written extensively on British History and the monarchy.
His previous publications include *The Rise of England's
Maritime Empire* (Longman); *Henry VIII and his Queens*
(Sutton); *Power in Tudor England, Revolution in Religion:
The English Reformation 1530-70* (University of Wales
Press); *Politics and Nation England 1450-70* (Blackwell).
He is currently the director of the British Academy John
Foxe Project, who are producing a twenty first century
version of thye principle work, *The Acts and Monuments
of the English Matyrs* by John Foxe (1517-87)

PAUL CHESHIRE Paul Cheshire is a prolific writer. He
has written and contributed to many books on a wide range
of subjects, including science, monarchy, social history and
technology as well as magazine articles and partworks.
Recent books include *The Queen Mother* and *The Millennium
Collection* which covers one thousand years of British History.

PICTURE SOURCES

The Art Archive: Eileen Tweedy: 280-281,
284; Musee de Versailles/Dagli Orti: 273

Impact Photos: Michael George: 223 (t);
David Martin: 288 (tl)

Mary Evans Picture Library: 5, 7, 8, 9, 10-11,
14, 22, 23, 24, 30, 31, 34, 36, 37, 39, 40, 41, 44, 45,
48, 52, 58, 61 (t), 63, 68, 70, 73 (all), 74, 75, 82,
90, 103, 105, 114, 116, 121, 129, 130-131, 139, 140,
150, 152, 153, 155, 156, 159, 162, 171, 179, 180, 183,
187, 193, 194, 202, 203, 207, 210, 211, 213, 214,
216, 221, 222, 223 (b), 225, 226, 232, 233, 236,
238, 248 (t), 251, 255, 260, 262, 265, 270, 276,
283, 291, 292, 303, 316; Edwin Wallace: 16 (all),
80-81, 87, 102, 122-123, 126; Institution of Civil
Engineers: 47

National Portrait Gallery of Scotland: 71 (t)

Topham Picturepoint: 6, 28-29, 32, 43, 49, 53,
56, 59 (all), 61 (b), 71 (b), 78, 83, 93, 94, 97, 98,
106-107, 109, 110, 111, 115, 118, 120, 124, 125, 127,
128, 132, 133, 137, 141, 144-145, 146, 147, 160-161,
163, 166, 169, 174, 175, 181, 182, 184, 190-191,
199, 200-201, 204, 208, 212, 218, 220, 230-231,
235, 241, 243, 245, 246, 248 (b), 249, 252, 256,
258-259, 261, 268, 271, 274, 279, 282, 286-287,
288 (br), 295, 296, 298, 299, 301, 302, 304,
305, 307, 308, 309

INDEX